Because of his mother's circumstances, IAN GILL was conceived in a Japanese prison camp in Hong Kong in 1945 and born in New Zealand after liberation. With his mother, he spent his early life in England, China and Bangkok. After boarding school, university and joining newspapers in England, he worked as a journalist in New Zealand, Fiji, Australia, Hawaii (where he took a master's degree as a grantee with the East-West Center), Hong Kong and Singapore for 14 years. In 1985, he joined the Asian Development Bank, a multilateral financing institution with headquarters in Manila. Over two decades, he travelled widely around the Asia-Pacific region, writing and producing video documentaries.

Since 2006, Gill has returned to journalism and writing books. During his exposure to a wide range of countries, he has paid particular attention to cultural differences in attitudes towards race, class and gender and how they have evolved over the past two centuries.

Searching for Billie

*A journalist's quest to understand
his mother's past leads him to discover
a vanished China*

Ian Gill

BLACKSMITH BOOKS

For my mother Billie, my wife Jean, and our children
Brian and Sabrina

Searching for Billie
ISBN 978-988-75546-6-0

Published by Blacksmith Books
Unit 26, 19/F, Block B, Wah Lok Industrial Centre,
37-41 Shan Mei Street, Fo Tan, Hong Kong
Tel: (+852) 2877 7899
www.blacksmithbooks.com

Edited by Paul Christensen

Contents

THE NEWMAN FAMILY TREE

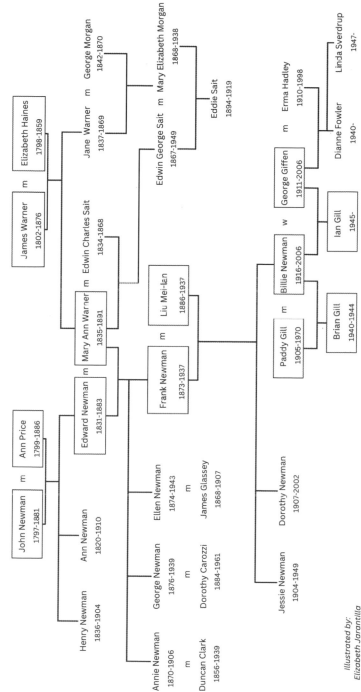

Illustrated by:
Elizabeth Jarantilla

A note on spellings

Several systems have been used over the years for transliterating Chinese characters into the Roman alphabet. The placenames in this book reflect the names and spellings commonly used in English at the time, many of which are different today. Some are listed below.

Old	New
Amoy	Xiamen
Canton	Guangzhou
Chefoo	Yantai
Chekiang	Zhejiang
Chengtu	Chengdu
Chungking	Chongqing
Foochow	Fuzhou
Hangchow	Hangzhou
Kiangsu	Jiangsu
Kwangsi	Guangxi
Kwangtung	Guangdong
Kweiyang	Guiyang
Mukden	Shenyang
Nanking	Nanjing
Peking	Beijing
Port Arthur	Dalian
Shansi	Shanxi
Shantung	Shandong
Shensi	Shaanxi
Swatow	Shantou
Tientsin	Tianjin
Tsingtao	Qingdao

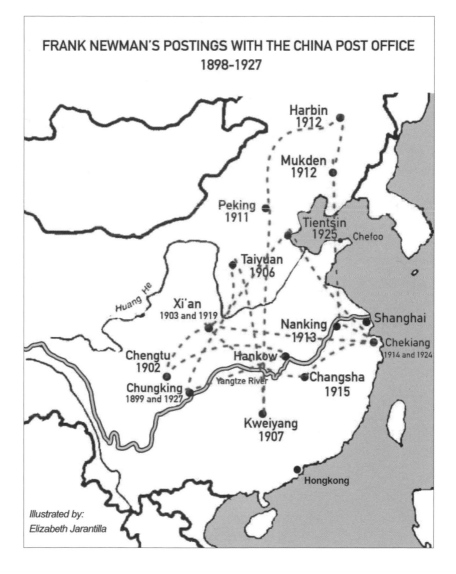

FRANK NEWMAN'S POSTINGS WITH THE CHINA POST OFFICE
1898-1927

Harbin
1912

Mukden
1912

Peking
1911

Tientsin
1925
Chefoo

Taiyuan
1906

Huang He

Xi'an
1903 and 1919

Nanking
1913

Shanghai

Chekiang
1914 and 1924

Chengtu
1902

Hankow

Yangtze River

Changsha
1915

Chungking
1899 and 1927

Kweiyang
1907

Hongkong

Illustrated by:
Elizabeth Jarantilla

Acknowledgements

I would like to thank the following for their help on this book and apologise to those whom I have inadvertently left out.

Family
Louise Mary (known as Marylou, and later as Billie) Gill (formerly Newman) (Switzerland); Dorothy (Dolly) Bido (née Newman) (Australia); Peter and Betty Bido (Australia); Graeme and Frances Clark (Australia); Duncan Clark (UK); Dianne Fowler (née Giffen) and Clarke Fowler (Canada), Frank and Norma Glassey (USA), Bob Giffen (Australia), Fred and Gudrun Giffen (UK), George Giffen and Erma Giffen (née Hadley) (Canada); Philip Giffen (Australia); Mona Granone (USA); Jenny and John Hall (UK), Charles and Jean MacKinder (née Giffen) (UK); Heather Nield (UK), Alan and Deborah Riddle (USA), Linda Sverdrup (née Giffen) (Canada); Bert Sverdrup (Canada), Marjorie Weatherley (née Giffen), (UK); David and Nadir Weatherley (UK).

Friends, Historians and Archivists
Australia: Henry Ching, Garry Dembon, Alex and Lynn Gordevich, Conner Hackett, Siaoman Yen and Richard Horsburgh, Robin and Bea Hutcheon, Stephen Hutcheon, Helen McNeale, Michael and Amber Moynihan, Samara Thomson (née Mavis Hamson), Bernard Whimpress.
Canada: John and Lynne Cole, Tim Cook, Gaby Gervais, Francis Lionnet, Bruce Murray, Robert Nield, Jim Wolf, Leila Wood.
China: Wei Chunyang (Victor), Stacey Ho, Yang Jang, Margaret Lin, Hao Youlin.
Denmark: Denise Yeoman.
Hong Kong: Tony Banham, David Bellis, George Cautherley, Gary Chan, Philip Cracknell, Professor Frank Dikötter, Angela Edgar, Mary Edgar,

Sylvia Edgar, Geoffrey Emerson, Reverend Ian Hadfield, Nick Kitto, Professor Catherine Ladds, Bill Lake, Lin Yutang, Janet and Victor Needa, Lynn Pan, Kevin Sinclair, Pete Spurrier, Jason Wordie.

Ireland: Campbell and Rebecca Black, Jeffrey Caine, Howard Davies, Donal and Kathleen O'Flynn, Dierdre Wildy.

Japan: John Carroll.

New Zealand: Professor James Bertram, Paul and Barbara Davidson, Miriam Duncan, Gavin Ellis, Fr Bruce England, Kate Fortune.

Philippines: Sydney Bates (née Larcina) and Charles Bates, Graham Dwyer, Jimmy Keir, Jay Maclean, Gilda Nanquil, Robert Salamon, Tuesday Soriano, Gina Tang.

Sweden: Professor Kingsley Bolton, Rosaleen Millar Kjellegård, Signe Kjellegård, Rydbert and Olle Rydbert.

Switzerland: Roger Diamond.

Taiwan: Spencer Moosa, Jimmy Wei, Lin Weibin, John C.H. Wu, Wen Yuan-ning.

Thailand: Vaudine England.

UK: Diana Anderson, Roy Anderson, Barbara Anslow (née Redwood), Jenina Bas, Alf Bennett, Professor Robert Bickers, Professor Charles Boxer, Reverend Alan Carr, John and Hiroko Charles, Professor James Cummins, Howard Davies, Nicola Davies, Karen Day, Brian Edgar, Gwenda Evans, Paul Ferris, Peter Hall, Hilary Hamson, Freda Ingham (née Howkins), Peter Ingham, Oliver Lindsay, Vivienne Lock (née Blackburn), Vanessa Morgan, Vickie Needa, Ian and Maureen Panton, Nina Quin, Mary Smalley, Claire and Nicolas Vafiadis, Gillian Woolley.

USA: Professor Dauril Alden, Frank and Norma Glassey, Emily Hahn, Professor Lane Harris, David Hill, Lois Larcina, Sarah McElroy, Cyril Reynolds, Jim Reynolds, JuDee Reynolds, Michael Towers, Carola Vecchio.

Author's Note

This book began with an almost surreal holiday with my mother Billie in 1975.

We met in Hong Kong that summer, when I was 29 and had been working as a journalist in Wellington for four years and she was 59 and about to retire from her job of running the Secretariat of the United Nations Disarmament Conference in Geneva.

My earliest memories were of an idyllic childhood in Bangkok from the early 1950s – just as, it turned out, her decade of turmoil and tragedy had ended.

During our reunion, she lifted the curtain on her early life in China – then shuttered from the outside world – and introduced me to a cast of extraordinary characters who had shared it with her. In Hong Kong, I met two elegantly dressed Eurasian women, 'Auntie Lois' and 'Auntie Mackie', who had been her best friends at school in Shanghai in the 1920s and 1930s. Billie also took me to Taipei to meet her erstwhile colleagues from Shanghai and Hong Kong who had fled across the Taiwan Strait as the Communists advanced to power in 1949.

They included journalist Spencer Moosa from her Reuters days and scholars Wen Yuan-ning and John Wu from the cultural magazine, *T'ien Hsia*, that she had helped to launch as office manager in 1935. Japan's war on China in 1937 had forced them to escape to Hong Kong, where they regrouped as a magazine and added an important function as an information office for the Chinese government. This arrangement lasted until Japan attacked Hong Kong in late 1941, leading to Billie being interned as a prisoner of war.

It was my first visit to Hong Kong and Taipei and I was struck by Billie's ease in environments that were strange to me, and especially by the warmth and respect people who had been senior members of the

Nationalist government showed her. Wen, though paralysed from a stroke, insisted on being dressed in a suit to meet the woman he had called his "right-hand assistant." It dawned on me that Billie was far more than a fiercely protective mother.

Before we left Hong Kong, she took me to the still-existing buildings of Stanley Internment Camp where she had spent nearly four years, experiencing starvation, the loss of her first son and an unlikely romance. We stood before the grave of my half-brother, Brian, where she told me, "You were two sons rolled into one," a remark I would not fully understand until years later.

During those 10 days, she gave me a tantalizing glimpse of her gilded childhood and her darkest years. When she suggested we work on an account of her life, I accepted readily, though not without apprehension. It was a unique opportunity to explore her rich and terrible heritage, which was mine, too. But I knew there would be challenges in writing such a book, not least because of the conflicts that had arisen between us since I reached adolescence, as well as the physical distances between us.

Nonetheless, Billie began dictating her memories into a recorder in Geneva and we would expand on these whenever we met, whether it was Hong Kong, where I got a job on a news magazine in 1978, or Singapore and Manila, where I subsequently lived.

Over the next decades, I met several more of her friends, including the American writer Emily Hahn and her husband, British intelligence officer-turned-historian Charles Boxer, and many of the women she had befriended in prison camp. In 1993, after China had reopened its doors, we returned to Shanghai together to recapture a world that, in the areas where she had lived, had changed almost beyond recognition.

Billie was desperate to learn more about her family – Frank Newman, an English postmaster, and Mei-lan, his Chinese wife – who had given her a cosseted upbringing and a privileged education in Shanghai's British schools. But they were of a reticent generation that spoke little of their past. Moreover, our search was confined mainly to the Births, Deaths and

Marriages records then at St Catherine's House, London. We finished a draft of our book in 2002, but shelved it for further improvement.

It was fortunate that we did so because it was only after Billie's death in 2006 that the exponential growth of the internet, plus some old-fashioned foot-slogging, led to the uncovering of much more of the history that had eluded her.

The online discovery of a card under the name Edward Newman, Frank's father, from the Carl Smith Collection in the Hong Kong Public Records, for example, yielded the strong connections the Newmans had for two decades with Chefoo, a small treaty port in northern China that Billie never once heard mentioned in the family home.

It was only through the digitized *North-China Herald* and China directories that one could piece together the amazing 30-year career of Frank Newman who had served the imperial Qing and, after the 1911 revolution, the Peking government, first in the customs and then helping to start China's first nationwide postal service in remote and often hazardous regions. It was a record all the more remarkable given that he flouted British social conventions, at risk to his career, by marrying a Chinese woman.

Billie would have been stunned to read of the court cases that revealed the fuller story behind Frank's separation from his family that had forced Billie to drop out of school and become a breadwinner. She would have been amazed at the exploits of Frank's parents, an iron-willed Malvern farmer's daughter and an intrepid London-raised seafarer, who had sailed to Hong Kong in the mid-19th century and ended up owning one of the best-known hotels on the China coast.

Research would also shed new light, though too late for Billie, on her husband and her lovers, revealing how their hidden sides had contributed to abrupt and puzzling break-ups that had aggravated her distress through the lack of closure.

It was both unsettling and liberating to discover that the reality was often different from what my mother – and I – had been led to believe.

The search ends with my meeting my father George – Billie's wartime lover – for the first time on a remote Canadian island and the impact this would have on Billie and me.

The family story, bookended by two strong women, portrays the evolving attitudes of society towards race, class and gender, as well as issues such as adoption and illegitimacy against the backdrop of China's turbulent century from the Anglo-Chinese wars to the advent of communism.

I must give thanks to those who provided breakthroughs at critical junctures. They include Tony Banham, Robert Bickers, Kingsley Bolton, Jeff Caine, John Charles, Henry Ching, Duncan Clark, Frances and Graeme Clark, Philip Cracknell, Brian Edgar, Geoff Emerson, Jenny Hall, Lane Harris, Robin Hutcheon, Siaoman and Richard Horsburgh, Nick Kitto, Robert Nield, Heather Nield, Victor Wei Chunyang and Jason Wordie.

1

Love Triangle

In 1861, Mary Ann Warner, a farmer's daughter from England's West Country, was trying to make it on her own as assistant manager of the Dock Hotel on Southampton's waterfront. Stepping out of the front door and crossing Canute Road, she looked out on two huge harbours, the Outer Dock and the Inner Dock, massive investments on which the town was gambling its future.

Mary Ann, 25 and single, was also taking a big chance. No longer in the first flush of youth, she had fled from her dominating father, a ruthless, philandering tenant farmer who, as was customary, was trying to marry off his daughters to much older men of means, rather than younger spouses of their choice.

A comely woman with dark eyes and shoulder-length tresses, Mary Ann had arrived by stagecoach from her village of Malvern Link, Worcestershire, alighted on the High Street, and crossed Porters Meadow (now Queen's Park), making her way between men in flat caps and jackets with leather elbows who were waiting hopefully to be hired to load and unload ships.

Southampton was bidding to transition from a sleepy spa resort into a bustling port and, as she approached Canute Road, Mary Ann saw on the right the customs house, which looked far too elegant for its prosaic purpose. Indeed, it had recently been converted from the Grecian-styled Royal Gloucester Baths, which had been built on the beach so that the ladies of society could bask in baths filled by incoming tides and reap the vaunted medicinal benefits of sea bathing.

On her left, she could see the source of Southampton's hoped-for prosperity – the terminus for the railway line from London, completed in

1840, which was bringing a steady stream of visitors from the metropolis in smoke-belching locomotives.

Mary Ann reached the corner of Royal Crescent Road where the Canute Castle Hotel still stands (though it is now a real estate business), with its octagon-shaped viewing tower on the roof.

Across the road were the grand offices, with arched entrances and Corinthian columns, of the Peninsular & Oriental Steam Navigation Company that was leading Britain into a new era of shipping, replacing wind-powered clippers with more reliable and faster iron hulks powered by steam engines.

Since winning its first major government contract in 1837 to carry mail to the Iberian peninsula of Spain and Portugal, P&O steamers were now making money carrying passengers and cargo as well. The company dominated the eastward routes and extended services to Alexandria in 1840, India in 1842, and Ceylon, Calcutta, Penang, Singapore and Hong Kong in 1845.

The new rail link had prompted the P&O to move its headquarters from London to Southampton, where it invested in offices, wharves and warehouses, as well as a school and housing for its employees and their families, and a laundry for the fleet's linen.

In response to the anticipated shipping boom, the port inaugurated the outer dock in 1843, which was immediately used by P&O steamships, and opened the inner dock in 1851.

It was undoubtedly the hope of becoming rich that enticed Harry Morgan into moving his family south in the 1850s from the pleasant market town of Stourbridge, Worcestershire, to run the Dock Hotel in this grimy dockland.

Handily for business, the hotel was right next door to the P&O Buildings. It was a stolid three-storey establishment, as tall as the P&O Buildings, and it confidently proclaimed its purpose by splashing "Dock Hotel" and "Morgan Family Hotel" in large letters across its stylish bay windows.

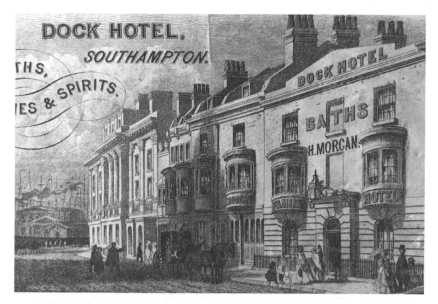

The Dock Hotel where Mary Ann worked. The P&O Buildings are on the left.

An 1859 advertisement shows prosperous-looking men in top hats and women in long dresses promenading in front of the Dock Hotel.

Unfortunately, Morgan made a big miscalculation. The elite preferred to stroll a few hundred yards and stay in hotels along the far more salubrious High Street, while the rougher trade headed for cheaper accommodation in the red-light district on the other side of the High Street.

And the bigger picture was not hopeful. Southampton, which had built its affluence on trading wool and wine across the Channel, could not match the industrial might of Manchester and the northern port of Liverpool.

Business was not taking off as Harry had hoped. On April 7, 1861, the national census taken that evening shows the Dock Hotel had only two boarders – a 23-year-old merchant from Hamburg, Germany and a 57-year-old man of independent means from Cheshire.

In fact, the staff easily outnumbered the guests. The Dock Hotel had five servants and two Morgan family members who managed the hotel –

Harry and his wife's brother, Alexander Barlow, 29, who, like Mary Ann, was an assistant manager. The other residents were Harry's wife Mary and their teenage sons George and William.

On top of lack-lustre business, disaster struck two weeks later when Harry died on April 19 at the age of 49. The loss would also increase the responsibilities thrust upon the capable Mary Ann.

Meanwhile, as one of the few personable women in a district of transient men, Mary Ann was catching the eye of suitors, including two who worked for the prestigious P&O.

One was Edwin Sait who, like Mary Ann, came from a farming village, South Bersted, but was making something of himself as a P&O engineer. He was showing the same potential as his enterprising father, who rose from agricultural labourer to coal trader and finally a farmer with 27 acres of land.

Mary Ann's other admirer was P&O steward Ted Newman, a London lad from the wrong side of fashionable Bloomsbury. Ted was one of 10 children born and raised next to the Rookery, a notorious slum depicted in stories by Charles Dickens and graphic drawings by William Hogarth.

Unlike Edwin, Ted had a rather ineffectual father. A daguerreotype of John Newman shows a man who looks quite distinguished, with an aquiline nose and bushy mutton chops, but he had never been much of a success as a maker of musical instruments, a brass worker or gas fitter and his final career as a licensed victualler at the Wheatsheaf pub near Clare Market had ended in disaster. After allowing a son to run the pub into debt, John Newman was declared bankrupt in 1861, a big disgrace. Adding insult to injury, the same son, Henry, also lost a well-publicized court case brought by a young woman claiming that he was the father of her child.

Ted Newman's father John, who died bankrupt

John Newman's strong and well-connected wife kept the family afloat, but the double public humiliation of financial ruin and moral shame drove the Newmans out of a neighbourhood where they had lived for decades – all 10 of the Newman children were baptized in their parish church of St Giles-in-the-Field. Ted's oldest sister Ann led the exodus, moving to Southampton after marrying a sailmaker the year her father's business failed. She would live only a few hundred yards from Mary Ann in the Dock Hotel and, later, she was followed to Southampton by two brothers, including Ted, two sisters and, eventually, her mother.

According to a cousin with knowledge of the situation, Edwin Sait and Ted Newman were best friends. Edwin, who became a chief cook, would have interacted with Ted the steward on their long voyages. It is clear from subsequent developments that both were very fond of Mary Ann, though it is not known how or if this love triangle affected their friendship.

What is evident is that Ted Newman was away a lot – one reliable source places him in Hong Kong as an administrative officer for a trading company, Margesson, in 1863, which indicates that he was plying the Far East route and sometimes took an onshore job, a common pattern of behaviour for mariners.

In any event, Edwin Sait, possibly because he was more home-based, was the first to win Mary Ann's affection and the two married in her home village at St Matthias' Church on November 1, 1864. Mary Ann's father, James, had been a church warden of St Matthias since its foundation 20 years earlier, but people in that tiny community knew that he was a hypocrite and a bully.

Even as he was giving away his daughter in church, James Warner, in his 60s, was having an illicit relationship with Rachel Ann Tudge, the 17-year-old daughter of a carter who rented a property on Warner's land. Furthermore, when young Rachel became pregnant, Warner sent her away to Claines, 10 miles away, where she delivered a baby son, who died soon afterwards.

Somehow, the spirited Rachel Ann managed to persuade Warner to marry her secretly at St Peter's Church in Birmingham but, when this became known, it caused a huge rift between the children of Warner's first and second families.

Nor did Warner's eyebrow-raising conduct end there. A self-made man who farmed land for the local squires and made sure they had pheasants to shoot in the hunting season, Warner proved so ruthless in protecting his land that he inspired both fear and scorn among the farm hands drinking in the local pub.

In 1837, the *Worcester Journal* reported that Warner had seen James Tyler, a labourer, carrying a withy pole (a frame to support crops) and, believing Tyler had stolen it from his hop yard, took him to court. Tyler challenged Warner to produce a witness who had seen him take the pole, which looked like any other withy stick. To Warner's embarrassment, the magistrates said they had no power to inflict a punishment on the offender as the price of the pole was under two shillings. In later years, Warner brought offenders to court for trespassing or stealing an apple or fish from a stream. He must have been a strong man, too, for in 1840 he reportedly hid under a hedge one Saturday evening and, after catching two men removing turnips from his land, hauled them off to court, where they were fined.

Back in Southampton, Mary Ann and Edwin set up home not far from the Dock Hotel, where she continued to work. When their son was born on January 17, 1867, Mary Ann broke with tradition by having the boy baptized Edwin George William, deliberately leaving out her father's name.

Later that year, Ted Newman – and possibly Edwin as well – took part in a highly publicized and costly adventure, the Napier Expedition. A conflict had broken out after Emperor Tewodros II of Ethiopia captured a handful of missionaries and British government representatives and held them hostage at his mountain fortress of Magdala. On August 21, 1867, Queen Victoria announced the decision to send a military expedition to rescue the captives. The task went to the Bombay Army under the leadership of Lieutenant-General Sir Robert Napier.

The mission involved transporting 13,000 British and Indian soldiers, 26,000 camp followers and over 40,000 animals, including 44 elephants to pull the heavy guns, from Bombay to the east coast of Abyssinia. Some of the P&O fleet and dozens of other vessels played their part. If Ted Newman was in Hong Kong, it is plausible that he took part in an expedition that was launched from India. If Edwin also took part, it could explain why he developed heart and liver trouble that would keep him confined to home for months.

Later that year, another misfortune struck the Dock Hotel with the death of Harry Morgan's widow, Mary, on October 23, 1867. This left her son George Morgan, now in his mid-20s, in charge.

Mary Ann's younger sister Jane was spending time in Southampton, possibly helping to look after Mary Ann's baby. Jane began a relationship with George Morgan and on March 10, 1868, the couple married at St Matthias, with the bride again given away by her father, James Warner.

With her sister now married to the hotel owner, Mary Ann's future appeared bright.

But, within months, everything fell apart.

After months of illness, Edwin died on August 26, 1868, at the age of 34, of vascular and hepatic disease. He left effects of under 200 pounds.

Mary Ann, already cut off from her father, now faced a bleak prospect. A single woman had few rights – she could not access bank credit, nor own a property – and now she had to hold down a busy job and raise a son alone.

In Hong Kong, Ted Newman heard of his friend Edwin's demise. A bachelor approaching 40, Ted had also recently attended the wedding of his good friend and P&O colleague, John Southan, and may well have thought of settling down.

He now did something that shattered Victorian decorum. Though the ground had hardly settled over his friend's grave, he proposed marriage to Mary Ann.

It is unlikely that Mary Ann, now approaching her mid-thirties, was swept off her feet by passion. She was by now versed in business and was adept at gathering intelligence through travellers at the hotel or ships' crews at the Dock Hotel's tap room on nearby Albert Road.

She knew that storm clouds were appearing over the Solent. She heard the rumours that P&O was harbouring serious doubts about its commitment to Southampton. The company was eyeing Liverpool, with its growing cotton exports to India, and also London, which was drawing increasing volumes of trade. It was becoming harder for P&O to be competitive in Southampton after adding the time and cost of moving goods back and forth to London.

Widows were supposed to mourn for two years, but Mary Ann made a quick decision.

Just as she knew Southampton was in trouble, Mary Ann would have been aware of the opportunities awaiting the bold on the other side of the world. She heard that Hong Kong, with its endless supply of labour from China, was doing well enough to open more hotels and boarding houses, including the new luxury Hongkong Hotel.

With her enterprising nature, Mary Ann would likely have earned her passage to Hong Kong as a stewardess. P&O was crying out for skilled women to service its growing number of female passengers in first class and Mary Ann would have been a godsend.

The Suez Canal was under construction but would not open until November 1869, so Mary Ann had a choice of taking the Mediterranean route to Alexandria, going overland to Suez and taking a ship from there to the Far East – or she could take the more hazardous route around the Cape of Good Hope with its notoriously stormy weather.

If Mary Ann worked her passage, she could not take her son. She left Edwin with Jane, who was now pregnant, probably with the intention of bringing him out later.

Though steamships were safer than clippers, hazards were not uncommon. She might have left Southampton on the SS *Travancore* on September 13 or on the SS *Carnatic* on October 10, 1868. A year later, the SS *Carnatic* ran aground on a coral reef in the Red Sea and broke up with the loss of 31 lives.

Mary Ann was also aware of the mysterious disease in Hong Kong that was killing many young soldiers in Happy Valley.

But, as she left from the same port as the Pilgrim Fathers when they set off for the New World in 1620, she sailed with hope and, to judge from what she would do, probably even had a business plan.

2

Crazy-Brilliant Plan

On the face of it, Ted Newman's steady career and Mary Ann bringing up the children suggested that he was the principal partner and she was the supportive wife. But when details of their crazy-brilliant plan to get rich emerged, it was clear she was the driver.

Mary Ann's plan may have been taking shape even before her iron-hulled steamer nudged its way between three-masted clippers and Chinese junks as it approached the P&O pier in Hong Kong on a winter's day in early 1869.

She was likely awed by the miles-long procession of elegant residences and grand offices that occupied every inch of prime real estate as far as she could see. But she may well have also felt disheartened. In less than 30 years, the population of this far-flung British outpost had grown to 120,000, four times that of centuries-old Southampton, and its impressive façade of commercialism made it obvious she was too late – the *taipans*, and the *hongs* (business houses) they commanded, had already driven up land prices far beyond what an ordinary working couple could afford.

As she stepped onto the wharf of P&O's two-storey headquarters, called *tit hong* (iron company) by the Chinese because of its cast-iron veranda, she saw the sedan chair carriers beckoning to her to take a ride up the steep hill, coolies with bent backs pushing wheelbarrows and carts and hawkers jostling to sell items she had never seen before.

Amid all this hustle and bustle, she inhaled an exotic mix of smells from spices and night soil – and perhaps a whiff of the money to be made in this entrepôt centre. She was one of only a few hundred European women in Hong Kong's capital of Victoria, and her gender and class counted very much against her in her determination to make a fortune.

But soon she would determine how she was going to do it.

Meanwhile, there were pressing practical matters to attend to. She was 34, a comely widow in the "wild east" and she needed to become "respectable" quickly. So, on March 29, 1869, she and Edward Newman married at St John's Cathedral, a fine structure in old English style near the seafront. They stood in front of the colonial chaplain, the Reverend W.R. Beach, who had taken up his post only four months earlier after working as a missionary in Tientsin.

He no doubt wanted to share his exciting news: the Duke of Edinburgh was soon to visit Hong Kong and the Reverend was in charge of the church services to honour his royal highness and was even planning to put out an illustrated publication to mark the event.

She, however, probably wanted to ask him about Tientsin, which the British, French and Russians had added to the small list of treaty ports in northern China.

As they recited their vows, they were fanned by a large overhead punkah, whose strings were being pulled back and forth by boys sitting outside the church.

They moved into the spacious staff quarters provided by the P&O at one of town's highest points – Old Bailey Street which, at 300 feet above sea level, had panoramic views of the town, the harbour and the hills beyond.

Their neighbours included Ted's colleague and friend, John Southan, the company store master, whose recent marriage may have encouraged Ted to settle down at the age of 38.

Mary Ann might have been initially shocked to realize that, right across from their home at 11A Old Bailey Street were the high walls of Victoria Prison. From the earliest days, after raising the Union Jack at Possession Point in January 1841 to take the island, the British were vastly outnumbered by the Chinese and, ever fearful of a riot, the stern first chief magistrate, William Caine, had chosen for his offices an elevated site that was protected by rocky ravines on two sides.

Mary Ann would step outside to see Indian Sikh guards taking out gangs of Chinese prisoners – who bore wooden stocks around their necks, with signs bearing their name and crime – to parade them outside the Man Mo temple on nearby Hollywood Road.

But, with the police headquarters also nearby, Old Bailey Street could nevertheless be considered one of the safer spots in the crime-infested colony. It wasn't the most exclusive neighbourhood – Eurasians and Macanese were also residents – but it overlooked the European quarter and had panoramic views of the harbour and the distant hills of Kowloon.

It took less than 10 minutes to walk down the hill to Pottinger Street, with its irregular stone slabs for steps, which was the unofficial dividing line between the European and Chinese communities.

On Queen's Road, Ted turned left for the *tit hong* building but, if Mary Ann was pursuing her plan – and they were certainly trying to accumulate savings – she might have turned right where she would have soon found a job in a hotel, possibly at the Hongkong Hotel, the colony's first luxury establishment which had opened the previous year at the corner of Queen's Road and Pedder Street, overlooking the harbour. Its management would have snapped up a capable and personable European woman who did not consider it beneath her dignity to work.

Before the end of her first year, Mary Ann received devastating news from home – her younger sister Jane died of apoplexy on December 18, 1869, at the age of 32. Jane left a one-year-old daughter, Elizabeth Mary, and had also, presumably, been keeping an eye on her nephew, Edwin, the little boy Mary Ann left behind.

It's doubtful whether Mary Ann returned to England because she became pregnant around the same time. Nearly ten months later, the Newmans' first child was born on September 28, 1870; they made the announcement in the local newspapers and telegraphed it to England. The baby was named after their mothers – Annie Elizabeth Victoria. A few months later, Mary Ann took her daughter to the studio of William Floyd at the corner of Wellington and Wyndham Streets and posed for a winsome photograph with Annie on her lap.

Mary Ann and Annie

This image, which Mary Ann sent to her family, is significant – and also misleading. At 36, she does not submit to the more conventional portrait of a wife standing beside her seated husband. Her handsome face looks directly at the camera with the faintest of smiles reminiscent of the enigmatic Mona Lisa. Thick locks flow over her shoulders as she sits, in a dark full-length gown, with a white collar around her neck, holding Annie around her chest with one hand and playfully holding her fingers with the other. It projects an impression of a caring mother but her eyes betray the ruthless determination she inherited from her father.

Around this time, Ted also had a formal portrait taken, presumably to reflect his soon-to-be-assumed role. It is full of contradictions.

Taken against a backdrop of a faux Grecian column with an ornamental balustrade, he is almost slouching against the pillar. He might be striving for a formal look, but his appearance betrays carelessness. His cape-like frock coat falls to one side, revealing part of a waistcoat and the tail-end of a light-coloured scarf.

He is holding a hat that looks like a boater, rather feminine, more suited for a

Ted Newman

sporting occasion. Is this a sartorial gaffe or is he sending a mocking message? His body language is clear, however. Edward rests his right arm, cocked at the elbow, on his hip and, in his long trousers, he crosses his right leg over his left, with the tip of a black shoe pointing downwards. It is a jaunty, even insouciant, pose. The cousin who showed the author the photo commented that he looked like a "spiv."

As a P&O steward, Ted could have been working on routes nearer home between Hong Kong and Amoy, Swatow and Foochow. Since they were exploring opportunities, Mary Ann may well have accompanied him on some trips.

Ted was promoted, first to clerk and then to Assistant, a senior position, but he was able to track goings-on in other ports through P&O agents.

In June 1870 a massacre of French priests and nuns in Tientsin, the gateway port to Peking, shocked the foreign community throughout China. Angered by rumours that the nuns were removing the eyes of orphan children to use for medicinal purposes, a Chinese mob burned down Catholic institutions and foreign buildings, including Tientsin Cathedral and four British and American churches. The crowd murdered two French consular officials and raped, mutilated and killed ten nuns. The final death toll, including Chinese Christians and three Russian traders mistakenly thought to be French, was 60.

The outrage had consequences in other ports. As a result of sharply raised tensions, the French established a naval command centre at the nearby port of Chefoo, which guarded the entrance to the Gulf of Chihli. As a precautionary measure, Chefoo cancelled its annual horse race meeting that September and again the following year.

The Newmans took an interest in Chefoo because it was known as the Brighton of China due to its British climate, with summers that were warm but not hot and humid like Shanghai, and cold in winter but not enough to freeze the river as in Tientsin. It had potential as a spa resort, something with which Mary Ann was familiar.

Then, in August 1871, Chefoo suffered a blow. Warships from several countries had gathered in Chefoo Bay to enjoy a rowing regatta during a summer break from the blistering heat of other ports. It was a prestigious gathering attended by three admirals and the foreign ministers of Russia and America as well as the head of British trade in China, Thomas Wade. An American on the frigate *Colorado*, James Brooks, spent a week in Chefoo, staying at the Family Hotel, and was part of an experience that would affect the Newmans.

"Chefoo is the summer heaven of the Shanghai Hades," he wrote. "I feel as if I were in Paradise. I am revelling on the borders of the ocean surf, with nine American and European warships in the port, with their flags, all in sight of our fair and comfortable summer (Family) hotel. This fleet must have on board some twenty-five hundred Americans, French, Germans, and Russians, and they make Chefoo, otherwise desolate —

with not a road in it, or around it, for vehicles, and no communication but by sedan chairs — a very jolly place, at least for this summer. We go everywhere we can, by water. The coolies take us through the surf, in their chairs, to the boats, or, we get on the back of some lusty sailor, who takes pleasure in saving us from a ducking, as we go to visit the ships."

In the evenings, the crews dined at the Beach and Family hotels, with music played by the ships' bands. The two hotels, said Brooks, were "a mile apart, the one inaccessible to the other, in consequence of creeks to be waded, save in sedan chairs." Beyond the beach, he reported, Chefoo was a "little Chinese town, all mud and dirt."

Suddenly, an unseasonal and violent storm interrupted their sojourn. "Rain, rain, nothing but rain! A long, dry season has been followed by a severe rain," reported Brooks. "The builders here build of mud, and lime, and straw — much mud and little lime — and when a flood comes, such as we are having now, the mud washes away, and down tumble ceilings, and walls, and plastering, and everything else. Certain it is, our (Family) hotel is being washed down, and is running off into Chefoo Bay and, if it washes much more, we shall have to take to the *Colorado* for refuge from the flood."

This disaster for the Family Hotel turned out to be the opportunity the Newmans were waiting for. Ted, in touch with the P&O's shipping agent in Chefoo, Thomas Fergusson, knew it could not have come at a worse time, the height of summer, wiping out bookings for the rest of the season.

To make it worse, the wife of the German hotel owner, Alex Bielfeld, was pregnant and was due to give birth the following year.

Rumours began to circulate that the Family Hotel might be for sale.

The timing was fortuitous for the Newmans. They had saved hard and, if they needed a loan, help was near to hand as ties between the P&O and the recently founded Hongkong & Shanghai Bank were close. A brilliant young Scot, Thomas Sutherland, had been sent to look after P&O's Hong Kong operations and had, in fact, been on a P&O steamer in early 1864 when he came up with the idea of founding a bank in Hong Kong to finance ventures in China, a job hitherto monopolized by banks out of India. Sutherland founded the Hongkong & Shanghai Bank in 1865.

If the Newmans' scheme was to succeed, it would bring a big jump socially. Chameleon-like Mary Ann could handle the transition, but she wondered about her husband.

Ted had been a bachelor seaman for a decade, and it can be safely assumed he frequented the same haunts as other mariners, shady dives and brothels from Bombay and Penang to Hong Kong's Queen's Road. He may have had a steward's disarming manner, which he needed to fit into the world of business.

Mary Ann's view of the Central Praya, 1860s

In early 1872, Ted Newman applied to become a mason at the Zetland Lodge, possibly proposed by his friend John Southan, and was admitted as a full member on May 13, 1872. Joining the Freemasonry, which was open to people of all races, creeds and social stations, was an excellent way of making contacts.

The year 1873 opened full of promise for the Newmans. On January 30, their first son was born and given the names Edward Francis Southan. Ted also ignored the custom of giving his son his father's name, John, and opted instead to include his friend's name, Southan. Ted's father had died a bankrupt in a boarding house 14 months earlier.

Ted was meanwhile going up in the world; a notice that he served on a jury in 1873 stated that he was now an Assistant with P&O.

Then change came with dramatic swiftness.

With baby Frank less than six weeks old, the Newmans packed their belongings and left their relatively safe, settled life and headed for China. They were going in the opposite direction to the thousands of Chinese who were pouring into the sanctuary of Hong Kong, to make a new beginning in a land where anti-foreign feelings ran high.

On March 10, 1873, Mr and Mrs Newman, two children and a servant boarded a ship for Shanghai, according to a *Hong Kong Daily Press* report on passenger movements.

Mary Ann and Ted likely stopped in Shanghai for a few days to meet suppliers and arrange other business matters before taking another steamer to Chefoo, a further two or three days up the coast.

Within a short time, they were installed as new owners of the Family Hotel. Unlike the missionaries, diplomats and merchants they would meet, they were without the backing of a large organisation. It looked foolhardy.

3

An Idyllic Trap

The Newmans' scheme appeared extremely risky for other reasons, too. A map of Chefoo around that time showed that the Family Hotel was in an isolated location a mile to the east of the tiny foreign settlement – and everyone knows a hotel's success depends on location, location, location. Only after the author visited the area did the genius of Mary Ann become clear.

Although Chefoo (today known as Yantai) has expanded into a metropolis of seven million, the old foreign settlement at the bottom of the hill serendipitously remains well preserved.

At the hotel that stands on the site of the old French convent and school, local historian Victor Wei turned up unexpectedly and proceeded to adopt the author and his wife as descendants of the Newmans of the Family Hotel. Over the next few days, he and his history-minded friends provided such a warm welcome it felt like a homecoming.

Wei pointed out the customs quay where, in March 1873, Mary Ann and Ted disembarked from the lighter that had carried them from the steamer, rocking in the large bay, exposed to blustery winds sweeping across the Gulf of Chihli.

Coolies with long, plaited queues lifted their trunks and other luggage onto their backs while they climbed into sedan chairs beside the grey-stone custom house, with its roof of curved tiles, that is still there.

Then, as today, the Newmans entered the western side of a narrow isthmus that separated them from the bay on the other side.

Chefoo was a fishing village long before foreigners came trickling in after the capture of Peking by Anglo-French forces in 1860, bringing an end to the second Anglo-Chinese war, and the unequal treaties that forced open Chinese territories to outside trade.

The stench as they left the customs quay came from the Chinese quarter on their right where fisher families dwelt in cramped homes, with sewage streaming along outside gutters. The sedan carriers turned left and approached Beach Road with the European-style residences and shops that attracted curiosity from local residents.

The customs wharf where the Newmans alighted in 1873.
Postcard courtesy of Lin Wei-bin

Above Beach Road was a hill, topped by a lighthouse, with its green slopes occupied by the consulates of Great Britain, France, the United States, Germany, the Austro-Hungarian monarchy, Sweden and Norway, Denmark and the Netherlands. The diplomatic corps was not as numerous as it sounded, for one British merchant, William A. Cornabé, represented the United States, Sweden and Norway, while British acting consul William Marsh Cooper also served on behalf of the Austro-Hungarian monarchy.

At the other end of Beach Road, the Newmans found the Chefoo Club, which is still there. Before them was a bay with merchantmen and warships at anchor. As their eyes followed the long curving shoreline for a mile, they could just make out, beyond the church and the grey bean fields, a speck of white. This lone bungalow was the Family Hotel on which the Newmans were staking their future. He was 42 and she was 38. Did they imagine they were going to spend the rest of their lives there?

Chefoo's Beach Road in the colonial era. Postcard courtesy of Lin Wei-bin

Although foreigners numbered only in the dozens when the Newmans arrived, the community was far from close-knit. The largest group, the missionaries, was regarded by the others as a nuisance; they stirred unrest among the Chinese, the Tientsin massacre being an extreme example. Also in conflict were the traders like Fergusson, who campaigned to open up the entire country through railways and the telegraph and mines, and the diplomats who knew they had to tread cautiously as China was far from ready for such modernization. Somewhere in between were the Imperial Customs officers who represented the Chinese government, for which Customs raised vital revenue.

Within this maelstrom of opposing interests, the Newmans had to work quickly on a property that had been severely damaged from the ferocious storm of 19 months earlier. They managed to re-open before the summer season. On June 14, 1873, the following announcement appeared in the newspapers: "Chefoo Family Hotel. Edward Newman, manager. This hotel is now open. Ladies or families desirous of rooms to be reserved for them are requested to make early application to the Manager. The Culinary department will be carefully attended to and supervised by the Wife of the manager. And the wines are of the choicest quality and were shipped direct from London to this Hotel. The hotel has been thoroughly done up and no expense has been spared in perfecting the arrangements. An Ice House has been erected immediately adjoining the premises. First Class Return Tickets, Shanghai to Chefoo and back – Taels 30 by the S.S.N. Co's and N.S.C. Co's boats."

The Family Hotel in the early days when it was a single-storey structure.
Courtesy of Graeme Clark family

Though Ted was officially manager, the venture relied heavily on Mary Ann's expertise and cool head.

The location was still puzzling until Victor Wei took the author to the hotel that stands on the exact spot previously occupied by the Family Hotel. From the hotel entrance, the view ahead was a sandy beach. "This is still the number one beach in Chefoo," said Wei.

This was a major part of the location's appeal but the main one revealed itself in an article in the *North-China Herald* in 1877: "It is now an accepted fact that if Shanghai residents are to preserve their health, they must annually quit the settlement for a month or six weeks. The conditions of life are unfavourable to continuous residence and August and September regularly witness an exodus of foreigners to Chefoo or Japan."

Mary Ann's market was not the passing local traffic but the well-to-do women and their children who sought a respite from the blistering heat of Shanghai and Peking.

And she knew, from her days in Malvern and Southampton, exactly what women at leisure wanted. In Southampton, they had paid to sit in bathing huts, waiting for the tide to bring in the sea. Here, they had a gently sloping beach where children could frolic safely at all times.

Moreover, its isolation was Mary Ann's trump card – the English ladies could play tennis, take picnics, go for walks and boat rides, all far from the inquisitive eyes of the locals. The only Chinese were her hotel staff and those who swept up seaweed from the beach.

There was another important advantage: the pristine water from their wells was of the highest purity in Chefoo, according to an analysis reported in *The China Medical Missionary Journal*.

The Newmans already knew that Chefoo was never going to succeed as a trading centre. Originally, it was thought the town might be the gateway for the populous, though still largely unknown, Shantung Province.

After the early rush, however, opium was a declining import and the Chinese did not have an appetite for British cotton. As for exports, local junks carried most of the beancake and beans. Within a few years, the Shanghai-based firms had pulled out, leaving only a handful of foreign traders.

Besides, the only way in and out of Chefoo was a dirt track usable only by mules and horses, and no effort was made to improve this. In addition to the Chefoo Club, the British built a racecourse – not far from the Family Hotel – but they never set up a fully-fledged municipal council or defined boundaries.

Mary Ann knew that, as long as she could attract out-of-town ladies, with plenty of repeat business, she would prosper. The local market provided an abundance of fresh fish, beef, mutton, eggs, milk and all kinds of vegetables and fruit, to ensure a delicious cuisine and she kept a close eye on their stocks of fine wine. Kobe, the Japanese city mentioned by the *North-China Herald* as competition, posed little threat as it drew men seeking sinful pleasure; and she did not want the rough trade of sailors.

With her acute knowledge of what women wanted, her personality and eye for detail, Mary Ann managed every facet from the staff and the food to the décor and the bedsheets. She was the power behind the throne.

Her strategy paid off as they added another floor to the hotel, possibly with financing from the Hongkong & Shanghai Bank, represented in Chefoo by Fergusson. A postcard from around 1880 shows the Family Hotel as a two-storey structure with a red roof and portico entrances. The expansion doubled its capacity to 34 bedrooms in addition to the "commodious" drawing and dining rooms and spacious verandas overlooking the sea. Not only did the hotel never lose money, it made enough profit in the summer months to tide them over the winter when it closed.

At the British consulate, the Newmans likely met Augustus Raymond Margary, an interpreter whose fate would affect their lives. Two years later, Margary was on an expedition in far western Yunnan, exploring trade routes to Burma, when he was killed by tribesmen known to be hostile to the Chinese government. After a period of stability in Anglo-Chinese relations, the murder caused a major diplomatic rupture and brought threat of another war. Britain's trade minister in China, Thomas Wade, had approved the exploratory trip and now seized upon the murder to demand reparations and concessions. Some of the difficult negotiations took place in Chefoo's Beach Hotel and ended with the Chefoo Convention in 1876.

The talks brought to town Sir Robert Hart, the influential Irish Inspector General of the Imperial Maritime Customs Service, who would have a direct impact on the careers and lives of the Newman progeny, including the girls.

In the 13 years since the Tsungli administrative office, in charge of Chinese foreign policy, had replaced the brilliant but arrogant Horatio Lay with the unassuming Hart, the Irishman had become trusted by the Chinese to represent their interests and was reputed among the British as the most reliable contact for anyone wishing to deal with China.

In 1854, during the Taiping rebellion, a triad-related group, the Small Swords, had seized control of the Chinese city of Shanghai, next to the International Settlement, and driven out the Chinese customs collectors. Worried that a failure to collect taxes might lead to a breakdown of the treaty system created after the first Anglo-Chinese war in the 1840s, diplomats appointed foreign customs inspectors to collect taxes as a temporary measure. This worked well and the Shanghai system was later extended.

Though the Tsungli administrative service headed the service, it appointed a Briton as Inspector General and gave him sole responsibility over his staff. Although the ultimate goal was to have the Chinese running the service, it started by necessity with a layer of foreign experts supervising and training Chinese staff who, it was well known, were prone to corruption as well as bullying by foreign merchants.

Hart, in order to improve efficiency and weed out corruption, made it a priority to personally vet every new staffer, westerner or Chinese. The seriousness with which he undertook this task was described by a later Inspector General, Lester Knox Little: "Hart's control of the customs staff was complete and autocratic. He was the only man in the service recognised by the Chinese government and, as such, was alone responsible to his employers for its operations. He hired, promoted, transferred, rewarded, punished, and discharged the staff of the Customs – foreign and Chinese."

At the Chefoo meeting, Hart had been brought in by the Chinese to advise their representative, Li Hung-chang. It was a delicate situation as his role put him in conflict with trade minister Wade, who had been personally involved in the Margary Affair. But Hart's calming influence helped find a peaceful solution, including opening up inland treaty ports on the upper Yangtze where Frank Newman would start his career.

As well as being busy with the hotel, the Newmans continued to expand their family. A month after their second daughter was born on February 27, 1874, Edward, probably accompanied by Mary Ann, walked up Consulate Hill to register Ellen Eliza Maude with the British consulate. Edward signed the registry together with William Cooper in the absence of his boss, William Lay. Cooper would tell people that Lay had been drinking heavily since being promoted to consul in Chefoo from Tientsin, where he had been vice-consul during the 1870 massacre and had taken charge after the French consul was killed. Lay and his wife had remained at the consulate while a Chinese crowd rioted and went on a killing spree. Afterwards, Lay's job included examining the bodies of the nuns who had been raped and mutilated. Lay's wife was sent home a nervous wreck while Lay was transferred to Chefoo. Within 30 months, however, Lay would be dead at the age of 40, leaving a widow and seven children.

"Chinese Cooper" – who became the interpreter after Margary – had also faced danger. He was stationed in Swatow in 1867 when armed men carrying flaming torches forced their way into his house at night. With his wife recovering from childbirth, Cooper fired at the intruders from his bedroom door, hitting two men and causing others to flee. Cooper's wife was sent home on medical advice.

Although such experiences reflected resentment against foreigners, Chefoo's lack of roads helped to insulate it from outside disturbances. Even so, the Newmans probably hired security guards and Edward might have slept with a gun under his pillow.

On October 4, 1875, Mary Ann delivered her second son who was registered as George James Thomas – again, Ted chose not to use his father's name. Two years later, in her 42nd year, Mary Ann gave birth to her third girl, Amy Dorothy Edith, on August 31, 1877, but the infant died a few months later.

At the consulate, the Newmans befriended Ary van Ess, the Dutch-born constable who, two decades later, would be a witness at Ellen's wedding. Van Ess would also investigate the mysterious death of a customs official found drowned and stripped of his valuables half a mile east of the Family Hotel.

Although vaunted for its health benefits, some considered Chefoo boring. Visitors complained in the newspaper that, apart from picnics, sea-bathing and a lawn tennis club, there was little to do. One complainant missed the "hucksters on European beaches." He thought the Chinese showed little initiative for making money as there were "no pretty sailing boats with gaudy flags, no woman offers chairs on the sand for cash, no girls with flowers, no ponies."

One writer even considered Chefoo claustrophobic, bemoaning that the range of craggy hills, "with its polypus arms, enfolds us till for want of roads we lament, 'I can't get out.'" Another critic was blunter: Chefoo "has a coast outline, excellent bathing, three hotels and nothing more."

While Mary Ann was in her element, one wonders how well Ted adapted to his new circumstances. He must have been proud of being a hotel proprietor, even if people knew his wife was the driving force. Like most British men in China, he may have been fond of alcohol and, surrounded by demanding and entitled guests, he may have missed his friends and adventures.

The Newmans would soon have met all of Chefoo's community through church services at St Andrew's, the horse races and regattas and cricket matches. Edward would surely have been a member of the Chefoo Club, but may have been self-conscious about his Rookery background.

One of their acquaintances was William Fuller, their neighbour between the hotel and the settlement. A versatile American, Fuller went to China as a missionary before turning to more secular activities. He was a storekeeper when the Newmans arrived and became a rival when taking over the Seaview Hotel. He was also an architect, building the lighthouse on Consular Hill and remodelling St Andrew's Church on the beach.

One resourceful missionary from whom the Newmans may have bought fruit was the American Protestant John Livingstone Nevius. After arriving in China in 1854, Nevius and his wife Helen travelled widely, setting up missions and schools and dispensing medicine in cholera epidemics before moving to Chefoo in 1871. By the following year, Nevius was introducing Western fruit such as apples and pears, laying the seeds for today's flourishing industry. Nevius also played a pivotal role in raising funds for the famines that afflicted Shantung Province in 1877 and 1889, the records of donors in 1889 showing a contribution of $5 from Mrs Newman.

Though it is not known whether Mary Ann or Ted were particularly religious, the unexpected arrival of one missionary was to affect their lives considerably. In 1879, James Hudson Taylor, founder of the London-based China Inland Mission, had fallen seriously ill on a voyage to China and was recuperating in Chefoo. He was walking along the beach near the Family Hotel with a fellow missionary, Charles Judd, when a farmer approached and asked if they wished to buy his bean field.

This encounter led to Taylor establishing the Protestant Collegiate School next to the hotel. The school would later be called Chefoo School and, after adding several imposing buildings in the mid-1890s, would be regarded as the finest school east of Suez, boasting alumni such as *Time* magazine publisher Henry Luce and writer Thornton Wilder. One writer said, "Echoing Eton, the buildings overlooked a river used for rowing competitions."

The Inland Mission's first building was a sanatorium on the other side of San Lane from the Family Hotel. Part of the hospital was used as a preparatory school, which opened in 1880 with three of Judd's sons as its only pupils. In January 1881, they were joined by Frank Newman, eight, and his brother George, five. Later, the school added a girls' section and Annie and Ellen, nicknamed Nellie, would attend. The school, with its classics-based curriculum, was a big step up from the parish and national schools that had been available to their parents.

On the face of it, the school had policies that appeared out of sync with its goal of converting the Chinese. For instance, although it was training missionaries to evangelize in China, it forbade the use of Chinese in school because the teachers did not want pupils talking in a language they did not understand. Many of its pupils who had learned Chinese from their *amahs* began to forget it.

Moreover, although the school had a sizeable Chinese staff, it generally barred Chinese teachers and pupils in order to protect the European children from the "polluting" environment of a field mission and its "unholy" and "vicious" sights and sounds. Ironically, such protections did not prevent the death of an early headmaster, Herbert Norris, who tackled a stray dog that wandered into the school, was bitten, and contracted a fatal dose of rabies. Frank's schoolmates included the mixed-blood children of a teacher, George Parker, who had married a Chinese girl. Perplexing to some, this situation provoked a debate that led to the school shutting its doors to non-whites.

Although boarders experienced severe pangs of homesickness, the Newman kids, living next door, were spared this – and they kept their fluent Chinese.

In August 1883 Chefoo was abuzz with preparations for a VIP visitor – Sir Harry Parkes, the British Minister Plenipotentiary in Peking. With their vested interests, the Newmans followed political developments and few were closer to what was happening than Sir Harry.

The British Consul, Byron Brenan, organised a delegation of British notables to meet Sir Harry, who was due to arrive on the Royal Navy's HMS *Vigilant* on September 16.

Ted Newman would surely have wanted to be on this distinguished list, which included the Reverend Charles Scott, Bishop for North China, as well as Fergusson and Fuller.

It is not known if Ted made the list for, on August 13, as he rose to cope with the busy day ahead, he experienced a sharp pain in his chest, collapsed, and died.

The death notice appeared in the *North-China Herald*: "At Chefoo Family Hotel, on the morning of the 13th of August, of Apoplexy, Mr Edward Newman, to the great grief of his widow and family." He was only 51. His gravestone in the settlers' cemetery on Temple Hill stated, without effusion: "In memory of Edward Newman of the Family Hotel who departed this life on August 13th 1883. Thy will be done."

Mary Ann apparently did not consider selling out and returning to England with her young children. Her father had left her nothing when he died in 1876 and the farm in Malvern Link was being run by the local farmer whom her younger sister Ellen had married under pressure from her ailing father.

Besides, her children were receiving a first-rate education on their doorstep. At 48, Mary Ann chose instead to bring out her first-born, Edwin, from England to help run the hotel. Edwin had apparently not had a happy childhood – a newspaper reported he had run away from boarding school at 14 – and he accepted the offer.

He was 17 when he arrived in Chefoo, a bright and self-reliant youth, and his name duly appeared in the local directory as manager of the Family Hotel. Although he would stay for half a dozen years, Edwin seems to have wanted more than tiny Chefoo could offer. Considering he would choose to be an architect, it is possible he was influenced by the Newmans' architect neighbour, Fuller.

Edwin had also kept in touch with his cousin, Elizabeth, daughter of Mary Ann's sister Jane, who had been orphaned (as had he, in effect). In 1890, Edwin left Chefoo for Canada via Hong Kong. A clipping from the *Vancouver Daily World* shows Edwin left Hong Kong on the ship *Abyssinia* on April 6 and arrived at Vancouver on May 21, in the company of the Duke of Connaught and his wife and "114 Chinese and 10 Japanese in steerage."

The departure of Edwin, whom she had left behind as a baby, must have been a blow to the over-worked Mary Ann, but it was not the only one. Her son Frank showed little interest in the hotel beyond helping out now and again and, by 1889, he was working with Fergusson the trader.

His outlook may have been expanded by Fergusson, a resourceful man who was pushing for a railway from Chefoo to Jinan, capital of Shantung – a project, however, that was welcomed by neither the British legation nor the Qing.

Meanwhile, the Family Hotel had become an institution on the China Coast. A missionary journal in 1891 advised readers to book in advance at "the Family Hotel kept by Mrs Newman" as demand for rooms was high.

Her parents had lived to a good age and, in her healthy location by the sea, Mary Ann, now an established businesswoman, would have wanted to live long enough to see her daughters married to men of social standing and her son become a merchant prince.

But the strain of running the hotel took its toll. On August 24, 1891 – at the height of the season – she succumbed to heart failure.

The *North-China Herald* reported her demise alongside a report that Chefoo's hotel keepers were complaining it had been a bad season and was likely to remain so if the steamers maintained their "prohibitive rates" for foreign passengers.

Without its matriarch, what would happen to the Family Hotel – and the children? In November 1891, the hotel was put up for sale. It seems that neither Annie, 21, nor Frank, wanted to take the helm.

One of the sale notices offers a possible clue as to why the Newman children wished to be rid of their legacy. It referred to the property as a "sanatorium," suggesting it had become more like the China Inland Mission hospital across the lane.

However, there were complications on the sale. Mary Ann had divided the estate equally among her five children and, as three were minors, they required trustees to act on their behalf, which delayed matters.

In the meantime, Chefoo's social scene was livening up, with a group of young men establishing the Savage Club, which staged musical and theatrical events that allowed the young of both sexes to come together.

In its well-attended first theatrical performance on February 19, 1892, a young Irishman named James Glassey, "in the garb of old Erin, sang 'Mister Malcahy, Esquire' in a rich and genuine brogue," reported the *North-China Herald*. Son of a ship's master, Glassey had joined the Chefoo customs as an entry-level Watcher months earlier in June, 1891.

A few days later, on February 27, Glassey sang, "A Trueborn Irishman," and also "cleverly acted," according to a reviewer, "the part of an Irish apothecary's assistant in the one-act farce, My Turn Next." In the same production, Miss N. Newman – this would have been Nellie – played "Marche des Troubadours" on the piano and sang "Let Me Hear Thy Voice Again," according to the Chefoo correspondent, who included the whole programme in his write-up.

Glassey's more senior colleague, Duncan Clark, who had joined the Customs in 1890, was making the acquaintance of Nellie's sister Annie, who was having difficulty coping at the hotel after her mother's death.

Annie had been well educated next door while the rough and worldly Clark had started working in the Glasgow docks from age 12 following the early death of his father. Despite their differences in age and background, Annie married Duncan on April 6, 1893 – 17 months after her mother's demise – at St Andrew's Church by the beach, in a ceremony officiated by the Reverend M. Greenwood. She was 22 and her thin frame was dwarfed by the big and burly Duncan, who was 36. Her brothers and sister, plus James Glassey, attended the ceremony.

A few months later, Annie's younger brother George was, at 18, clearly impatient to leave because he sailed for Canada to visit Edwin. The *Daily Colonist* reported that the steamer *Mogul*, after a rough voyage in the north Pacific, "arrived in Vancouver in mid-November with two saloon passengers, including Mr Newman who is joining his brother in New Westminster."

On July 20, 1893, Chefoo experienced a thunderstorm of "unusual violence (which) did considerable damage to the crops, and caused the death of one native woman," according to the *North-China Herald*. Its report continued, "The Family Hotel had a providential escape from a serious accident. It was about half-past five o'clock that the storm broke out, and the guests at the hotel were for the most part in their bedrooms, when a succession of appalling thunderclaps caused consternation among the ladies and their children whose alarm was greatly increased when a louder clap of thunder shook the house and the lightning at the same time seemed to envelop the building."

It seemed like an omen.

On June 1, 1894, the *North-China Herald* reported that the Family Hotel had been sold off to a syndicate of Chefoo and Shanghai residents who were anxious to keep the hotel going. "The price of 19,300 taels," the newspaper noted, "does not seem excessive from a commercial point of view as, even during the worst of its vicissitudes, it seems it has more than paid its expenses."

Three days later, on June 4, 1894, Nellie Newman, aged 20, tied the knot with James Arthur MacFarlane Glassey, 26, at St Andrew's. Soon afterwards, the Glasseys left for Swatow where James would take up a promotion to third-class tidewaiter (customs officer).

Thus, less than three years after her death, Mary Ann's legacy was sold off, her daughters were married, and two of her children had left Chefoo.

Mary Ann was interred next to Ted on Temple Hill. A photograph shows Frank, in a three-piece suit and a flower in his buttonhole, leaning on her imposing grave, which was topped by an ornamental urn. Inscribed on her tomb is a verse from Isaiah 33:17: "Thine Eyes Shall See the King in his Beauty; They shall behold the land that is very far off."

Mary Ann had followed her lodestar, but it had turned into a trap from which her children sought to escape. Curiously, Frank never mentioned his life in Chefoo to any of his children and the reason for this glaring omission – whether the memories were too painful or too happy – remains a mystery.

Frank stands by the graves of his parents Edward and Mary Ann Newman
in Chefoo. Courtesy of Duncan Clark family

4

From Smuggler Chaser to Postmaster

After a mission school education and two years with Fergusson – his mother may have wanted him to become a merchant prince – Frank Newman joined the Imperial Maritime Customs in Chefoo as a Watcher, the lowest rung on the ladder, in mid-1892.

He was 19 years old and would spend the next 35 years in service to the Chinese government, first with the Customs and then with its offshoot, the China Post Office.

There is little question that Frank's appointment and subsequent transfers and promotions within the Customs and later to the China Post Office would not have happened without the scrutiny and approval of Robert Hart.

The Inspector General's style of management was highly personal. As Ex-Commissioner Paul King wrote, in a 1924 pen portrait: "Hart is not a polished man of the world: 'favorita succeeded favorita' at his court (without scandal, though), he was a small, slender, iron clad autocrat, held grudges, and treated his British employees well or badly just as he pleased."

Hart had strong connections with Chefoo. It was a ferry ride from Peking and he had at his disposal a bungalow on the Commissioner's property, where his wife Hester spent summers in the late 1870s.

He would have known that Frank possessed assets that he prized but found elusive among his officers – a mother-tongue fluency in Chinese and an ability to get along with the locals.

Hart might have been perplexed as to where to place Frank. The foreign staff were sharply divided between "indoor men," an elite corps of administrators recruited from minor public schools in England through

Hart's London office, and the "outdoor men," who carried out the hard labour of inspecting cargoes and combating smuggling and were drawn mostly from the working-class sailors and adventurers who turned up on the China Coast. The indoor men disdained their outdoor colleagues and the groups did not mix socially.

In Hart's eyes, Frank would have been disqualified from an indoor position as he was not from a public school in England and, importantly, had question marks hanging over his family. Hart placed a premium on heredity, commenting on one Belgian candidate for an indoor position, "Like all men who make their way up from nothing he is, of course, without that foundation of character which heredity really gives: the responsibilities of position through three or four generations and the amenities of respectable life give form and solidity to the nebulae with which 'the first of his name' cannot help starting," he surmised. "It is a mistake to help them up too high."

Frank's mother owned one of the town's highest-profile businesses and Frank had been educated at one of the best schools east of Suez. It was somewhat bizarre that Frank would not have been accepted into the Customs' indoor club, let alone the Chefoo Club, but some might have regarded Frank, raised entirely in Chefoo, as "not quite pukka," as he had not been shaped by the ethos of empire-building or the inbuilt sense of British superiority.

When Frank was hired, the Commissioner of Customs in Chefoo was Jim Carrall, whom Hart described in his diary as "a prim, selfish, thick-headed prig," but whom he nonetheless appointed Acting Commissioner in 1890 because Carrall's wife Emma was a close friend.

Sporting prowess was highly valued among the British and it is possible Frank's skill as an oarsman eased his entry into Customs. Within weeks of joining, he created a sensation at Chefoo's autumn regatta, a highlight of the sporting and social calendar.

On September 7, 1892, after days of continual rain, the weather cleared for the big day, reported the *North-China Herald*, which covered the event extensively.

Visiting ships were anchored in the bay, including the custom ship, RC *Lingfeng,* gaily decorated with flags, on which its "genial" Captain Thomson and his officers welcomed guests while a band from the HGS *Leipzig* played and crew served cakes and refreshments.

Spectators milled at the Family Hotel, which was handily located in front of the starting point for the races.

The Customs teams were favoured as their outdoor men rowed as part of their duties in inspecting merchant ships for contraband.

Soon after the races got under way after 2pm, its Chinese six-man team broke one of its oars and had to abandon the two-mile race.

But the Customs' honour was upheld when its European team, including Frank, won the half-mile contest for the Merchant Steamers' prize in their boat *Omnibus.* In an astonishing display of strength and stamina, Frank went on to win three more races, two of them over half a mile, in his dinghy, *Agnes.* The *Herald's* correspondent made special mention that the *Agnes* was an "exceptionally well-built little boat," built to Newman's design.

A photograph of the *Omnibus* crew shows the men standing against a wall mounted with their long paddles. With arms folded across their chests, they are wearing caps, vests and long white pants. Fair-haired Frank has a slim build but disproportionately bulging biceps.

His fellow oarsmen include James Glassey, a 24-year-old Irishman, with a slight smile over a moustache, and Duncan Clark, 35, a burly Scot with a dour expression and a thick, drooping moustache. Both would soon become Frank's brothers-in-law.

Two months later, Clark and Glassey were in the Customs crew that rowed out to rescue people from the barque *Stanfield* in a gale that had wrecked the American barque *Escort* seventy miles west of Chefoo. A newspaper reported that "the kind and helpful services of Customs Commissioner Carrall and his officers in preventing loss of life on the *Stanfield* have already been reported to Her Majesty's government" and, as a result, Clark, Glassey and the rest of the crew were awarded Gold Medals by the British government's Foreign Office.

Chefoo's Imperial Maritime Customs rowing team in 1892: Frank Newman (far left), James Glassey next to him, and Duncan Clark far right. Photo courtesy of Duncan Clark

Frank's work in clamping down on smuggling had its exciting moments, too. In one incident, recounted by Duncan Clark's grandson, a Customs crew chased a Chinese gang across Chefoo Bay. "The Chinese threw overboard a rope with sealed tins attached to it. The Customs crew stopped their pursuit to examine the suspected contraband and the smugglers got away. They took the cans ashore and found they were filled with human excreta. The Chinese had a sense of humour."

In July 1894 war broke out between China and Japan over Korea, which was under Chinese control but had coal and iron resources coveted by the Japanese. Since the Meiji Restoration, Japan had undergone rapid industrialization and, though many expected China to win with its greater numbers, Japan's superior military technology carried it to victory after victory, ending with landing in the Chinese port of Weihaiwei, only a few miles east of Chefoo. As well as agreeing to cede more territory, China agreed to pay war reparations in the Treaty of Shimonoseki, signed in April 1895, which included an exchange of agreements at Chefoo's Beach Hotel.

Despite the war, the Chefoo races took place as scheduled a few weeks later. The three-day meeting in September drew gentlemen jockeys and spectators from other ports. "The Taotai [a high provincial officer] and suite and almost the whole community were present," reported the *North-China Herald.* A band from an American flagship played music as the sun shone on Bluejackets and Chinese soldiers in "quaint uniforms" and the ladies in "magnificent" costumes.

The Customs Commissioner was now Matthew Boyd Bredon, Hart's son-in-law, whom he had installed after Carrall fell seriously ill in March 1893. Bredon was a race steward as well as owning several horses at the meeting.

"The genial Commissioner," said the *Herald,* "after winning (the Taotai's Cup) with Bismarck, donned a tall white hat, upon which he received the cordial congratulations of his friends."

Frank Newman, now 24, was also competing, not only as a jockey, but as owner of a grey, Blossom. A photo of a moustachioed Frank holding the reins of a horse shows him attired as a gentleman jockey with buttoned jacket, white pants and dark shoes.

On the first day of the meeting, Blossom came second in the Russian Navy Cup, beating the Bredon horse, Brian Boru, into third place. On day two, in the Consolation Cup, the same horses and jockeys raced over the same distance but this time Brian Boru was first past the post, beating Blossom into second place.

Any rivalry was dropped in one race, however, when Frank rode Bredon's horse Buffalo Bill in the Consular Cup, though they finished out of the top three. Blossom was a hard-working horse, garnering three second places and one third under jockey J. Pike, whereas Bredon's stable captured eight first places, two seconds and three thirds.

It must have appeared incongruous for some to see an outdoor man competing against the Commissioner, but some already suspected that Frank was destined for higher things.

A letter from Robert Hart penned to his confidant and London Commissioner, James Duncan Campbell, on May 26, 1896, contains an intriguing mention of Newman. Hart wrote, "I am sorry for Smith's health and Simpson's failure. Would the second Simpson pass I wonder? I wonder de B. gave you a non-English speaking man. No room for Mr Newman."

Gentleman jockey Frank Newman raced against his boss. Photo courtesy of Duncan Clark

Only two Newmans were listed in the service, Frank and his brother George in Shanghai. Whether or not this was a reference to Frank, Hart did find room for him a few months later when he promoted Frank to third-class tidewaiter, effective September 1, 1896, and, more importantly, transferred him to Hankow.

It was a big move as Frank had to ferry down to Shanghai before boarding an American steamer for the weeks-long, 500-mile journey up the Yangtze River deep into central China.

It was a cultural shift, too, for he was entering western China, where he would spend the next decade. Over a millennium, the Hui people, descendants of Persians, Arabs and Mongols, had migrated along the Silk Road and intermarried with Han Chinese.

Hankow was the furthest Yangtze port reachable by ocean-going vessels and the commercial gateway to nine central provinces. Frank found the city was recovering quickly from the Taiping rebellion that had halved its population and reduced it to rubble. It had 300 foreign residents – though many were tea traders from Shanghai who came only for the season – and its bund of imposing buildings and willow trees stretched for half a mile. The posting gave Frank his first significant exposure to Russians, major traders in this tea-growing terrain not far from their homeland.

Following its victory over China, Japan was pressing for a concession in Chungking, which prompted demands from other treaty powers. The Germans signed for a Hankow concession in October 1895, followed by the Russians and the French the following year. With foreign trade growing apace, Frank had his work cut out for him.

China's defeat had another consequence that would affect young Frank. Hart had pressed the Chinese for years to open a national postal service and now found the Qing government more receptive, especially as a means to raise revenue and pay off the Japanese indemnity. Various postal systems were in existence – the Customs had its own courier service, foreign post offices dispatched mail from the treaty ports, and the Chinese government had a horse post system for official mail, but the system Hart proposed would be the first for the general public.

As Hart's plans to set up the China Post Office neared fruition, Frank was transferred in 1897 to Chungking and promoted to first-class tidewaiter. This involved another logistically daunting move as Chungking was a further 600 miles up the Yangtze – and no steamer had yet navigated the treacherous upper reaches, which were too shallow in winter to protect against hidden rocks and overly fast in summer with the snowmelt from the Himalayas.

Proceeding upriver after Ichang, Frank stood on deck to watch the muddy brown river squeeze between towering, narrow gorges and turn into boiling rapids and whirlpools. On some stretches where the junk could not proceed on its own, long chains of near-naked, chanting trackers pulled it from the riverbank.

After an exhausting months-long journey, Frank reached the end-of-the-line in the treaty port network and gazed up at a mountain city, perched atop a rocky peninsula. On disembarking, he was carried up long flights of steep, slippery steps, jostling with other sedan-chair bearers, only inches from a precipitous fall onto the rocks below. With crenellated walls hemming in 300,000 people, Chungking looked down upon the Yangtze and Kai-ling rivers swirling at its base.

Visitors complained of hot, damp summers and raw, chilly winters. Thick fog enveloped its craggy hills from November to March. The fattest creatures were the rats that fed off the sewage left in crude ditches until rain washed it away.

Chungking was the hub for Sichuan, a prosperous and self-contained region of dizzying cliffs and fertile valleys. Frank arrived to find only a handful of foreign diplomats and merchants, with most agencies being represented by Chinese.

He would have met Archibald Little, the British merchant who had come to China in 1859 as a tea taster, had set up a trading company, and was determined to build the first steamship capable of navigating the upper Yangtze.

Chungking had become a treaty port in 1890 but when Little arrived at Ichang with a steamer the year before, the Chinese threw up objections, such as claiming that monkeys would roll down boulders onto the decks or that navigation would displease the deities which had placed rocks in the river.

Despite this, Little designed and financed the *Leechuen*, a twin-screw steamer of nine tonnes which, though it had to be pulled along some of the rapids, arrived at Chungking on March 8, 1898, to a reception by the Taotai, salutes from Chinese gunboats and firecracker explosions.

That year, Frank was among 24 foreigners who were detached, along with 357 Chinese, from Customs to serve in the new Postal Department. The new service was under the auspices of Customs and officers were supposed to do double duty for a while, much to their resentment.

Frank took up his new position as assistant postal worker officially from January 1, 1899, shortly before his 26th birthday. Despite his title, he oversaw the new office and had two assistant Chinese clerks, Sieli Kavoli Chieu and Yu Shun-foo. The Post Office had a similar structure to the Customs so, in just over six years, Frank had moved from the bottom to a rank equal to an indoor man, with the attendant social status and pay.

Having lobbied for the Post Office for so long, Hart wanted to introduce the system quietly and develop it slowly as he did not want to overburden the Customs, wanted to learn as he went, and did not want to overspend. Moreover, he knew the French wanted to control the Post Office and the Tsungli administrative office agreed to this in 1898.

In the early years, the Imperial Post Office focused on establishing accounting procedures, setting postal rates, and recruiting and training Chinese staff. Crucially, it sought to forge an identity as a postal service for the Chinese, no easy task when locals saw white faces and questioned whether this was a state-run institution for their benefit or another scheme instigated by foreigners.

It was soon clear that the Post Office needed many more Chinese and it would also help allay suspicion to liaise with schools for recruitment and to appoint senior Chinese as inspecting clerks, the eyes and ears of the postmaster in each district. Their job was to visit and inspect branches and agencies and box offices (outlets that only sold stamps and received letters but not parcels).

Frank was now "a big shot." In reporting on the inauguration of an 80-bed London Mission hospital on December 23, 1899, the *North-China Herald* referred to "Postmaster Newman" as one of the dignitaries in a group that included senior Chinese officials, foreign consuls and the acting Customs commissioner.

But even as Frank attended the opening ceremony in a room bedecked with yellow silk ribbons, he knew an anti-Christian movement was under way that would make life much more difficult for foreigners.

In Frank's home province of Shantung, where Germany had staked claim to Tsingtao and the surrounding area as reparation for the murder of two German missionaries, Chinese groups were torching churches and killing Chinese Christians. After years of increasing foreign demands and extortion of privileges, this escalation sparked the Boxer Rebellion, which would spread rapidly to other parts of the country. The upheaval, which drew millions of supporters, would also deal a heavy blow to the burgeoning Post Office in the north, with the destruction of offices and facilities along the railway line between Peking and Shanxi Province.

Of pressing concern, however, was the threat to the personal safety of Hart who was in the Peking Legation when, in June, some 20,000 Boxers, who practised martial arts and believed they possessed magical powers making them impervious to bullets, assembled outside, calling for the annihilation of the foreigners.

German soldiers under Minister Clemens August Baron von Ketteler captured a Boxer boy in the legation and executed him. This caused thousands of Boxers to burst into the walled city, burning Christian churches, sometimes with victims inside. British and German soldiers shot and killed several Boxers, further stoking up the Chinese and pushing the Qing government towards supporting the Boxers.

On June 20, the Boxers killed Baron von Ketteler as he was on his way to negotiate with them. This triggered a siege of the legation – where 1,300 foreigners were in a compound fortified by a small garrison – that lasted 55 days and included an onslaught on residences. Hart saw his house torched and his papers destroyed. His death was announced in *The Times* on July 17 – and was not retracted until nearly three weeks later.

Around this time, an historic event took place in Chungking. Archibald Little had built a commercial steamer, the *Pioneer*, that could carry 50 tonnes of cargo as well as passengers and he had found a partner in Captain Cornell Plant, an experienced navigator. When Plant steamed into Chungking on the *Pioneer* that June, the entire foreign community was there to greet him and the commercial lifeline he had brought.

But soon afterwards, the *Pioneer*, under instruction of British consul Michie Fraser, was commandeered by the Royal Navy to evacuate the foreign community because of the perceived threat of a Boxer invasion. The British population of Sichuan was transported downriver for three weeks. In the event, no threat arrived. The consul was criticized for "running away," but he was not penalized for playing it safe.

Though the Boxer rebels did not reach Chungking, the siege in Peking had a direct impact on Frank.

A French Customs official, Théophile Piry, had stayed in the British legation with his wife and children throughout the siege and became close to Hart. After the siege was lifted, Piry took special leave and, upon his return in October 1901, Hart put him in charge of the postal service. Piry would take over an infant service closely dependent on the Customs and turn it into an independent and modern organisation. Frank's future, especially when he broke the rules to marry a Chinese girl, would depend very much on Piry.

5

A 'Scandalous' Marriage

Most of the early foreigners who joined the Post Office quit or were removed within a few years. Loneliness and mental exhaustion caused health problems, and many did not like the long hours, frequent transfers to isolated places and the rules prohibiting marriage for five years. Others were transferred or fired for marrying local women or having a problem with alcohol.

"Essential to their occupational survival was the ability to adapt to China, master classical and spoken Chinese, and function within the British-style civil service system where individual initiative was often met with suspicion or outright hostility," wrote Lane Harris in his thesis on the China Post Office.

Frank was temperate and hard-working, but he had an independent streak and would shock the British community by blatantly ignoring some of its firmly held social conventions.

In Chungking's tiny foreign community, Frank may have befriended Archibald Little and his wife Alicia not only because they were a mine of local information, but because they shared curiosity about their surroundings. An author and social activist from Madeira, Alicia had come to China in 1887, despised foreigners who did not bother to learn Chinese, and was campaigning for social reforms including a ban on foot-binding, a subject that would interest Frank personally. Alicia liked to travel and take photographs and, though she was welcomed in some homes, she was pelted with earth at others, reflecting the deep suspicion in which white faces were held.

A Chinese paper reports that Frank was also involved in setting up a match company in Chungking in 1899. Since the Qing government held a monopoly on the manufacturing and selling of matches, they might have been making use of Frank, as a government representative, to promote investments in one of their ventures.

When Théophile Piry took over the postal service in 1901, he began a process of rapid development, slashing postage rates to attract business and quickly expanding the number of offices to extend the postal network. Considered, even by his critics, as a clever and capable expert who could solve the most complex postal questions, within three years Piry expanded the Post Office to 1,319 establishments, handling 66 million articles over a network of 33,000 miles.

Frank Newman was part of this expansion drive and in 1901 was tasked with opening an office in Chengtu, a further 270 miles upriver. It was so remote that a poet observed that getting to heaven was easier.

Surrounded by a rich plain, Chengtu was an ancient imperial capital to which the Empress Dowager had fled in 1900 when matters became too troublesome in Peking. It was well preserved with three sets of walls but, despite its beauty, there was little incentive for a foreigner to live there.

The river journey was dangerous. The British consul Alex Hosie, one of the first men Frank would have met, had been shipwrecked on the way to Chengtu, losing most of his effects. The nakedness of the river crews made it disagreeable for European women. Moreover, Chengtu, despite lying beside the shallow Min River, which joined the Yangtze 150 miles downstream, was not a treaty port so there were no customs staff to boost the foreign presence.

Hosie, who was there because the British and French were interested in the region bordering Yunnan and British India as a passageway to the north, complained that Chengtu was depressing, lonely, and his accommodation unsuitable. He had left his wife in England, as did several of his successors.

According to Chinese sources, "the postal branch office in Chengtu was first established in 1901, led by British man Frank Newman as the first bureau chief, located at a small room house in the north street of

Shuwa." It opened with three Chinese personnel: Yang Shao Quan, Newman's assistant; Zhu Pu Sheng, who handled mail and packages at the window; and Zeng Fu as mailman.

After being promoted to inspector from district officer, Frank left Chungking with a glowing tribute in a letter signed by 36 members of the foreign community and published in the *North-China Herald,* saying of him that "no community in China could have been better served by a more obliging or painstaking officer."

To advertise their services in Chengtu, Yang and others stood outside the office, banging gongs and shouting slogans. They soon ran into trouble and, following complaints, the Governor of Sichuan, Chao Erh-sun (Zhao Erxun), ordered the new office closed.

It turned out to be a misunderstanding. The sound and tone for "posts" and "oil" were identical, so the public thought they were selling vegetable oil and suppliers complained. "One local oil company thought that the postal office was monopolizing the vegetable oil industry. The Governor sent men to close down the office after three days, and staff members were forced to move to a hotel," said the Chinese report.

Frank went to call on Governor Zhao to resolve the issue. "Zhao saw Newman, a foreigner, coming in a big carriage to talk to him. Zhao dared not to neglect him, plus he feared it would stir up diplomatic issues, so he immediately commanded that the postal office be re-opened," concluded the report.

Clearly, Piry believed that Frank had diplomatic skills for he was sending him to a city with a recent history of anti-foreigner violence. In 1895, rioters had burned and looted missionary buildings in and around the city. Missionaries took refuge in the magistrate's administrative office and were put on trial for drugging and murdering Chinese children to use their eyes, hearts and other body parts for medicine. They were acquitted, but the evangelists, including a group from the China Inland Mission, remained unpopular.

While some foreigners became alcoholics or went mad in remote outposts, Frank found happiness in Chengtu.

A studio photo of Frank Newman

Likely through work, Frank befriended a prosperous merchant named Liu and visited his home where he met his family. After a while, Liu was not the only reason for Frank's visits. He met Liu's daughter, a sweet and lively girl whom he found enchanting. Like many girls from the privileged class, she also had bound feet, a status symbol.

Frank courted her for a year, indicating a traditional process. He might have used a matchmaker and could have written formal letters to the bride's parents to request betrothal and marriage. There would have been an exchange of gifts.

Frank knew full well the price he would pay in terms of his career if he married the girl, whom he called Mei-lan after his mother. The British believed their authority was derived from their whiteness and, while they might tolerate their countrymen enjoying informal, discreet relationships with local girls, marrying one would make Frank an outcast and cause him to be fired or ruin his chances of advancement. Some Chinese, too, would have been horrified at such a union, believing that miscegenation might produce deformed children.

The wedding took place in 1903 when the bride was 16 and Frank was 30. It was an unusual, hybrid occasion, a Qing ritual in a church. Mei-lan was carried in a sedan chair and arrived late. She wore a ceremonial Mandarin gold and black jacket, intricately embroidered – which now hangs framed in the author's home – along with a red (for luck) pleated skirt. Frank was

*Mei-lan's gold-threaded
wedding jacket*

dressed in a dark suit and a starched shirt with a butterfly collar. A tea ceremony followed at Frank's home.

Frank's wife was inscribed into his brother George's family Bible as "Manchu Princess," indicating a high status. A cousin said that Frank began dressing much better after his marriage and wore an air of prosperity.

The couple would have engaged staff, including a cook, Dor-tze, who had a stooped back and was a wizard of the wok, capable of whipping up a full array of spicy Sichuanese dishes.

Despite their privilege, Frank and his wife lived in the sanitary conditions that prevailed in most of China. There was neither electricity nor an indoor toilet, and water had to be boiled to avoid endemic disease. Summer brought the threat of cholera.

Into this environment, the couple welcomed a baby daughter, Jessie, the following year. Jessie would resemble her father more than Mama, as Mei-lan would be known, and would receive a sound education in Shanghai and speak English as her mother tongue. Despite this, the British would relegate her to a low status as a Eurasian.

It is not known how Piry or Hart regarded Frank's marriage officially but the evidence suggests they might have been privately sympathetic. Piry had suffered from intense loneliness during a posting at Pakhoi (in Kwangtung province) before returning to France with a young bride, a cousin, with whom he started a large family. It is worth noting that, during his ample spare time at Pakhoi, Piry translated a Chinese novel as he knew that a command of the Chinese language and culture could enhance his career.

Hart had even more reason to be understanding. Early in his career, the Irishman had a long, affectionate – and clandestine – relationship with a Chinese woman, Ayaou, with whom he had three children. He sent her away only because of the damage it would do to his career if the relationship became known. At the age of 31 in 1866, he returned to Ireland on leave, met a lively 18-year-old-girl, Hester, proposed to her the day after, and was accepted. Although Hester returned to China with him, she later took their children back to Europe for their education and would separate from Hart for nearly 17 years.

Frank made no secret of his marriage. Lane Harris, a historian on the China Post Office, said, "From what I can tell, E.F.S. [Frank] was an extraordinarily liberal and generous man. He was bucking convention in China long before it was socially acceptable, but his open-mindedness may also have limited his career prospects. He spent the bulk of his career in the most undesirable locations (the Upper Yangzi ports, Guizhou, Shanxi, Shaanxi, Hunan) and never seems to have been appointed to any of the 'plums' in the service for very long."

This is true, but Frank had already worked in Chungking and Chengtu and, given that he became a published scholar and noted collector of Chinese antiquities, may well have regarded his job as an opportunity to explore the path less travelled. After all, he accepted such assignments without apparent complaint for the next 24 years.

Newman had the typically peripatetic career of a postal service pioneer, moving around so much that the Post Office staff directories, by necessity out of date by a few months, sometimes show him in more than one place in any given year.

Frank published an article on China's ancient coins in this 1927 issue of The China Journal of Science & Arts

Along with rapid expansion, Piry began re-organising districts and postal routes to meet Chinese needs, which meant setting up post offices in provincial capitals and dividing districts into subsections. A key part of this strategy was to make use of existing or planned railways, with many new branches placed in towns with railway and telegraph facilities.

A 1905 service directory shows Frank as a district inspector in Hsian (Xi'an), capital of Shensi Province, which means he could have been transferred from mountainous Sichuan to the parched plains of northern China a year earlier.

The starting point of the Silk Road network, which stretched westwards 4,000 miles to Turkish Anatolia, Xi'an had a large Muslim population. As the capital to 13 dynasties, Xi'an was also rich in historical relics, which suited Frank well. He acquired a rare coin – a *Guo bao jin kui zhi wan* (国宝金匮直万) from the Xin Dynasty – which local farmers had unearthed in 1901. Frank later sold the coin, which is now in the National Museum of China in Beijing.

Of Frank's work in Xi'an, the local correspondent of the *North-China Herald* wrote in 1905: "I ought long ago to have referred to the great improvements here during the last two years, and to the work done by Mr Newman who has, by much hard work, got the local system into good order. Among other improvements he has made, Mr Newman has moved the Post Office from a dark tumble-down building on a back street to a large new building, conveniently situated."

It was also in Xi'an that Frank did something else that the British community found unacceptable.

From his home, he could hear the screams of a young girl who was being beaten by a neighbour, a trader who had acquired her in the Gobi Desert. One day, Frank could stand the cries no longer and he approached the merchant, handed over a large sum of money and brought the girl home. He called her Dorothy and entered her in his travel document as his daughter. Dolly, as she was nicknamed, was thought to be of Russian origin.

Frank's next posting, soon afterwards, to Taiyuan, capital of neighbouring Shansi, was challenging. In a province impoverished by civil war, drought and famine, Taiyuan had also seen anti-Christian and anti-foreign feeling reach a peak on July 9, 1900, with the beheading of 44 foreigners – missionaries and their families – at the official residence of Governor Yuxian, a militant who had months earlier been moved from Shantung after foreign diplomatic pressure. By the end of the summer, more foreigners and up to 2,000 Chinese Christians met their deaths, some at the hands of mobs.

All this occurred while China was at war with the foreign powers. At the time of the missionaries' executions, a multinational expedition was heading towards the imperial capital and entered Peking on July 14, 1900. They ransacked the city before proceeding to Taiyuan, slaughtering many on the way. Yuxian was executed in 1901 as a reprisal.

Many post offices and facilities were destroyed and could not be rebuilt before the new governor, Cen Chunxuan, could offer protection. Before Frank went to Shansi, two senior Chinese clerks, brothers Deng

Weifan and Deng Weiping, went to Taiyuan, Dingzhou and Zhengding to investigate whether the new governor would take steps to ensure the safety of post office officials, to promote the new service over local alternatives, and to house its offices in local administrative buildings.

An important task in Shansi was to build the post office's Chinese identity; the influential Chinese newspaper *Shenbao* carried articles praising it as an important part of the central government's reforms.

Frank did his best to boost the Post Office among foreigners. The Taiyuan correspondent of the *North-China Herald* wrote in 1906, "Until recently, the work of the Imperial Post Office has been entirely carried out by Chinese clerks, but a definite advance has been made this year. The advent of the provincial superintendent, E.F.S. Newman, was a clear indication of the growing importance of the Shansi work, and the sure prospect of a complete organisation.

"Communication has now been established between most counties and the capital. The branches in the less important stations are naturally not in a high state of efficiency. However, with increase in mail matter, there will come the possibility of better staff. At present, the branch offices are worked by local tradespeople. Since Mr Newman's arrival, wooden boxes for receiving letters have been distributed over the city in most cases fixed onto walls in prominent places."

In January 1907, Frank was transferred 1,000 miles southwest to Kweichow, a region of mist-enshrouded karst mountains and scattered communities, many of them Hui and tribal minorities. Traditions were enduring and it took longer for Newman and his staff to convince locals to switch over from older postal systems.

Sometime the following year, around the time that Robert Hart left China, technically on leave but in fact for the last time, Frank also took home leave to England, possibly going overland via the trans-Siberian railway.

One problem was that, much as he might have wanted to, he could not take his wife or children, as Mei-lan's bound feet made it impossible for her to walk easily or very far.

In striving to turn the post office into an independent and modern organisation, Piry learned from postal services in other countries, especially France, and possibly he asked Frank to help in this respect during his long leave. There are few details of Frank's activities in England. Probably he visited family in Southampton where three of his paternal aunts, Ann, Eliza and Ellen, were running or living in boarding houses.

After the distances and vistas of China, he would have found Britain small – one and a half Englands, for example, could be squeezed into Shansi Province.

One event he attended, as a member of the prestigious Royal Geographical Society, was its meeting in London on May 11, 1908. It was chaired by Sir George Goldie, known for his explorations of the lower and middle Niger in Africa. It is not known if Frank wrote anything of his own experiences but in 1923 the *China Journal* featured a photo of a giant salamander with the caption: "The accompanying photograph, which was taken by Mr E.F.S. Newman of the Postal Service, is of an enormous specimen that was taken in Kweichow Province, in the Chin Ho, near Kwei-yang Fu. This specimen measured five feet, nine inches."

Frank knew that, while he was away, momentous changes were taking place in China with the steady drumbeat of uprisings and protests signalling the decline of the Qing Dynasty that had ruled since 1644.

It would have also been a sad personal journey as Frank mourned the tragic early loss of two close family members back home.

6

Rich Annie, Poor Nellie

Sisters Annie and Nellie Newman were born within three and a half years of each other, grew up in the same home by the sea, attended the same school next door, and married within 14 months of each other, both to outdoor customs officers who were colleagues.

That one sibling became wealthy while the other met severe financial difficulties reflects how life in China could offer unexpected opportunities while disease and death lurked around every corner.

Annie Newman had not been married long before she realized she had made a mistake. As a single young woman, she needed someone to lean on after her mother died and the canny, powerfully built Duncan Clark seemed like a man who could protect her.

Poker-faced Duncan was from a poor subsistence-farming family on the Scottish island of Islay and had made his way after losing his father at the age of five and serving a tough apprenticeship in the Glasgow shipyards from an early age. After sailing to China, he joined the Chefoo Customs as a tidewaiter in 1890 and, as a bachelor, sowed his wild oats in the Chinese quarter.

Annie gave birth to her first child in July 1894, but the boy died after two weeks. However, she became pregnant again a few months later and thereafter gave birth to six children at frequent intervals.

She was unhappily married and watched her siblings leave Chefoo one by one while she remained with her unpolished husband, who had little prospect of advancement.

Then an unforeseen opportunity presented itself.

During the 1894-95 Sino-Japanese war, Japan captured nearby Weihaiwei (Weihai) on the northeastern tip of the Shantung peninsula, directly across the Pechihli Gulf from Port Arthur. Between them, the ports controlled access by sea to Peking.

Japan succumbed to international pressure by withdrawing from Weihaiwei in 1898, whereupon the British pressed China into leasing the territory to them as a naval base because Russia had earlier leased Port Arthur to extend its railway network – which already traversed northern China – down the Liaotung peninsula.

As soon as they heard of British plans to establish a northern naval base, Annie and Duncan saw a once-in-a-lifetime opening. He knew about shipping and she had run a hotel, and they had some of her capital.

They trekked 60 miles along a rough military road to Weihaiwei, with Annie perched on a makeshift seat straddled between two donkeys while Duncan strode alongside. It was a genuine "gold rush."

The British raised the Union Jack on Liukungtao, an island in the middle of Weihaiwei's large natural harbour, on May 24, 1898. The Clarks arrived at Liukungtao to find that, as well as sharing the salubrious climate of Chefoo, their new home had other similar features such as a waterfront location and low, bare hills at the back.

The Clarks opened the island's first business as a general merchant firm providing food, water and coal for the Royal Navy's China Fleet which would move up from Hong Kong every summer from April to October. Other navies, from the United States, the Austro-Hungarian Empire and France, would also visit.

For Annie, it was the Family Hotel all over again. They pulled down some bungalows and built the Island Hotel, a grand establishment that opened in 1900. Many years later, a second floor would be added.

There can be little doubt that Annie, whose fluent Chinese was better than Duncan's and who had her mother's ease in handling locals, would have been crucial to the firm of D. Clark & Co. as it grew and widened its activities.

When bands of Boxers roamed around Shantung, torching churches and killing Chinese Christians, the Clarks would have been concerned lest the violence reach Weihaiwei.

By June 1900, 20,000 Boxers were outside Peking's legation quarter, calling for the extermination of foreigners and Chinese Christians.

At this point, another break appeared – and Duncan seized it.

The British, with their army engaged in the Boer War in Africa, had created the First Chinese Regiment in Weihaiwei in 1898, with 1,000 Shantung Chinese to quell any local uprising without bloodshed.

Now the Chinese regiment was mobilized – and it was the Clarks who chartered and provisioned a vessel to transport the troops northward.

Not only that, but Duncan accompanied the force, which arrived at Tientsin on June 24, 1900. Disappointingly, the regiment would not be used in the relief of Peking but was given tasks like tending to the wounded or clearing the dead. Nonetheless, the regiment lost two officers and 21 men, including nine who died in an accident while disposing of gunpowder seized from the Boxers.

Still, Duncan's initiative cemented his relationship with the military as well as the navy and, as Weihaiwei became a supply and hospital base, he scooped up more contracts.

In January 1902, the former Hong Kong Colonial Secretary James Stewart Lockhart took over as Commissioner of Weihaiwei, marking the change from military to civilian government. Some hoped Lockhart, a noted Chinese scholar as well as a respected administrator, would turn the town into a bustling Hong Kong.

As with Chefoo, however, such hopes soon proved unrealistic because of the largely dry and rocky hinterland and lack of roads. Again, as in Chefoo, this would not matter much to the Clarks for, with its British climate, Weihaiwei was already regarded as a health spa and holiday resort with football and cricket grounds, tennis courts, sailing, and a sandy beach for bathing.

Clark's firm was by now advertising itself as a manufacturer of aerated water, land agent, grower of foreign fruits and vegetables, supplier of bunker coal and freshwater to steamers, and provider of ferry launches. It also operated the British Post Office and, in 1903, added a silk factory to its enterprises.

In 1904, the Clarks established a free school for Chinese boys in English instruction which would also provide workers as they helped develop the town's tourism potential.

Annie's expertise would have been required in 1906 when, with the disbanding of the Chinese regiment, they converted the officers' quarters and regimental mess block into Clark's Mainland Hotel.

Their summers were hectic, but the Clarks were now prosperous and would winter in Scotland, where Duncan began buying properties, including a mansion on the island of Eriskay, though Annie disliked the place.

On one trip to Scotland in 1903, they hired a nanny, Catherine MacGregor, as Annie was pregnant and would give birth to her fourth child, also a Duncan, on September 16. Catherine was a schoolteacher around the same age as Annie.

Two years later, another battle on the geopolitical stage brought business for the Clarks.

Japan, which had contributed to the international force against the Boxers, was increasingly agitated over Russian encroachment in southern Manchuria, which now reached the Liaotung peninsula, too close for comfort to Korea, which Japan had annexed. In 1904, Japan attacked the Russian fleet without warning and, the following year, Russia sent its Baltic fleet halfway around the world to take on the Japanese navy in the Tsushima Strait, not far from Weihaiwei. In the battle of Tsushima on May 27-28 – which some rank as the most significant since Nelson's victory at Trafalgar – the Japanese scored a decisive victory, destroying two-thirds of the Russian fleet.

The defeat of a European power by an Asiatic nation shocked the world and changed the balance of power in East Asia. It also brought a large increase of trade to Weihaiwei as cattle, mules and provisions were in great demand by combatants.

In early 1906, Annie Newman, at 36, found herself pregnant for the seventh time in 12 years.

A few months later, Duncan received news of another pregnancy, that of their Scottish nanny, Catherine MacGregor.

This alarmed Duncan since, if news of an illegitimate child got out, it would upset his wife and could lead to the cancellation of lucrative contracts with the elite of Weihaiwei.

On October 26, 1906, Annie gave birth to a son, Alastair, on Liukungtao. It took Duncan a week to register the birth on November 3 and he may have been distracted for he failed to notice that his son's name was misspelt as Alaister in the Weihaiwei registry.

It was chilly and Annie, exhausted by the delivery and her numerous other demands, caught pneumonia. Despite being attended by the island's medical doctor, Dr H. Hickin, she failed to recover as she had done on previous occasions.

Three weeks later, on November 16, 1906, Annie died of broncho-pneumonia, aggravated by nephritis, a kidney infection. She left six children, the eldest being 11.

According to one cousin, Duncan would blame Alastair for his wife's death and would treat him so badly that the two would eventually go their separate ways.

Annie's death opened up the possibility that Duncan might marry Catherine MacGregor. But Duncan had a dilemma – he could hardly remarry so soon and, besides, people would calculate that Catherine's baby had been conceived many months before Annie's demise.

Thus, when Catherine delivered a son, Eric, on March 18, 1907, it was recorded on his birth registration that he was 'Illegitimate' and the space for his father's name was left blank. For the unmarried mother and her child, the stigma would hover over them for the rest of their lives.

Eric was born at Glenlyon House, Glenorchy, the home Catherine shared with her widowed mother, also called Catherine, who would not register her grandson's birth until two months later.

It is not known whether Annie knew of her husband's infidelity.

Catherine MacGregor left their son in Scotland, to be looked after by his grandmother, when she rejoined Duncan in China.

No doubt Catherine would pressure Duncan into making an honest woman of her, but remarrying so soon after Annie's death would cause tongues to wag and there was also the matter of how marrying the nanny would affect his children by Annie.

Duncan complicated matters further by getting Catherine pregnant again in Weihaiwei in early 1909.

Catherine would not have wished to have a second child out of wedlock, but Duncan evidently did not wish to marry her on Liukungtao, where he had a reputation to uphold.

Towards the end of 1909, Duncan took his family, plus nanny Catherine, to spend Christmas in Scotland. From Shanghai, they boarded the newly-launched Japanese mail ship, *Miyazaki Maru*, for the journey to London. They had first-class cabins.

On November 19, two weeks before reaching their destination, Catherine, now 40, began to feel contractions. By day's end, she had delivered a second son, Evan.

It is not known whether Duncan and Catherine tried to keep the drama from the children or whether they were successful. Had Catherine managed to conceal her pregnancy with a full but loose-fitting Victorian dress? Did Duncan arrange for Catherine and their newborn son to stay in their cabin until they docked on December 4?

Christmas came and went and, six weeks later, Duncan finally married Catherine, not in her home town of Dalmally, but in Glasgow, on February 2, 1910.

Though Catherine was now Mrs Clark, she left Evan behind with her mother as she accompanied Duncan back to China. Predictably, the marriage would cause friction between Duncan's first and second families, with the ex-nanny caught in the middle.

Eighteen months after their wedding, at the age of 42, Catherine delivered a third son, Ewan Roy Stewart, at Liukungtao on January 13, 1912. Though this would deepen the family divide, it did not stop Duncan from continuing to expand his business empire.

In time, he would acquire his third hotel, King's, on the mainland, giving him a monopoly on local hotels.

He became a pillar of the community, serving in Weihaiwei's municipal administration as well as holding positions in various clubs, before retiring to his palatial mansion on the isle of Eriskay where he died at 82.

Soon after Annie's death in 1906, her sister Nellie was going through testing times in Shanghai where her husband James Glassey was seriously ill.

Nellie had suffered a great deal since her wedding in Chefoo in 1894 when guests had tried to gloss over the fact that she was six months pregnant.

They were posted to Swatow (Shantou), where James was a third-class tidewaiter, in a coastal area with many bays, estuaries and islands where nefarious activities such as opium smuggling and the coolie trade could be carried out by Chinese and foreign merchants with minimal official interference. It was also close to the fiercely anti-foreigner mainland. Nonetheless, the Glasseys were part of the foreign community on Double Bay Island, where Nellie gave birth to a daughter, Eileen Margaret Ann, on September 17, 1894 and a son, Frank Edward, on July 7, 1896.

Around 1900, they were transferred to Amoy (Xiamen) where James was a second-class tidewaiter. Amoy stayed remarkably free of serious disturbances, even during the Boxer Rebellion, and its large foreign community on Kulangsu Island had a comfortable club, with a small theatre, where James might have sung, and its own daily newspaper, the *Amoy Gazette*.

Nonetheless, this was also where Nellie had the misfortune of delivering babies who did not survive beyond infancy. Most heartbreakingly, their daughter Eileen died on December 29, 1901, at age seven.

Life was expected to improve when they moved to the International Settlement in Shanghai, where James became an assistant examiner. They joined a family celebration in 1904 when George Newman, 24, married a schoolteacher, Dorothy Carozzi, 20, at Shanghai Cathedral in a ceremony officiated by the dean, James Glassey; another Customs man, Albert Henry Budgen, signed the registry.

In April 1905, Nellie Glassey attended a Customs Ball where dozens of officials and their wives dressed up in costumes such as an Imperial Dragoon or a Lady Mephistopheles. Nellie went as a Swiss girl.

Notably missing among the husbands, however, was James Glassey, who was on unattached leave from Customs due to illness.

Even though James was ill, he and Nellie conceived another child before he died at their home at 131 Range Road, Shanghai, on September 15, 1907, of blackwater fever, a complication of malaria. James was one month shy of his 40th birthday. Nellie might have learned she was pregnant only a few weeks beforehand.

The financial consequences of losing James were immediate and, adding to her misery, were reported in excruciating detail by the local newspaper.

In one case, a cook, who was not named, sued Nellie for non-payment of $148.45 in wages and spending for provisions while in her employ, a Shanghai court heard on December 27, 1907. Mrs Glassey told assistant judge F.S.A. Bourne that she had paid the plaintiff until two days after her husband died and then had told him she could not pay more and asked him to keep an account and she would settle later. The cook said his wages were $18 a month and that, when he started work on June 29, there were three people in the house. In September, there were 10 people in the house (presumably family and friends had come for the funeral). Defendant and plaintiff were back and forth, arguing about the minutiae of expenses for a rickshaw and an egg and it became clear it was less about money than principle, for the cook had threatened to report her to the British consulate and she had told him to go ahead. The judge found in the cook's favour for $72.60 and costs of $14.25.

Three weeks later, on January 18, 1908, Nellie again appeared before Judge Bourne in a dispute with another employee, Sze Ah-kur, over wages due of $17.25. Mrs Glassey sent a medical certificate to show she was too unwell to come to court. The judge told the plaintiff that Mrs

Glassey had paid the sum to the court but was alleging he was guilty of theft in another court. She would be given one month to bring that case to conviction in a mixed court and if, by that time, he had not been found guilty, the money would be paid to him.

One week after this case, Nellie gave birth to her second son, Cyril Herbert Glassey, on January 25, 1908.

It is highly likely that one of Nellie's brothers, Frank or George, came to her rescue during this period.

Not long afterwards, probably with the help of family, Nellie landed a job in Japan teaching English to the children of a Japanese baron with connections to a shipping line. Nellie took her baby, Cyril, but left 11-year-old Frank Edward with one of her brothers until he could go to boarding school in Hong Kong.

It was perhaps just as well that Nellie left China at a time when it was approaching a period of unusual political turbulence that would affect Frank Newman in particular.

7

Surviving Revolution

Frank Newman returned to China with a broader perspective gained from his long leave in England. He had a better understanding of how tiny England had led the world with steam engines and other technology that enabled it to exert such a powerful influence on the other side of the world.

He also arrived home to find much had changed while he was away and had to confront events that brought his professional and personal conflicts into sharper focus.

Frank had always been acutely aware of his ambiguous position as a white man working for the Chinese government. He also knew that he would have to make decisions on how to raise his two non-white daughters in a British community that equated whiteness with superiority.

He was appointed Deputy Postmaster in Peking, where he would have been apprised of events that threatened the very foundations of the Post Office. In 1909, a Minister of Posts and Communications, notorious for his antipathy towards foreigners, tried to extend his control over the Post Office that would have meant reducing Théophile Piry to an advisor and replacing the entire foreign staff.

Piry fought back hard, arguing that the Post Office, which handled the transfer of funds as well as mail, needed to be above politicking and that foreign control was essential in maintaining this independence.

Piry also realized that the Post Office had to sever its umbilical cord with Customs and, after skilful negotiations with a new minister, he achieved both his key goals. In May 1911, it was agreed that the Post Office would separate from Customs and become part of the Ministry of Posts and Communications – but also that the new Post Office Directorate, as it would be called, would be headed by a Chinese director, although Piry would be allowed to keep absolute control as Postmaster General.

This settlement would save the Post Office when the 1911 revolution began a few months later.

After decades of putting up with Qing corruption and inefficiency, subjugation by western powers and Japan, rising poverty and growing exposure to modern schools of thought, the first Chinese uprising took place at Wuchang on October 10, 1911. It was quickly followed by spontaneous revolts around the country.

That same month, in Xi'an, where Newman had recently worked, native Hui Muslims joined the Han Chinese revolutionaries in storming the Manchu fort and killing most of the city's 20,000 Manchus.

Sun Yat-sen, the reformist leader of the Nationalists, was in America at the time but returned to China and was elected provisional president of the new Chinese Republic, based in Nanking, on January 1, 1912.

Sun was a western-educated intellectual from the south who sought to modernize China with wholesale import of western ideas and technology, from railways and the telegraph to education.

However, his major weakness was the lack of an army and he had to make a deal with the northern military strongman, Yuan Shikai. On February 12, the Emperor, the six-year-old Puyi who was controlled by the Empress Dowager, abdicated. Sun resigned as president of the republic and Yuan was elected his successor on February 14.

Yuan would need financing but, fortunately for the Post Office, the Qing, just before it was toppled, had approved a policy for foreign commissioners to continue the collection of customs duties and deposit them in foreign banks, putting them out of Yuan's reach.

Nonetheless, Yuan's rise would usher in a chaotic era where a fragile republic tried to emerge amid a power struggle between warlords in the north and the nationalists in the south. As different "government" representatives tried to take over the Post Office, Piry held the line by declaring it to be "provisionally neutral."

Frank Newman escaped much of the tension between Peking and Nanking as he was posted to Harbin and later Mukden in the far northern region of Manchuria, sandwiched between Russia and Japan, where he had to deal with the consequences of a larger power struggle.

After China's defeat by Japan in 1894-95, Russia wrested a concession from the Qing to build the China Eastern Railway (CER) as a short cut linking the Russian cities of Chita, in Siberia, and the far eastern port of Vladivostok. The route meant traversing northern China via Harbin.

Russia claimed extraterritorial rights for the wide zone covered by the CER, placing it outside Chinese jurisdiction and making it Russian territory, not only for railway employees but for hundreds of thousands of travellers and settlers, Russian and foreign.

The railway network was T-shaped, with Harbin at the point where the southern track began its route to Changchun, Mukden and the strategically vital, ice-free Port Arthur.

If Frank had taken his family with him, they would have enjoyed the benefits of a thriving, cosmopolitan, business-minded city, though they would also have had to endure winters so cold that the Songhua River would turn to ice.

Japan, however, viewed Russia's eastern expansion with alarm, and the CER would spark the Russo-Japanese conflict in 1905. Japan shocked the world by defeating the Russians in the Battle of Mukden, which involved 600,000 combatants, before crushing its navy in the Tsushima Strait.

The Japanese would use Mukden as their base while Harbin continued to prosper as Russians continued to arrive. From the railway station where Frank would have arrived, it was a short walk to St Sophia Cathedral, built in 1907 and a focal point for Orthodox Russians, and the Pristan district with its fine shop windows displaying the latest fashions from Paris as well as banks and theatres. An imposing, ochre-coloured China Post Office, built as a two-storey building in 1914, still stands. Frank may have stayed in Noviy Gorod (New City), with its tree-lined streets, elegant mansions and foreign consulates.

Russian rail employees were well paid and enjoyed free accommodation and firewood, long holidays and medical care. It seemed as if the good life would last forever but, within a few years, the revolution in Russia and the establishment of the Soviet Union would change everything.

From Harbin, Frank was transferred to Mukden, which the Japanese occupied after their 1905 victory and took over the railway between Changchun and Port Arthur, renaming it the South Manchuria Railway.

By the time Frank arrived, however, Chinese warlords had taken back the city, and changed its name back to Shenyang. Yet within a decade, the Japanese would be back in force to use the city as a springboard for their occupation of Manchuria.

With the revolution causing many foreign staff to quit the postal service, Frank's chances of promotion improved and he was sent to Nanking in the south as Deputy Postmaster in 1913.

Once the base for Taiping armies, Nanking was not previously considered for a treaty port even though it was less than 200 miles upriver from Shanghai. But after the Taiping rebels were defeated with heavy loss of life, the British and French had arrived in 1865 to stake out their concessions.

With rail links to Shanghai as well as a river that could accommodate the largest ocean-going ships, foreign businesses appeared in Nanking, along with imposing government buildings like the Post Office.

However, 1911 brought a major setback when a rebel army laid siege to the city, destroying the Manchu quarter. The surrender of Imperial forces was followed by widespread looting and damage.

In 1913, when Frank arrived to improve postal facilities along the 60-mile stretch between Nanking and Wuhu, an army mutiny turned into a rebellion against the central government. Loyal government troops eventually took back the city from the mutineers, but at a great cost of lives, including women and children.

In contrast to his early rise, Frank had seen postal colleagues overtake him in the promotion stakes but, in 1914, he obtained a long-awaited promotion when he was appointed Acting Postal Commissioner of Chekiang Province, only a short distance from Nanking.

He moved to its capital of Hangchow, only 100 miles south of Shanghai, to which it was linked by rail and the Grand Canal.

Decades earlier, the Chinese had resisted British requests to swap Hangchow, an enormous and wealthy city, for less successful treaty ports, but it was the Japanese who staked their concessions after their 1894-95 victory.

Its foreign settlements were unhealthy and it was not until 1911, three years before Newman's arrival, that the first non-Japanese foreign trader arrived to take up residence.

It was an easy trip to Shanghai and Frank might have gone to the International Settlement there in October 1914 to join the crowd that waved goodbye to over 100 British men, including some from Customs, who left from the Bund to join up for the war that Britain had declared on Germany a few months earlier. Even if he had considered such patriotic action, Frank at 41 was too old.

In the meantime, Piry continued to improve and expand the postal services. When there were conflicts between the central government and regional forces, such as during the Second Revolution in 1913 or the Protect the Constitution War of 1915, the Post Office managed to keep both its territorial and administrative integrity by remaining an "impartial" institution.

In May 1915, an ailing Piry handed over control of the Directorate General of Posts to Henri Picard-Destelan, another Frenchman, who became Associate Director General, the new designation for Postmaster General.

Although Picard-Destelan would be criticized for lacking Piry's vision, he would preside over the most profitable era in Chinese postal history.

It was under Picard-Destelan that Frank was appointed, in September 1915, as Acting Postal Commissioner to Changsha, capital of Hunan Province, nearly 600 miles to the west in central China.

One of the benefits for a commissioner was that Frank and his family were entitled to a large house on Orange Island, across the river from the Customs House and Post Office in the walled city of Changsha.

Frank was 42 and knew he had disappointed Mei-lan, 28, by not giving her more children. His frequent travels and long absences had also left her lonely in places where other foreigners would have ignored her.

He was now in a high-ranking position, yet once again he would be unafraid to do something that would make his wife happy, but would shock Changsha's small foreign community.

8

Edwin Goes to War

As Frank was settling in at Changsha, no doubt reading news of the war and discussing it at the club, his half-brother Edwin Sait in Canada was feeling the shock of seeing his only son join the army to fight in Europe.

The three brothers had kept in touch, and George had stayed with Edwin on his first trip to Canada in 1893. Edwin was the only one among the brothers who had produced a son.

At the outbreak of war a year earlier, Edwin was a portly, middle-aged architect with a successful business in New Westminster. A self-made man at 47, he lived in a comfortable three-level, wood-framed home with his cousin Elizabeth, whom he had married, and their son and two daughters.

He and Elizabeth had long put behind them their childhoods as "orphans" and were focusing on his work and their teenage children.

Business had been kind. After fire devastated two-thirds of its downtown in 1898, New Westminster had seen a furious boom in business and construction and Sait, who had won a competition for rebuilding Government House in Victoria, had his own architects' office by the mid-1900s.

The Great War pulled in Canada as part of the British Empire. The huge but burgeoning colony of less than eight million people did not have much to offer – only a small navy, an army of 3,000 soldiers and a few militia units.

But English-speaking Canada had strong ties to Britain, and Prime Minister Robert Borden pledged to provide a Canadian Expeditionary Force (CEF) of 25,000 soldiers.

Caught up in patriotic fervour, 35,000 men volunteered, including veterans of the Boer War. In October 1914, as the first contingent of 30,000 left for England, Sam Hughes, the minister of militia and defence, addressed them: "Some of you will not return, but the soldier going down in the cause of freedom never dies. Immortality is his."

The 1st Canadian Division arrived in France in early 1915 and, in its opening combat at Ypres that April, came up against the Germans' first poison gas attack.

Back home, Edwin's son Eddie joined a batch of volunteers. When Eddie arrived at the Vancouver recruiting station on October 19, 1915, for his medical examination, his record described him as a 20-year-old clerk who was five foot six inches tall, weighed 147 pounds and had light brown hair and brown eyes. One official noted Eddie had a slight stammer and recommended that he see the dental corps. Eddie signed up as a private with the 72nd Battalion, also known as the Seaforth Highlanders, of the CEF's 4th Division.

After initial training, the Seaforth Highlanders departed Halifax on the SS *Empress of Britain* on April 23, 1916. For much of the journey, they were under threat from German U-boat torpedoes until they disembarked at Liverpool, England, on May 7.

When Eddie was stationed at the Canadian base of Bramshott Camp, Hampshire, "khaki fever" was sweeping English army towns, referring to young working-class women, including prostitutes, who pursued uniformed men for alcohol and sex in alleyways and parks.

Perhaps after seeking to lose his virginity before going to war, Eddie entered Connaught Hospital on May 20 with gonorrhoea. He developed German measles as well and was transferred to an isolation hospital. The rubella cleared up, but he needed a further 17 days at Connaught before being cleared of venereal disease. As punishment, he was docked $21, or two-thirds of a private's monthly pay.

By now, he had seen the returning wounded and the reality of the carnage in France was sinking in. On June 26, Eddie wrote a will, leaving everything to his mother.

A month later, Eddie went on a drinking spree and damaged government property in his barracks for which he was sentenced on July 21, 1916 to Field Punishment (FP) No. 2, a forfeit of 28 days' pay and a fine of $6. Punishments in the army were more about discipline than fairness, and FP No. 2 involved brutally hard physical work.

Three weeks later, on August 14, Eddie landed in France with his battalion and marched to the Somme, where French and British troops had been fighting Germans across a 25-mile front since July 1. The scale of casualties had been horrific; the first day of the Somme had seen nearly 20,000 British soldiers die, with three times that number wounded.

The Canadian Corps entered the fray in mid-September, rotating its four divisions. By mid-October, it was the turn of Eddie and the 4th Division.

Back in Vancouver, Edwin was agitated. Perhaps Eddie had left home after a spat with his father, who now felt guilty. Perhaps Edwin knew his son had issues with discipline that would land him in trouble.

Just as Eddie was readying for battle in Europe, Edwin, now 49, did something quite extraordinary. Exactly one year after his son enlisted, the man who had grown up without a father set off to follow his son to war.

With his wife and daughters likely pleading with him to stay, Edwin left his home at 316 3rd Avenue, New Westminster, and presented himself at the army recruiting station on October 19, 1916. The attestation form for Edwin George William Sait shows that he lied about his age, stripping off seven years to claim that his birthday was January 17, 1874. The form noted that his "apparent age" was 42 and his hair was "iron grey." His vision was 20/30, with a "slight defect, but not sufficient to cause rejection."

Soldiers were required to be between 18 and 45, but thousands lied about their age – the oldest recorded member of the CEF was 80, while the youngest was ten – and, with the government calling urgently for more fighting men but new entries plummeting, recruiters were often flexible.

6th Field Company Canadian Engin **ORIGINAL** No. 2005475

ATTESTATION PAPER.

CANADIAN OVER-SEAS EXPEDITIONARY FORCE.

Folio. .

Original

QUESTIONS TO BE PUT BEFORE ATTESTATION.
(ANSWERS)

1. What is your surname?	S A I T
1a. What are your Christian names?	Edwin George William
1b. What is your present address?	316 3rd Ave New Westminster B.C
2. In what Town, Township or Parish, and in what Country were you born?	Southampton Hants England
3. What is the name of your next-of-kin?	Elizabeth Mary Warner Sait
4. What is the address of your next-of-kin?	316 3rd Ave New Westminster B.C. *(Canada)*
4a. What is the relationship of your next-of-kin?	Wife
5. What is the date of your birth?	17th Jany 1874
6. What is your Trade or Calling?	Architect
7. Are you married?	Yes
8. Are you willing to be vaccinated or re-vaccinated and inoculated?	Yes
9. Do you now belong to the Active Militia?	No
10. Have you ever served in any Military Force? If so, state particulars of former Service.	No
11. Do you understand the nature and terms of your engagement?	Yes
12. Are you willing to be attested to serve in the CANADIAN OVER-SEAS EXPEDITIONARY FORCE?	Yes

DECLARATION TO BE MADE BY MAN ON ATTESTATION.

I, Edwin George William Sait, do solemnly declare that the above are answers made by me to the above questions and that they are true, and that I am willing to fulfil the engagements by me now made, and I hereby engage and agree to serve in the **Canadian Over-Seas Expeditionary Force**, and to be attached to any arm of the service therein, for the term of one year, or during the war now existing between Great Britain and Germany should that war last longer than one year, and for six months after the termination of that war provided His Majesty should so long require my services, or until legally discharged.

Edwin G.W.Sait (Signature of Recruit)

Date October 19th 1916   (Signature of Witness)

OATH TO BE TAKEN BY MAN ON ATTESTATION.

I, Edwin George William Sait, do make Oath, that I will be faithful and bear true Allegiance to His Majesty **King George the Fifth**, His Heirs and Successors, and that I will as in duty bound honestly and faithfully defend His Majesty, His Heirs and Successors, in Person, Crown and Dignity, against all enemies, and will observe and obey all orders of His Majesty, His Heirs and Successors, and of all the Generals and Officers set over me. So help me God.

Edwin G.W.Sait (Signature of Recruit)

Date October 19th 196   (Signature of Witness)

CERTIFICATE OF MAGISTRATE.

The Recruit above-named was cautioned by me that if he made any false answer to any of the above questions he would be liable to be punished as provided in the Army Act.

The above questions were then read to the Recruit in my presence.

I have taken care that he understands each question, and that his answer to each question has been duly entered as replied to, and the said Recruit has made and signed the declaration and taken the oath before me, at Vancouver this Nineteenth day of October 1916.

C.G.Henshaw J.P. (Signature of Justice)

M. F. W. 22.
400M.—1 -15.
H. Q. 1772-30-861.

Middle-aged Edwin Sait lied about his age on his attestation form

Although middle-aged Edwin was two inches shorter than his son at five feet four inches, he was 20 pounds heavier at 165. He had a scar over his right eye and a tattoo on his left forearm. Edwin was recruited as a sapper in the 6th Field Company of the Canadian Engineers.

In France less than two days later, at 12.06pm on October 21, 1916, Eddie and the CEF's 4th Division attacked the Regina Trench on the slope of a ridge running from the village of Le Sars to Staufenfeste, close to the German fortifications at Thiepval. After heavy artillery support, the 4th captured the remaining parts of the trench on November 11. The effort cost the 4th Division 4,311 casualties, but Eddie was unhurt.

That winter, the Canadian Corps, having given up 24,000 men to the Somme, rebuilt its battalions. Even during this period, however, they harassed the Germans with "trench raids."

The Canadians had become adept at these night attacks, which were designed not to hold ground but to create havoc, keep the enemy off-balance and undermine morale. In fact, a rivalry sprang up between Canadian units as to which could cause the most disruption.

In the early spring of 1917, to break the trench deadlock, the Canadians began planning an audacious campaign to take the four-mile-long Vimy Ridge near Arras, northern France.

As a softening-up exercise, leaders of the 4th Division proposed a "reconnaissance in force," which would turn out to be the largest Canadian raid to date. The division commander was Major-General David Watson, a former newspaper editor who had come up through the ranks, and his top staff officer was Edmund Ironside, a confident, forceful man who stood six foot four inches and had the nickname 'Tiny.' Many considered Ironside to be effectively the one in charge.

They assembled 1,600 men from the 54th, 72nd, 73rd and 75th Battalions, with the goal of taking Hill 145, the highest point on Vimy Ridge and fortified by interlocking machine-gun nests, barbed wire and dugouts. British and French troops had failed to capture it and, since conventional means had not succeeded, Watson decided to use poison gas.

Eddie and his fellow infantrymen were told the gas would wipe out the enemy so they were likely to meet only dead Germans.

They needed a strong wind to carry the gas to the heights of Vimy Ridge, but they were unaware of the arguments raging between their leaders. One battalion commander was urging that, since the wind was unpredictable, they should postpone the raid, while another was warning that his troops had no experience with gas.

Ironside refused to consider a delay. Attack groups moved to the front and, by the night of February 25-26, 15 tons of gas in 150-pound canisters were waiting for release by the men of Special Gas Company "M."

On that cold night, Eddie lay in the mud for hours as the raid was delayed because the wind was too weak or blowing in the wrong direction. They could hear, from the other side of No Man's Land, the Germans taunting them to come over the top, so they had lost any element of surprise.

A German artillery barrage punctured some Canadian gas canisters, releasing a cloud that killed one soldier through suffocation. Still, the plan remained unchanged. The raiders were instructed to wait for the second of two gas clouds to float over the Germans before advancing.

A stiff breeze arrived at 3am on March 1, bringing the decision to release 1,038 cylinders of White Star (chlorine and phosgene). The gas carried to the opposing lines, but found the enemy prepared. They replied instantly with an artillery attack that punched holes in several phosgene canisters, gassing Canadians.

Forward observers reported to division headquarters that the anticipated slackening in enemy fire as Germans were supposed to drop dead was not happening.

Soon after 5am, the second cloud of gas was discharged and the raiders steeled themselves to follow it 40 minutes later. The gas moved slowly uphill, hovered, and then drifted back as the wind changed.

Nonetheless, the Canadians went "over the bags" on schedule. As they crossed a terrain of craters, rats and barbed wire – all brightly lit by enemy flares – they were met by withering fire from the German trenches.

During the battle, the Germans used their respirators while some Canadians, blinded by bullets and gas, removed their masks, turned green, vomited and screamed. The next morning, a German officer walked into No Man's Land, holding up a white flag, to offer a respite for the Canadians to collect their wounded and dead.

As military historian Tim Cook concluded, "The division's staff officers had little understanding of how chemical agents worked in battlefield realities, so the conception was flawed from the start. This was the single most self-destructive Canadian raid of the war."

Eddie survived a battle that claimed a 43% casualty rate but he was severely gassed. He spent time at the Canadian hospital at Dannes-Camiers on March 5 before being shipped back to England to recuperate over several weeks at Brown House Hospital, Guildford; the Royal Herbert Hospital, Woolwich; and the military hospital at Epsom.

R. 140. Name SAIT. Edwin, Unit 72nd.Battalion. Next of Kin Canada.		Rank **Private**				Reg. No. 130104	
Date 1916.	Movement	Place	Casualty	List No.	Notified N/K O.	W.O. List	
21-5.	Conn.Hos.Aldershot.		N.Y.D.	10.			
27-5.	Isol.Hos.Aldershot.		Rubella.	10.			
5-6.	Conn.Hos.Aldershot.		N.Y.D.	B32.			
22-6.	Discharged.		V.D.G.	B36.			
1917. 8-1.	No.7 Gen.Hosp.St Omer.		?,Mumps,slt.	A111.			
16-2.	Discharged.		Jaundice.	A14?			
5-3.	22 Gen.H.DannesCamiers.	Gas Poisng.sev.		A155.	M81.		13-3.
10-3.	First Line.H.Clandon Pk.Gldfrd.	-do-	slt.	B157.			
20-4.	Can.G.H.Woodcote Pk.Epsom.	-do-	"W"Dcs./	B191.			
11-5.	*Discharged*			B234			

Eddie's war record shows he was gassed

On May 3, 1917, not knowing that his son was convalescing, Edwin Sait left Halifax on the SS *Justicia* and would spend months training in Seaford, England, before being transferred to France towards the end of the year. Eddie was still complaining of shortness of breath when he was sent back to France on July 18, 1917.

Survivors of the gas raid remained bitter and distrustful of their officers. After another drinking bout, no doubt, Eddie faced accusations of "wilfully damaging government property." He was sentenced, on November 22, 1917, to 28 days of Field Punishment No.1. This meant being tied to a gun wheel or a fence for two hours a day in addition to hard labour. Soldiers referred to FP No.1 as "crucifixion."

Just three days earlier, on November 19, 1917, Edwin Sait followed his son to France, arriving at the Canadian General Base Depot in Etaples, between Calais and Boulogne. As a sapper, Edwin was both a fighting man and an engineer, with duties that included digging ditches, repairing roads, assembling bridges, tunnelling, mining, laying tramway tracks, setting up water points and disarming booby traps.

Now 50, Edwin was affected by the bitterly cold and wet French winter. He complained of lumbago, specifically pains in his left arm and right leg, including the knee. His arm and leg would frequently "go lame," according to one report. Edwin also had severe bowel problems, though they eventually disappeared with treatment.

1918 opened with no end to the fighting in sight. With the United States expected to enter the war, the Germans, boosted by 50 divisions transferred to the western front after the Russian Revolution, began their Spring Offensive on March 21. They sought to break through Allied lines, defeat the British Army and push the French into seeking an armistice.

They retook lost ground and gained new territory, but suffered heavy casualties and their supply lines of food and ammunition could not keep up with their fast-moving stormtroopers.

In July 1918, as the Americans arrived, the Allied commanders switched from defence to offence. French Generalissimo Ferdinand Foch planned an assault in the Amiens region of northern France to protect the vital Paris-Amiens railway. The Canadian Corps, by then much feared by the Germans, were part of his strategy.

In early August, the Allies made false moves by day to distract the enemy while stealthily shifting into Amiens 100,000 troops, thousands of field guns and howitzers, more than 600 tanks, and 2,000 aircraft.

Learning from earlier years, the Allies combined air and ground power more effectively and their artillery was more flexible and accurate.

During the moonless night of August 7, the Battle of Amiens opened with the Royal Air Force squadron laying smoke screens over the battlefield, adding to a heavy mist.

At 4.20am on August 8, 900 Allied guns opened fire as Eddie Sait advanced towards the German Fourth Army on boggy terrain in thick fog.

The Germans, outnumbered and unprepared for the scale and efficiency of the offensive, surrendered in their thousands. German General Erich Ludendorff described it as "the black day of the German Army in the history of this war." He was referring not to the casualties and lost ground, but the mass surrender.

By day two, August 9, the Canadian push was slowing down while the Germans resisted. Exploding shrapnel caught Private Eddie Sait's right arm, shattering the humerus and taking muscle, too. Despite the pain, Eddie felt relieved. He was now certain to be sent home.

Amiens proved a turning point, marking a decline in Germany's military capacity and the Allies' growing superiority in materials, tactics and technology.

On August 16, 1918, Eddie returned to England on the hospital ship *Carisbrook Castle*. While his division fought at Cambrai and Mons before the war ended on November 11, 1918, Eddie spent months in hospitals in Manchester, Epsom and Buxton.

After an operation to clear out debris, he exchanged his plaster cast for a sling. Doctors examined the break in his arm and considered joining it with plating or a graft.

A medical report dated May 3, 1919 noted a "marked stammering" in Eddie's speech and that his nervous and cardiovascular systems had been affected. He was two pounds lighter than his enlistment weight.

In France, sappers like Edwin, who was now plagued by haemorrhoids, were building crossings and bridges to help the Allied push towards Germany.

When the war ended, the soldiers faced months of frustrating waiting as the authorities repatriated more than a quarter of a million Canadians.

In May 1919, six months after the Armistice, Eddie was invalided to Canada. His father waited longer in France before returning to England around August 1919, but at least he knew his son was alive.

Now a corporal, Edwin was processed at the Canadian camp at Witley before leaving from Tilbury for Canada, where he was demobbed on September 20, 1919, after nearly three years of service. Edwin wasted no time before visiting Eddie, who was laid up in Shaughnessy Hospital, Vancouver, awaiting tests. His arm was badly broken, but his life was not in danger, and the family was looking forward to Christmas.

A lame arm was an impediment to a career, however, and Eddie submitted to another operation on August 25 to "dovetail" the separated bones in his arm before they could be rejoined.

Eddie was "well-nourished and robust," according to a report when he was admitted to Esquimalt Military Hospital on October 9 for another operation.

Surgeon Dr McTavish wired Eddie's bones together on October 31. At first, the surgery proceeded well.

"I pared both ends of the bone, sawed a wedge-shaped piece of upper fragment, dovetailed the lower fragment into the upper," reported Dr McTavish. "Ends slipped together and wired into position. Muscles sutured over it. The muscle spiral nerve, where it was fibrosed, resected, and ends sutured. Fascia sutured."

As the operation came to an end, the anaesthetist drew the doctors' attention to the patient. Eddie had stopped breathing and his face was deep blue and suffused. The doctors pulled out his tongue and began artificial respiration. They injected him with $1/30^{th}$ grain of strychnine. When Eddie's pulse still failed to return, they opened his abdomen and massaged the heart. This did not work, either.

After surviving trench warfare and gas, Eddie's heart gave out at the age of 25. A post-mortem determined that "the patient died of heart failure under anaesthesia and that everything possible was done for his welfare in pre-operative treatment and at time of operation."

His family buried him in a military grave at Fraser Cemetery, New Westminster. They carved a simple inscription on his stone: "Dear Eddie Rest in Peace." There were no more male heirs in Mary Ann's family.

9

A New Baby

The Hunanese, women as well as men, are renowned for having an independent spirit and a fiery temperament, like their spicy food.

Their antipathy to outside influence was such that, in 1895, Robert Hart wrote to his London-based confidant, James Campbell, "Changsha, the capital of Hunan, is the real centre of everything that's anti-foreign."

That began to change after Changsha became a treaty port in 1903 with the signing of the China-Japan commercial treaty. A customs house opened, and diplomats and businessmen soon appeared in significant numbers.

However, the city's relations with foreigners received a blow in 1910 when a starving woman drowned herself because a greedy merchant refused to sell her rice at a price she could afford. Long-simmering resentments against the Qing exploded into three days of rioting in which mobs set fire to government buildings, including the administrative office; the arson extended to foreign pontoons and hulks off the bund. This led to an exodus of foreigners to Orange Island (Ju Zi Zhou), a narrow, three-mile sandbar that lay in the Xiang River between the walled city and the nearly 1,000-foot-high Yuelu Mountain on the eastern bank.

The unrest anticipated the overthrow of the Manchus but, in fact, when the revolution broke out in nearby Wuchang the following year, Hunan crossed over to the Republican cause readily and with little bloodshed, apart from a few heads of resisting officials being impaled on spikes. Notably, the local residents treated foreigners with courtesy during the crisis for, apart from being chauvinistic, the Hunanese were receptive to new ideas and appreciated the railways, steamers, electricity and modern education the westerners brought with them.

The customs house in Changsha was burned down in 1910

Compared to the baking red deserts of Shensi and the freezing winters of Manchuria, Changsha, surrounded by flat, fertile plains and mineral-rich mountains, was a haven where Frank could keep his family with him. The climate, as noted in a directory of 1918, was "excellent" and "there is no great heat here, the summer is short, and there is no malaria, the poisonous mosquito not existing here."

With his scholarly bent, Frank would have appreciated the nearby Yuelu Academy, the ancient seat of learning, while Mei-lan loved the city's elegant buildings, electric power, public gardens, paved streets and enticing shops that reminded her of Chengtu.

Hunan's rich minerals explained why Frank's neighbours included executives of the American company Standard Oil, whose grand homes and expansive lawns still exist, as well as German mining engineers eyeing the zinc and iron ore potential of the mountains.

The British consul was Victor Savage, a long-time resident of China, who complained that he missed the dignified, courteous officials of the imperial era and now had to deal with "hot-headed, half-educated students," as he called the new Japanese-influenced generation of office holders.

The Customs Commissioner, R.A. Currie, had also been in China a long while and had risen through the ranks after joining as a Watcher a few years before Frank. His grand riverside residence has also survived.

Fortunately, Dorothy, or Dolly, whom Frank had rescued in Xi'an, painted a picture of their life in Changsha for the author when he visited her in Sydney in the 1990s.

"We had a big, beautiful place near the river, and we had this German family, a wife with two girls and a boy called Charlie, staying with us," said the diminutive, sprightly Aunt Dolly, who was in her 80s when she gave the author a tearful hug, saying, "I used to cuddle you when you were two years old."

She recalled her father's morning ritual. "There would be Chinese staff lined up in blue-and-white sailor uniforms and they would row him out to a motor launch to take him to work. If there was a flood, the water would come up to our steps and he would climb onto the boat."

As well as Changsha, Frank's duties covered other provincial centres, including the upriver trading town of Yochow (Yueyang), beside the vast Dongting Lake.

"My favourite photograph was taken on the doorstep of our Changsha home with all the German family and myself, and little Charlie next to me," said Dolly, sighing as the picture had long been lost. The only one missing in the photo was Jessie, who was sent to St Joseph's Convent in Shanghai for schooling.

"Mama [Mei-lan] didn't speak much English, but she was a beautiful woman, dressed in Chinese clothes, and she used to play mahjong and have parties with the servants."

Beyond their sandy shore, trouble was brewing. Sun Yat-sen had fled to Japan after relinquishing the presidency but he returned to regroup his Republican government in the south and challenge the warlords who controlled much of the rest of the country.

In 1913, governors of several southern provinces revolted against Yuan's Beiyang government and supported Sun's Nationalist Party (the Kuomintang). This "second revolution" failed and, as Hunan had sided with the nationalists, Yuan sent troops to replace its popular provincial governor, Tan Yankai, with his own non-Hunanese appointee.

When Yuan went too far and declared himself Emperor, Hunan troops forced out Yuan's governor and brought back their former leader. Province after province rebelled and Yuan was facing calls to resign when he died on June 6, 1916.

A few weeks after Yuan's death, Dolly was at home when the front door opened to reveal a slender Chinese man, dressed in a traditional gown and holding a basket that contained a small white bundle. The swaddling was peeled apart to reveal a tiny Chinese baby girl. She was clutching a toy pussycat with a bell attached to its collar; a piece of paper beside her noted she had been born 40 days earlier, on June 14.

"Mama gave a big smile as she took the baby in her arms," recalled Dolly. They nicknamed her Marylou, and Frank arranged for her to be added to his British travel document, probably by Consul Savage.

Thus did Marylou acquire the British nationality that would shape her fate. "Mama told me I was a gift from heaven. From that moment, I was rarely out of her sight."

Marylou had arrived, as the Chinese say, in interesting times.

It was not long before Marylou displayed her Hunanese willpower in a strange way. Mama told the story that when Jessie, who must have been there on holiday, brought home a doll, Marylou pushed it off the table and broke it. When Jessie slapped her, Marylou rolled her eyeballs and fainted and, on coming to, found Mama scolding Jessie severely.

After this, Marylou would swoon to get what she wanted. On one occasion, she was unconscious for such a long spell that her worried father was rowed out at midnight to a visiting British gunboat to fetch the ship's doctor. This might have been the *Thistle,* which was assigned to protect British interests in various ports, including Changsha.

Though Changsha had much potential for prosperity, it continued to be ravaged by battles between north and south.

The Beiyang generals who followed Yuan were also bent on dominating the south and, in the late summer of 1917, northern troops marched to Hunan to replace Tan Yankai.

The power struggles went back and forth. With the help of troops from Kwangsi and Kwangtung, the Hunan army pushed northern troops from Yochow in January 1918.

Settling differences among themselves, the Beiyang army commanders now assembled nearly 150,000 troops for a counterattack in March. They recaptured Yochow in mid-March and reached Changsha on March 26. Attacking other key locations at the same time, they forced the overwhelmed Hunanese army into retreat.

They now proceeded to target civilians with atrocities – killing and robbing, mutilating and raping – on an unprecedented scale.

On February 22, Frank Newman gave a talk on ancient Chinese coins at the Changsha Friday Evening Club. A month later, he and assistant Liu Yao Ting found themselves in the middle of mayhem.

He reported to the Directorate General of Posts, to Picard-Destelan, on March 27: "The looting proceeded all through the night, right up to practically noon next day and was carried out most systematically. The city today is in a most deplorable condition. There is not a shop, both large and small, that was not cleaned right out of everything movable, nothing but the empty shelves remain, to bear witness of the thoroughness in which the looting was carried out."

Frank and his staff did, however, take action to protect the post office.

"I took every precaution to have the two sets of heavy doors at the entrance, as well as the back entrance, heavily barred and shored up with heavy beams against probable attack," he wrote. "The Post Office most happily was not touched, although all the shops round about it were cleaned out, owing to the prompt arrival of the northerners on Tuesday at noon, otherwise I believe the Post Office would have shared the same fate as the shops if they could have forced a way in."

A week later, on April 5, 1918, Frank reported, "The demand for money orders since the arrival of the northern troops at Changsha has become very great. During the last three days, there has been remitted at the head office alone over twenty thousand dollars, and still they come. The office is simply packed from early morning to after three o'clock with soldiers demanding money orders (to remit their plunder to their families in the north), fighting and struggling as to who should be served first. It became so bad that I had to apply to the governor for a guard to keep order."

At the British consulate, Consul Savage, responsible for British lives (and Norwegian, too), remained stoic during the crisis, but admitted the continuous rifle fire deprived him of sleep and brought him to close to "hysteria." He was glad to leave Changsha soon afterwards.

The overloaded trains carrying northern troops damaged the rail line as well as other infrastructure and repairs could not be carried out. As one report noted, "Owing to financial and other difficulties due to the European War, no further work on the railway is being undertaken at this end."

Not surprisingly, for security reasons, Frank decided to move his family to Shanghai.

Shanghai, which the Yangtze River reaches after travelling 4,000 miles from the Himalayas through the vast Chinese hinterland, was by far the largest and richest of the treaty ports. As the Great War ended in 1918, leaving swathes of Europe devastated, Shanghai was on the cusp of becoming one the one of most populous, cosmopolitan and exciting cities in the world.

Merchants and adventurers arrived from all over the world and the Chinese fled to the

Frank Newman as he looked around the time the family moved to Shanghai

enclave to escape from lawlessness and poverty.

As a centre of commerce and culture, it boasted the best schools and hospitals as well as the liveliest night life. It was the dream post for foreign staff of Customs and the Post Office.

Although he was never posted to Shanghai, Frank set up home for his family in the International Settlement's northern district, which was popular with foreigners and close to the Chinese quarter of Paoshan.

Their new home was 2 Boundary Lane, a narrow path between the main thoroughfare of Range Road, where Frank's sister Nellie and James Glassey had lived, and bustling Haining Road. Their neighbours had names like Youngson and Allenspach, and Marylou was soon playing hopscotch with an English girl called Mary.

For Mei-lan, mahjong parties and the Chinese theatre – her great passions apart from her family – were a short rickshaw ride away. By this time, Frank was one of the Post Office's most experienced officers and had repeatedly shown his worth under challenging circumstances.

In March 1919, Frank, now 46, was dispatched as Postal Commissioner to Shensi Province where he had helped to establish the postal service 15 years earlier.

It was also during this volatile stage of his career that Frank would find solace in another woman's arms.

10

Warlords and Nuns

Though Frank never landed the plum post of Shanghai, he paid a large part of his salary to settle his family there. It proved a worthwhile sacrifice for, while his older brother Edwin was embroiled in the Great War devastating Europe, and warlords were dividing China sowing chaos and misery, Shanghai's foreign concessions were prospering.

It also helped that his younger brother George was working in the International Settlement, making good money as a trader for Lavers and Clark. Its principal, Percy Lavers, was from Chefoo, where he had been appointed young George's trustee after his mother died. Frank hoped George would help out in family emergencies, though it turned out George had domestic problems of his own.

Since the death of the autocratic Yuan, the *junfa* (warlords) had carved China up into largely independent regions without an effective national government.

The Beiyang government in Peking claimed to represent civilian rule with a parliamentary system, but it was really a front for whichever warlord faction was in power. Despite this, the foreign powers recognized Peking's authority and their merchants paid massive duties and import taxes, which the warlords pocketed.

In the south, Sun Yat-sen, standard bearer for Western-style Republicanism with his "three principles" of nationalism, democracy and improving the livelihood of the people, was preparing an army in Kwangtung Province to rid the country of what he called "a single den of badgers."

The Post Office strove to remain neutral but would remain in the sights of both the warlords, who coveted its assets, and the nationalists, who wanted its foreign staff replaced by Chinese.

Nationalism received a boost in Peking on May 4, 1919, when thousands of students protested against the unfairness of the Treaty of Versailles that allowed Japan to keep parts of Shantung Province which they acquired from the Germans at the onset of the Great War. Both China and Japan had fought with the allies.

The May Fourth Movement sparked demonstrations around the country, including in foreign-dominated Shanghai, where it led to a general strike of merchants and workers, showing that patriotism enjoyed support from the masses as well as the intellectuals.

Because of its proximity to Peking, no province was more of a hotbed of warlord intrigue than Shensi, where Frank returned as Postal Commissioner in March, 1919.

Much had changed politically since his previous posting in the early 1900s. Yuan's death had left a power vacuum and his former henchmen had grabbed different parts of the national army and were now rivals.

The warlords sought to preserve their territory and maintain a balance of power, alternately siding with, or turning against, each other to prevent any one faction from becoming too powerful.

Throughout his tenure until November 1922, Frank had to deal with the warlord version of musical chairs involving the Anhui, Zhili and Fengtian cliques.

When he arrived, Shensi's military governor was Ch'en Shu-fan, backed by the Anhui group which had overthrown the civil governor, Lu Chien-chang, three years earlier. Ch'en kept control of the strategically important Xi'an and the Wei Valley until May 1921 when Peking replaced him with a Zhili general, Yen Hsian-wen. After Yen committed suicide a few months later, he was succeeded as military governor by Feng Yuxiang, a former Anhui man who switched to the Zhili side after his uncle and mentor, Lu Jianzheng, was executed by Anhui warlord Xu Shuzheng. In mid-1922, the Zhili faction defended Peking from an attempted takeover by the northern Fengtian clique which, after Frank left, would return to expel the Zhili group and retake Peking.

In Shensi, a vast, largely arid area where poverty was high, Frank strove to keep the Post Office neutral while maintaining vital mail and remittance services between the provincial centres and Peking.

Private enterprises also provided remittance services, but they were profit-oriented, charged exorbitant fees and focused on big traders. The Post Office, however, offered money order and parcel post services to the public at reasonable prices and helped to foster economic growth as well as removing social inequalities.

Picard-Destelan believed the Post Office helped to hold the country together during these tumultuous times. "It is impossible to conceive to what extent the course of the country's history would have varied had not the National Post existed in such a state of development," he wrote. "The unifying influence of the National Post is undeniable."

But the warlords also caused severe problems as they could not pay their soldiers, who were often recruited from gangs of bandits or forcibly conscripted from villages, and allowed them to plunder the peasantry. The *North-China Daily News* reported in 1921 that in Shensi, robbery, violence and rape were terrorizing farmers.

The troops depended heavily on the railways for transport and on the Post Office to send funds, ill-gotten or not, to their families. But the Zhili clique, for example, threatened to kill railroad workers if they went on strike while bandit soldiers robbed isolated post offices and rural couriers. In 1916, brigands killed 25 postal couriers and stole from over 400 others.

In addition to such demanding duties, Frank had to deal with the famine that devastated Shensi and neighbouring provinces in 1921 as the Post Office played a key role in relief efforts.

For his pains, the Peking government honoured Frank twice, awarding him the Fifth Class of the Order of the Excellent Crop (also known as the Order of the Precious Brilliant Golden Grain) in 1917, and the Fourth Class of the same order two years later.

Because of his position, Frank likely met Feng Yuxiang, the warlord who would cause his downfall a few years later. A tall man who led an austere life, Feng was known as the "Christian General" as he had been baptized a Methodist and encouraged his troops to find Jesus and sing hymns. Feng, regarded as an anti-imperialist patriot, was noted for his highly disciplined troops who paid for requisitions and rarely abused civilians. Nonetheless, Feng avenged his uncle when his soldiers pulled Xu Shuzheng out of his train and shot him in the back of the head.

Meanwhile, at her Boundary Lane home in Shanghai, Mama presided over a household of servants, including a baby *amah* for Marylou. Mama, with warm chestnut eyes and raven hair rolled into a bun, was a simple, big-hearted woman, always ready with a sweet for children. Marylou never heard her speak ill of anyone.

Mama was a captive of her bound feet

But her bound feet forced her into a restricted existence. "She couldn't walk normally. She hobbled. We always had to wait when she came down the stairs or whenever we went anywhere," said Marylou. "In the evenings, Mama would sigh with relief when her bandages were taken off and she soaked her feet in warm water."

Electricity and running water had yet to come to Boundary Lane and coolies came to the cobblestoned lane at dusk with long poles to light the gas lamps. The hot water coolie brought boiling water in buckets dangling from a pole across his shoulders to fill two large Soochow jars, which were painted with white storks against a brown background. Marylou's first memory of pain was when scalding water splashed her accidentally.

Downstairs, the family slept on a large, charcoal-heated *kang*, which also kept the house warm in winter. "I may have been an unlovely baby, but Mama worshipped the ground I stood on and never let me out of her sight," said Marylou.

Mama took her to mahjong and the Chinese opera and silent movies on North Szechuan Road. She laughed and cried at the opera but Marylou, sitting on her lap, covered her ears against the clanging of gongs and cymbals. She did, however, relish the dumplings, sweet soybeans and sesame cakes that attendants brought during intervals with hot, scented towels to wipe her fingers.

Improving railway connections enabled Frank to return to his family quite often and a frenzy of cleaning and cooking would precede his arrival. Marylou especially loved Chinese New Year as Frank would stay for several weeks and there were feasts and firecrackers and she would kowtow to her elders to collect red packets containing silver dollars.

Frank and Mama treated each other affectionately and Marylou never heard them quarrel. Neither could she recall her father raising his voice or drinking too much. He treated the servants with respect, told her to tell the truth always, and to treat others as she would wish to be treated. Once, when she tired during a walk, he placed her in a rickshaw but insisted on striding beside it rather than joining her, saying that no human being should work as a beast of burden.

Guests packed the dinner table when Frank was home. One frequent visitor was a heavily pock-marked brother of Mama, whom Marylou called Jieu Jieu (meaning "uncle"). Jieu Jieu frequently told the story of how he had nearly been buried alive after contracting smallpox. "I lay so still that people thought I was dead, and they had dressed me in burial clothes when I suddenly sat up," he said. "They looked at me as though I was a ghost who had come back to haunt them."

When some European neighbours looked askance at the medley of occupants and visitors to No 2 Boundary Lane, Marylou would later recall, emphatically, that her father "didn't give a hoot what anyone thought about his relationships."

After Marylou started attending St Joseph's, where the nuns had taught her older sister Jessie to sew beautiful embroidery and sing an enchanting solo *Stabat Mater* in church, Mama put Marylou in a carriage with a *mafoo* (groom) who wore a white cone-shaped hat. In winter, Mama wrapped her daughter's hands in a muff, with a tiny hot water bottle inside, and placed a small brass brazier with hot coals under her feet.

The convent school gave out ribbons as prizes every week – red for class work, brown for French and white for general conduct. As often as not, Marylou would jump into Mama's waiting arms, clutching a red ribbon for being top of the class.

From St Joseph's, Marylou moved to the junior section of Shanghai Public School for Girls (SPG) at Boone Road. Before it was taken over by the municipal council it had been built as a school for Eurasian children by a Scottish philanthropist, Thomas Hanbury. The classrooms were in a Victorian red-brick building and, said Marylou, the school hired "the best teachers from England"; and errant pupils had to stand in front of a grandfather clock in the entrance hall as punishment.

After Shensi, Frank was sent to Hangchow, where he had also worked previously. He was on the move during this period, with one service directory placing him in Hangchow until October 1926 while another put him in the Russian Concession of Tientsin in 1925.

This means he was in or near the centres of power – Shanghai, Nanking and Peking – when Chiang Kai-shek, a professional soldier who had assumed the Kuomintang leadership after Sun Yat-sen's death in 1925, began his 18-month Northern Expedition against the warlords.

Frank moved the family from the northern district to a three-storey house on Rue Lafayette in the French Concession, which had become Shanghai's premier residential district. The house had a small garden with a swing. Marylou recalled it as the grandest of their Shanghai homes. "We had hot running water from taps and beds with spring mattresses," she said. "We had sofas and armchairs and an open fireplace in the living room, and we had salamander stoves in all the rooms, beautiful Peking carpets, blackwood and rosewood furniture. and mirrors encrusted with soapstone."

Frank filled his study with "fabulous" curios and stored others in crates in the basement. They included Tang, Sung and Ming vases, bowls and figurines, a few early Han bronzes, and a pair of Ming lacquer vases. "Dad would have friends over and would ask me, because my hands were tiny, to pull the stuffing from the Ming vases," Marylou said. "He had a splendid coin collection, laid out in trays, each coin having its special place in a wooden cabinet custom-built by a local carpenter. He would talk about the burial sites where some of them had been found." A *wan min san*, a decorative umbrella, stood open in the room. Chinese characters were sewn onto loose panels that hung from its edges and represented the people who held him in esteem. It is thought to have been an appreciation of Frank's help during a famine.

The study had a sacrosanct atmosphere and Marylou recalled her father sitting in a chair and telling her something she never forgot: "You're smart enough to be a lawyer, Marylou."

Frank Glassey, Frank's nephew whom his sister Nellie had named after him, came to stay. He had left Shanghai for America as a 16-year-old and joined the Merchant Marine. "Frank was five feet nine inches tall, had blue eyes and his resemblance to my father was astonishing," said Marylou. "He lived with us for six months and created such a flutter among Jessie's girlfriends. My father adored him. So did Mama. So did we all. I was always happy when he took me for long walks in the French Park near our house. I learned how to play rummy from him."

Frank's younger brother George also came often. "Uncle George emigrated to Canada but stayed with us after he told us his wife had died. He taught me cribbage. He eventually got a job as a purser with Butterfield & Swire and left." In fact, George made another trip to Canada from Shanghai at age 46, declaring in an immigration form that he was carrying $3,500 and intending to retire. But his wife developed mental health issues and would be confined to an asylum.

Meanwhile, Marylou's older sister Jessie had developed into an attractive young woman with a keen sense of fashion. She kept European magazines and a Chinese tailor would come to the house and make dresses in the latest Paris styles, keeping aside material for matching shoes. When the "permanent wave" arrived in Shanghai, Jessie was one of the first to have her straight black hair curled and coloured. Mama recoiled with disapproval when Jessie brought home a flimsy black lace bra and panties.

Marylou would sit in a corner of the living room during Jessie's afternoon tea parties while she and her Eurasian friends danced the waltz and the foxtrot to Red Seal records on the gramophone. She recalled how good-looking some of the Eurasian boys were.

Dolly, several years older than Marylou, was a sweet, affectionate girl though she lacked any academic inclination. Frank would find her a job as a nanny with a rich American family and Dolly went with them when they moved to France.

Marylou was not close to Jessie and felt her sister was jealous of the attention Mama gave her and that their father was sending her to the prestigious Shanghai Public School for Girls.

One day, "Jessie and her boyfriend took me to French Park near our house and told me to play in the sandpit until they came back," recalled Marylou. "I was with other children but, one by one, they left with their *amahs* until I was the only one left. It got darker and darker and I didn't know how to go home. I didn't even know my address. It wasn't until eight or nine that night when Jessie went home and Mama asked where I was. Jessie had gone to the French Club and played tennis and had completely forgotten about me. I saw lanterns and heard my name being called and they found me screaming. After that, they drummed my name and my address into me."

Jessie had at least one European boyfriend but a serious, bespectacled Eurasian began making regular appearances at the dinner table.

Jimmy Jamieson Ellis worked in the advertising department of the *China Press* and was one of four sons, all good-looking, of a former Jardine Matheson agent at Ichang.

Jessie with one of Shanghai's first permanent waves

Soon afterwards, the Newmans moved to a terraced house at 3 Kiangwan Road, near Hongkew Park and the North railway station. This was where, Marylou recalled, Jessie and Jimmy held their reception after getting married on June 26, 1926.

Jimmy's family was present, along with many Eurasian guests, and Frank proposed a toast to the happy couple. Amid the milled guests, Jimmy suddenly crumpled to the floor, his champagne glass shattering.

Frank took charge, kneeling down and feeling Jimmy's pulse. Jimmy was not a big drinker and it was clear that something was seriously wrong.

An ambulance took him to hospital, where he was diagnosed with scarlet fever, a disease with no known cure except rest.

The following month, on July 27, Chiang's National Revolutionary Army began its Northern Expedition. By October 10, it gained control of Wuhan which it declared as its provisional national capital.

In early January 1927, following anti-foreign agitation in Hankow, the British evacuated their citizens and returned the concession to China a month later. In March, Chiang's army entered Nanking and took part in the rioting and looting of foreign properties.

Thoroughly panicked by such events, the British in Shanghai rushed in 20,000 troops to erect barricades and sandbags in the International Settlement. As Nationalist troops arrived at North railway station in March, Frank returned to move his family once again. Amid the rush, Dolly recalled putting on mismatched shoes while Marylou remembered a barbed-wire barricade near Garden Bridge manned by British "Tommies", who waved them through.

The Post Office came under severe pressure. In several provinces, including Shensi and Sichuan, anti-imperialist forces of the Nationalists and the Communists were openly protesting foreign control and foreign employees in the China Post Office, particularly by forming labour unions inside the Post Office.

On the east coast, Picard-Destelan was negotiating to hand over control of the entire Post Office to the Nationalists.

In Shensi, warlord Feng Yuxiang, with whom Frank was acquainted from earlier days, had changed sides again and thrown his weight behind the Nationalists. He sent his political head, Jian Youwen, to take control of the Xi'an Postal Service Administration, which was chaired by Frank Newman.

Jian pushed for the dismissal of foreign officials, including Frank, as well as replacing the postal Blue Sky flag with a White Sun flag. However, since the service came under the Directorate General of Posts in Peking, such moves would have been deemed illegal by some. Peking responded by transferring Frank to Chungking.

But in Chungking, where he had been acclaimed three decades earlier, Frank found himself increasingly beleaguered. He was subjected to anti-imperialist criticism from the newly-formed labour union in the Sichuan Post Office.

Trapped between his duty to stay and the need to leave for his personal safety, he wrote on 6 March, 1927 to the Directorate General of Posts in Peking, saying he had received a warning from the British Consulate about possible threats to foreign lives and property and he was preparing to evacuate from Chungking.

Then, on April 30, the *North-China Herald* reported that he and a Dr McCartney, a well-loved American physician and long-standing resident, were being "hooted" by a crowd in Chungking, with the doctor being stoned.

In a story handed down to the author's cousin Duncan Clark through his father, Frank Newman believed he had no option but to resign – and did so in dramatic fashion.

"According to my father," said Duncan, "Newman had fallen out with his superior officer so he got a shotgun, took the shot out of the cartridges, and went to the office and pretended to shoot the officer, who promptly fell back over his chair in shock, thinking he was dead. I suppose that was Newman's idea of a joke."

This action appeared out of character for a man known for his ability to handle people, but it reflected his frustration at being forced out of an organisation to which he had given decades of service.

He was not alone. With the Nationalists bent on taking over the Post Office and dismissing its foreign employees, 19 of the 131 foreigners serving in the Post Office in 1926 were dismissed or left the service in 1927 and an additional 28 would leave between late 1927 and early 1928.

Feng and Jian would clear the roads to Peking of warlord troops and the Northern Expedition would end with the conquest of the city on June 8, 1928.

In Shanghai, Jimmy had left hospital and was back with Jessie at Yuyuen Road, a quiet, leafy street in a residential area. The doctor told the family that Jimmy's condition was still serious and that he needed to rest and stick to a strict diet.

As a semi-invalid, however, Jimmy complained of being bored and began going to the office to see friends. Sometimes, he rang to say he would not be home for lunch and it would transpire that he had joined his friends for one of his favourite meals of Porterhouse steak. Jessie and Mama chastised him and urged him to be more careful.

Their entreaties were to little avail, however. Jimmy's condition worsened and he lapsed into a coma. He was taken to Shanghai's Country Hospital, where he died on July 12, aged 27.

The Ellis family organised the funeral but when Jessie tried to contact her father, they could not find him. Colleagues said he had left the postal service but no one seemed to know where he was. Jessie's grief was compounded by a loss of face.

One hundred days after Jimmy's death, Jessie had a curious experience, according to Marylou. "That night, all the lights suddenly came on and Jessie's dog, a lovely Airedale that slept on an armchair in their room, started wagging its tail as, according to Jessie, Jimmy came into their room. Jimmy went over to the dressing table and played with Jessie's manicure set. He came and stood by the foot of her bed and said, 'Goodbye, Girlie' – that was his pet name for her. Then he walked out of the room. We all woke up because of the lights and Jessie calmly told us, 'Jimmy came to say goodbye.'"

Frank's whereabouts were still unknown by then but, when he was found, the family could hardly believe their ears.

11

The Russian Woman

Marylou never did discover why her father did not show up for Jimmy Ellis's funeral and, if Mama and Jessie eventually found out, they did not tell her.

The answer lay in a manifest of the RMS *Empress of Canada*, one of the Canadian Pacific Steamships' ocean liners plying between Asia and North America.

When Jimmy died, Frank was not even in China. He was thousands of miles away in America – on a trip that would include Canada and Britain.

And he was not alone.

The manifest showed that E.F.S. Newman, 54, Postal Commissioner, was accompanied by his "wife", Nina Kovaleva, 25, born in Sevastopol, Russia, and his "daughter", Kira, six, born in Harbin, China.

This revelation, assuming Kira was Frank's daughter, means that she was born in 1921 and that Frank had known her mother for some time earlier.

Frank was based in Shensi during that period, though he took leave to see his family in Shanghai. The fact that Kira was born in Harbin suggested Nina had returned home to her parents for the delivery. In addition, Nina's birth in Sevastopol suggested that her family had moved from the Crimea to Harbin at a time when there was only one compelling reason a Russian would do so – to seek employment related to the China Eastern Railway. Russia was building the railway through Manchuria in northern China to link Chita with Vladivostok and Port Arthur in the Russian far east. Russians flocked to Harbin, which was the hub of the system.

Kira's birth, five years after Marylou joined the family in Changsha, placed Frank in a quandary, with two families to support. He was a decent man with a deep sense of responsibility and the thought of abandoning either of them was anathema.

He stayed with his Chinese family, installing them in a grand home in the French Concession and provided for them into the 1930s, including paying for his clever Marylou to attend the highly regarded SPG.

It's not clear where Nina and Kira lived. She had a mother and possibly other family, too, but Frank surely supported her as well.

When Frank met Nina, the position of Russian émigrés in Harbin and other parts of China had become especially precarious. The tens of thousands of Russians who migrated to Harbin for the massive railway project from 1897 were joined by many more thousands who fled the Russian civil war following the Bolshevik revolution of 1917.

Then, in 1920, China ceased to recognize the White (anti-Bolshevik) Russians while ending Russian extraterritoriality in the China Eastern Railway zone – thus leaving White Russians in Manchuria stateless. Without official documentation, White Russians found it very difficult to find work. Men were forced into menial occupations like doormen or bouncers while women had to work as dancers or "escorts" to survive.

When Frank left the Post Office abruptly in April 1927, events showed that he wanted a break from China.

While he could not take his disabled wife Mei-lan even if he had wanted to, he knew Nina was desperate for a passport. Frank came up with the idea of renewing his passport and applying for "legitimate" travel documents for Nina and Kira at the same time, claiming they were his wife and daughter.

Records show that Frank, Nina and Kira collected their passports in Shanghai on May 14, 1927, and two days later, picked up tourist visas for the United States.

Around two weeks later, they embarked on the *Empress of Canada* in Shanghai, which left Hong Kong on June 1 and docked at Seattle, Washington, and Victoria, British Columbia, some three weeks later.

What were Frank's plans? Information that Frank provided to immigration officials in the United States and Canada shows that he was carrying $11,000 and he and his "family" intended to spend up to two months in America before proceeding to Canada. He also stated they would cross Canada by rail and sail to Britain as part of a world tour.

Frank with Nina and Kira, circa 1927, courtesy of Alan Riddle

For obvious reasons, he did not mention his Chinese family. Instead, he named his nearest friend/relative in Shanghai as his son-in-law, John Ellis, residing at 14 Kiu-Kiang Road.

Was he really cutting ties with his Chinese family or was he just telling a story to immigration?

Frank evidently wanted to help Nina and Kira get a fresh start – but where? In 1927, America was the world's leading economy though the boom years were tapering off. British Columbia, where Edwin and George lived, was plagued by long and bitter labour disputes. Britain was still paying for the effects of the war and going through a downturn.

In Shanghai, which was flourishing, Marylou was moving up from the junior to the senior section of the SPG, which was handily near where she lived.

Frank's decision to continue underwriting her British education would shape her future.

In a country where the vast majority of Chinese girls stayed at home until they married, the influence of SPG upon its pupils cannot be overstated. Under the purview of the Shanghai Municipal Council, SPG educated the children of foreign businessmen or professionals of 30 nationalities, including British, Indian, Portuguese, Russian, Japanese and Germans.

Chinese and Eurasian girls were generally not accepted – but the authorities made an exception for those with British fathers and names. Marylou's closest friends were Lois Kemp, daughter of a British sea captain and his Japanese wife, and Mary McIntosh, whose father was a Scottish police officer and mother was Chinese.

The headmistress, Miss A.S.M. Alexander, and the teachers were well qualified and British. Typically, they were single and recruited from England on expatriate terms, including travelling out first-class on P&O ships. The women were self-reliant and open-minded and many had a taste for adventure. They taught a British curriculum that included science as well as the arts and they encouraged British activities such as drama and sports.

As well as being academically bright, Marylou played hockey, representing the school as a fast and nimble centre-forward, netball and volleyball, and she swam. In a callisthenics display on Sports Day, she curled up into a ball to depict the last full stop as the girls formed the giant letters of S.P.G. on the sports field. Although she lacked Jessie's vocal talent, Marylou sang in the chorus in Gilbert & Sullivan productions such as *The Pirates of Penzance*.

In short, whether a girl was an Indian Parsee or an Australian Chinese – like two of Marylou's friends in another class – she soon developed into an SPG girl, shaped by the English language and a peculiar mix of history, hockey and Gilbert & Sullivan. An SPG graduate was confident and possessed of an inquiring mind and independent spirit that would enable her to make something of herself in a man's world.

Calling themselves the Three Musketeers, Marylou, Lois and Mary hung around together after school. By the 1930s, Shanghai was one of the world's largest and most cosmopolitan cities, with grand hotels and modern department stores that flaunted the latest merchandise. In their uniforms of white blouses and sky-blue tunics, the girls would walk down the main thoroughfare of Nanking Road, browsing at the Wing On or the Sincere store and slurping noodles with iced tea at the popular Sun Ya restaurant.

Sweet-natured Lois blossomed into a slender teenager with doe-like eyes and milky complexion while the older Mary, vivacious with bold dark eyes, made them giggle with worldly "wicked" stories.

They watched Hollywood's silent classics with Charlie Chaplin and Laurel and Hardy. When the first "talkies" arrived, Marylou heard the tinkling of water being poured into a glass by Al Jolson in *The Singing Fool*.

Hollywood brought on-screen romance. Once, Marylou encountered a star in the flesh. In December 1929 she was among those given a half-day off to see Mary Pickford at the Majestic Theatre.

She watched transfixed as the movie star, who was promoting the first Oscars on a world tour with Douglas Fairbanks, glide down the spiral steps of the lobby with her peach-like complexion and blonde curls. "Her perfume stayed with me until I got home and I gave my hand for Mama to sniff," recalled Marylou.

Marylou learned that relationships in real life were rarely like those on the silver screen. Mary's father, a burly, ginger-haired sergeant at Sinza Road police station, asked her to take something to her Chinese mother in Chapei, the Chinese quarter. Marylou and Lois went with her in a rickshaw. Once outside the foreign settlements, the streets became narrow and congested, with more than a whiff of offal and night soil.

When they alighted, Mary led the way through a wooden moon gate into a courtyard and found her mother, younger sister and baby brother in a drab, dimly-lit room. In one corner was a *modung*, a covered wooden bucket. Mary's mother, thin and dressed in a padded jacket and black pants, greeted them shyly. Mary scooped up her little brother and held him tightly.

Mary McIntosh went to work as a taxi dancer after her Scottish father abandoned his Shanghai family

Mary said her father was being posted back home and had promised to take her with him. When, soon after, Mary failed to appear at school for several days, Marylou and Lois took another ride to Chapei to see if she was all right. Mary told them her father had left, saying he needed her to stay behind to look after her mother and siblings but would send her a ticket to England as soon as he could. The ticket never arrived; letters from her father dried up and Mary went to work as a taxi dancer in a night club, where she fell in love with a Basque jai-alai player.

Lois took Marylou to her home at the end of the tramline beyond Avenue Edward VII in the French Concession. Her English father plied a ship between Shanghai and Kobe where he had met "Auntie", as Marylou called her, a tiny Japanese who wore brightly-coloured kimonos and took short, dainty steps around a spotlessly clean flat. The captain, a tall, greying man in his fifties, sat in a chair, silent and stern-looking, waiting for his next assignment. "Auntie" told Marylou the captain had been in love with her best friend in Kobe but, after her sudden death, had turned his attention to her.

When Marylou next visited Lois's home, the captain was away and she met a tall, handsome Japanese man with a clipped moustache, sitting on a tatami mat. Oji-san, or "Uncle", rose and bowed deeply, with a military bearing.

Lois soon had a boyfriend named Joe. Joe's parents, said to be of Spanish and Jewish blood, had been killed in a car crash when he was 15 and he was looking after his younger siblings. Joe, with unruly hair and bulging eyes, was leader of a gang that was engaged in activities he referred to as "rackets."

Lois had other suitors, but Joe was persistent. When Lois went to the cinema with a boy on a motorcycle, they emerged to find the bike scattered in pieces on the pavement. When Lois introduced Joe to her parents, the captain was not happy that Joe had no steady job and told Lois he was not welcome. Undeterred, Joe climbed a drainpipe to her first-floor bedroom.

With a long face, Lois told Marylou she was pregnant. She was nervous about telling her father and asked Marylou to accompany her. Lois told the captain that she and Joe were in love and wanted to marry. Her father asked what was the rush when she had not finished school.

When Lois explained the reason, he started shouting while Auntie cried. He reminded Lois he had forbidden her from seeing Joe and she would have to accept the consequences. He told her to leave. Marylou helped her friend pack a suitcase and took her to stay with Joe.

Marylou also had a suitor, Bertie Anderson, who had a Swedish father and Chinese mother, and had a steady job as a clerk with the Shanghai telephone company. Considerate and well-mannered, Bertie had thick glasses and was small. Marylou wondered whether he asked her out because she was the only girl shorter than him.

On Saturdays, he took her for a drive around the Rubicon, a stretch of countryside beyond Hungjao, ending up with an ice cream soda with friends at the Chocolate Shop on Nanking Road. Their outings ended with a peck on the cheek. Once, in a movie theatre, Bertie reached over to hold her hand, but Marylou withdrew it quickly. He was a nice, dependable boy, but she felt no sparks.

By the early 1930s, Chiang and his Nationalists governed much of the country, and he was implementing national modernization programmes while his brilliant, glamorous wife Mei-ling focused on schemes to improve the lot of women.

The Generalissimo's control, however, did not extend to Manchuria, which the Japanese were making moves to occupy, or the mountainous areas of Shensi, where the Communists were waiting to make their move.

In 1931, the Japanese, ever keen to extend their rule, especially over resource-rich territories, were involved in a "provocation" called the Mukden Incident.

This began when a Japanese army lieutenant dynamited a track of the Japanese-controlled South Manchuria railway near Mukden on September 18, 1931. Blaming Chinese dissidents, the Imperial Japanese Army launched a full-scale invasion of Manchuria, establishing the puppet state of Manchukuo within months.

In early 1932, the Japanese became involved in the Shanghai Incident. This began with some Japanese army officers provoking anti-Japanese demonstrations in the International Settlement. On January 18, a Chinese crowd attacked Japanese Buddhist priests, killing one. Heavy fighting broke out between Chinese and Japanese troops and lasted for months before a truce was reached on May 5. The agreement called for Japanese military withdrawal and an end to Chinese boycotts of Japanese products.

These incidents drew international condemnation but Japan's militant faction grew more powerful and observers believed it was only a matter of time before Japan stepped up its incursions in China.

In the meantime, Frank had returned to China with Nina and Kira and, also around this period, he and Jessie were quarrelling a great deal, according to a cousin. Such arguments apparently did not take place in front of Marylou, for she was unaware of any rift.

It is not clear when Jessie found out about Frank's affair, but she would have been upset that her father, who was now retired, was squandering family money on a Russian mistress.

The family squabble burst into public view in 1932 with two court cases.

On April 9, 1932, the *China Press* newspaper, Jimmy's former employer, ran a headline: "Newman fined £50 by Haines. Heavy Sentence Given Briton For Falsifying To Get Passport." Newman had appeared in Shanghai Police Court, under bail of 1,000 (Shanghai) dollars, before magistrate C.H. Haines on a charge of obtaining a passport for himself and Nina Kovaleva, Russian, by representing the latter to be his wife. The magistrate stressed the seriousness of the offence against a British Parliament Act designed to keep undesirables from entering Britain. Newman's defence lawyer K.E. Newman (no relation) said his client was in "sheer ignorance" of the British Parliament Act and requested a light fine. The prosecutor, V. Priestwood, said that Newman had "deliberately cloaked the woman under the respectability of his wife," and he was not the ignoramus as portrayed and that it was clearly stated in red ink in all passports that heavy penalties would be meted out to such offenders. The magistrate, as a warning to the public and a lesson to the defendant, fined Newman £50 or $738 with an alternative of six months in jail if he did not pay the fine. Prosecution costs were set at $100.

A few weeks later, on May 23, 1932, the *South China Morning Post* in Hong Kong printed a report that E.F.S. Newman had appeared in Shanghai Police Court, again before magistrate C.H. Haines, this time being charged by Marion (an Anglicised version of "Mei-lan") Newman with desertion and non-maintenance. "Plaintiff said she did not wish to press the charge but she wanted alimony," said the report. "Defendant stated that he had made arrangements for the payment of $100 a month to plaintiff and he would sell his belongings to keep this up. Somebody had been pressing plaintiff to bring the case against him."

Haines adjourned the case for an hour to enable the parties to come to a settlement and the report continued: "When the court adjourned, defendant announced that an agreement had been reached by which he would assume plaintiff's debts and pay her $100 for maintenance. On this condition, the case was struck out."

One sentence was of particular interest – "Somebody had been pressing plaintiff to bring the case against him."

As Dolly was abroad and Mama still loved her husband, the one other person who had an interest in bringing such charges was Jessie.

Jessie was undoubtedly feeling insecure. She was a widow and knew it was difficult for a Eurasian to find a decent-paying job.

Mama had not been her cheerful self for several weeks when she asked Marylou to sit down as she had something important to say about her father. Marylou knew he had been away for a long time, but assumed it was because of his work. She had no idea he had retired. Nor had she any inkling of what had been in the newspapers recently.

Mama said that Frank was not expected to come home anytime soon, and the reason was that he had found a Russian girlfriend and was moving to Tsingtao.

After this came another blow. Mama said her father's monthly cheques had stopped coming and they were going to sell some of his curios, but they needed to cut down on expenses by not sending Marylou back to SPG. Marylou threw her arms around Mama's neck and they wept together.

Part of her knew she might not see again the man who had been a rock-like presence, even in his absence. She adored and respected him as a man and as a father and nothing would ever change that. In fact, when she looked back upon the family break-up decades later, she did not blame her adoptive father at all. On the contrary, she defended him stoutly, putting the blame on the Russian woman "with her wiles."

Another part of her knew it was the end of her wonderful childhood. She was in the lower sixth form with another year before the matriculation that might open the door to university and a career as the lawyer Dad once said she could be.

She did not know then but, even without matriculating, her father had already given her the key to her future. She was, after all, an SPG girl.

12

Breadwinner at Reuters

Once their father's cheques stopped coming, the family faced immediate money problems, more serious than 16-year-old Marylou realized.

A florid man with an authoritative manner and thick eyebrows and craggy nose arrived to buy Frank's curios. Crestfallen, Marylou watched as workmen carried out his porcelain bowls, bronze ewers, ivory figurines and carefully-wrapped coin collection. She recalled how lovingly he had handled them, how knowledgeably he had talked about them. It was as if they were carrying away her father piece by piece.

Even his armchair, the one in which he had sat and made her laugh by pulling funny faces – he was the only person she ever met who could make his upper lip wobble while keeping the rest of his face still – was carted off to the lorry.

The Jewish dealer argued with Mama about the Ming vases, but it was not about the price. Mama refused to sell them even though they were among the most valuable items. She knew how much her husband treasured them and she wanted them at home when he returned. The fact was that Mama believed deep down that he was having a fling and he would come back once it had run its course. Mama and Frank had never had a serious quarrel and she knew, even if he had long lost desire for her, that deep affection remained between them.

The sale was no doubt a disaster for the Newmans as the only person who could have obtained a fair price was Frank while, in his absence, Jessie seemed more concerned to make a quick disposal than to drive a hard bargain.

Even selling the collection was not enough as the family also had to move to a smaller, two-storey house in Dixwell Road in Hongkew with its growing Japanese community.

Jessie, who was working as a teletypist for Reuters news agency, seemed to accept their fallen state more calmly than Marylou expected.

"What's going to happen if our father never comes back?" Marylou asked.

"We should be all right now that we've sold his things," replied Jessie, lightly. Normally so practical, Jessie seemed unconcerned that the money raised from the curios would run out sooner or later.

It turned out that Jessie had a new distraction. A guest began appearing at the dinner table – a tall, sturdy English police officer with brooding good looks and more than a touch of vanity. Proud that he was from the London Metropolitan Police, Constable Albert Short was patronizing towards the local force and the Chinese in general.

Looking at Albert's vacuous eyes, Marylou wondered why he should feel superior, but it was clear that Jessie was madly in love with him. She became playful when he glanced at her, though Marylou noticed that Albert kept his own feelings well under control. Cloyingly, Jessie called Albert a "strong, silent type," but Marylou thought that he did not have much to say.

Jessie felt far more English than Chinese but she knew the stories about Eurasian girls who fell in love with British boys, who went on home leave and returned with English wives. Marylou knew personally of at least one rejected Eurasian girl who had swallowed Lysol with fatal results.

Just as Marylou was wondering what to do, a friend of Frank from the Customs, Bob McNeale, appeared. An avuncular, good-humoured man, he offered to underwrite a six-month course in secretarial skills and office management for her.

Marylou suspected he had been prodded by his young wife, Edie, who was Jessie's best friend from St Joseph's. A lively young woman, Edie was the daughter of an Irish priest and a Japanese consular official. Upon discovering that she was pregnant, her mother had gone back to Tokyo in disgrace. She had given birth but encountered so much prejudice in raising her mixed-blood daughter – in Japan, they called her a "half" – that she sent her back to Shanghai where the nuns educated her.

Marylou accepted Uncle Bob's offer with the promise that she would repay him when she could.

Bob McNeale paid for Marylou's secretarial course. He married Helen (left) after Edie ran off with a soldier

Corneck's Secretarial Institute turned out to be a large classroom, with a small adjoining office, in an old, shabby building. It was a no-frills learning place with about 20 desks, a table, and a gramophone player. Mrs Corneck, a brisk Eurasian woman in her mid-forties, was the sole staff.

Yet within these unadorned walls, Mrs Corneck performed daily deeds of quiet heroism.

The girls were mostly Eurasians but were unlike the girls Marylou had seen at Jessie's tea parties. Many were wan and thin and wore the same threadbare dresses day after day. For these girls, the course was a chance to land a low-paying job that would make the difference between a full and an empty stomach.

As well as running the institute single-handed, Mrs Corneck was a gifted and caring teacher. She taught rhythmic typing to music from the gramophone and she walked slowly from desk to desk, giving each girl attention and showing endless patience in coaxing some out of their shyness. She stayed behind to give extra coaching if it was needed.

Marylou learned that Mrs Corneck would allow those who were in financial straits to postpone paying her until they found a job.

Not surprisingly, the girls adored her.

Mrs Corneck never spoke about herself, but they would have been astonished if she had told her story.

Margaret "Daisy" Phillips was 21 when she married Warrington Corneck, a 38-year-old English master mariner from Devon, at Shanghai's Holy Trinity Cathedral in 1907. They had a son the following year but, not long afterwards, her husband went on a routine sea voyage – and simply disappeared. Nothing was ever heard again of him or the ship. It must have haunted Mrs Corneck that she could never bring closure to her grief, but she maintained an appearance of steadfast optimism.

Marylou responded to Mrs Corneck with enthusiasm and soon mastered Pitman's shorthand and was running her fingers along the Remington keyboard, typing 50, 60 and then 80 words a minute.

She became close to one of her classmates, a pretty, sweet-natured girl with sad brown eyes. Over tea at the Chocolate Shop, Lillian Faithfull told her that her English father had left his Chinese wife who was bringing up their two daughters alone.

At weekends, Lillian took her to the Erin Villa Club, run by a Filipino called Jock, who organised outings like bicycle rides and picnics for single Eurasian girls. It was a fun way of sharing information and contacts about jobs.

Lillian applied for a job as secretary in a pharmaceutical company and received a remarkable response, with the company sending a car to pick her up.

"I was so excited when the company rang and asked if I could go immediately. They sent a car and you should have seen my mother's face when a black limousine drew up outside our flat," she told Marylou. "I felt like a princess. When we arrived, I was ushered into this huge room where a fat Englishman sat behind the biggest desk I have ever seen. He was smoking a cigar and he looked up and said, 'Of what extraction are you?'

"He didn't even ask me to sit down. I told him my father was English and my mother was Chinese and that I had been educated in English schools. He said, 'So you're a Eurasian?'

"I told him I was and he asked, 'May I ask why you are applying for the job?'

"'My CV shows I have high marks from secretarial school and I live nearby. Would you like to see my references?'

"'No need, no need,' replied the man, waving his cigar. 'Thank you for coming. We'll let you know. The driver will take you home.'"

Needless to say, Lillian did not get the job, but soon found another.

When she brought her police officer boyfriend Bunny Judd to the Chocolate Shop, Marylou thought that, like Jessie's Albert, he was good-looking, though a slightly pointed chin gave him a sly look.

Bunny spoke of his night's work of moving beggars off the pavements, referring to them as "Chinese riff-raff." He did seem genuinely fond of Lillian and Marylou was delighted when Lillian asked her to be a bridesmaid at their wedding.

Marylou finished Mrs Corneck's course a month early and went to see Uncle Bob McNeale to hand over the unspent balance. He lived in one of the upper floors of the Customs House and she was surprised to see the door opened, not by Edie, but by a pretty girl she vaguely recognized.

When she said her name was Helen Toussaint, Marylou remembered that she had been at St Joseph's, too, and had been given the name Toussaint because she had turned up in the convent's revolving crèche on All Saints' Day.

Soon after this, Jessie asked Marylou to meet at her office so they could share a ride home. Sitting in a corner of the Reuters bureau on Avenue Edward VII, Marylou watched men with green eye shades clattering away on typewriters and walking over to scan the telex machines that were spilling out news from all over the world.

A balding, middle-aged man appeared and peered over his glasses at her. Mr W.R. Mowll beckoned her to come into his office where he asked about her typing and shorthand speeds. Reuters, he said, liked to engage members of the same family as this encouraged loyalty. Without further ado, he offered her a job as a typist at 50 yuan a month. The salary was paltry – a bowl of noodles at the Sun Ya cost three yuan – but Reuters was a prestigious company. Stunned, Marylou found herself accepting.

Jessie announced that Albert was being posted back to England. She didn't say anything else, but it was obvious that she hoped, even expected, that he would take her with him. Over the next few weeks, her moods swung between giddy anticipation and despondency.

Jessie followed her best friend Edie (on the left) to England. This photo shows them in Brighton

As Albert's departure drew closer, Jessie grew irritable, snapping at the slightest pretext. Then Marylou returned home to find that Jessie had locked herself in her room and could be heard weeping. P.C. Short had sailed without her.

A few weeks later, Jessie resigned and announced she was leaving for England. Mama turned almost translucent and could not hold back her tears as Jessie said she was following Edie, who had left Uncle Bob and run off with an English soldier called Ginger. Jessie did not say it, but Marylou sensed she hoped Albert would change his mind.

Marylou knew their combined income was barely keeping the family afloat and she thought Jessie was selfish to leave her as the sole breadwinner.

At Reuters, Louise – the grown-up name Marylou now used – stared at the cable she had torn off the teleprinter and frowned at the gobbledygook. When she showed it to Spencer Moosa, one of the senior staff, he explained the telegram office charged by the word and so reporters joined some words together and abbreviated others to save money. The result was "cablese".

Reuters' reporting staff was headed by British bureau chief Frank Oliver, who had followed Chiang Kai-shek on the march from Canton to Shanghai in 1927 and had been captured by the Communists and the Japanese, fearing for his life on both occasions before being released. Easily distinguishable by his ginger hair and intense blue eyes, Oliver summed up Chiang's rise with typical bluntness: "China was ruled by warlords. Chiang was the first man to bring unification to China either by forcing the warlords to join them or by defeating them." He would give Louise a reference, saying: "Your work will be your best recommendation wherever you go." It was advice that she followed throughout her career.

The international staff Louise worked with included a young American woman, Christine Diemer, and a Portuguese, J.J. Alderguer, but the one she had most contact with was Moosa, a tall, spare senior staffer who gazed at others over an imperious nose with an expression of amused tolerance. A hybrid of Jewish and Middle Eastern origins, Moosa held a British passport but confessed he had never been to England.

At first, Louise typed as the editors stood over her, dictating as they pulled stories off the wire. Adding flesh to the bones, the editors turned cryptic cables into a flowing narrative, at the same time pruning out speculation and unsubstantiated facts.

"When in doubt, leave out," Moosa said, pencilling thick red lines through copy. Louise learned how to tighten a story, eliminating repetition and superfluous words.

The editors dragged at cigarettes, glancing often at the wall clocks that showed the times in London, New York and other major cities. Reuters had a night shift and Louise did not understand why some editors preferred the "graveyard" shift, even drawing lots for it.

She soon discovered the reason. The journalists played hard as well and took full advantage of Shanghai's credit system. In the shops, bars, and even the brothels, they could sign chits for anything and everything. Bills were settled at the end of the month by *shroffs,* the accountants-cum-debt collectors.

It didn't take Louise long to realize that the *shroffs* came during the day – and that was why some editors sought to work at night.

Moosa, for example, had a fondness for Russian women and often ran out of money before payday. He had no qualms about borrowing from Louise even though she earned a fraction of his salary. Moosa coined the phrase, "Miss Newman is always good for five yuan," which became a standing joke. To his credit, Moosa always repaid her.

It was boom time for foreign and local journalists in Shanghai as China was increasingly in the focus of the world with Chiang Kai-shek's Nationalist government in Nanking facing increasing aggression from Japan and internal resistance from the Communists.

Whether Chinese or foreign-owned, Shanghai's newspapers were unabashedly partisan, pushing their proprietors' interests, and even some of the news agencies were far from impartial. China's Central News and

Japan's Domei were mouthpieces for their governments and frequently reported the same event quite differently.

One of Louise's jobs was to count the agency stories used by the Shanghai press each month. Reuters would always top the list above Associated Press, United Press, Havas and International News.

Louise was a quick learner and honed the writing and editing skills that would stand her in good stead. The editors relied on her increasingly and her work was deserving enough for her to be included under Reuters' news department as Miss L. Newman in the 1935 Shanghai directory.

She was proud of her work, but the tiny pay packet that she handed over, unopened, to Mama was not enough to support them.

They moved yet again to a smaller, cheaper house in Lansing Terrace, a lane off Dixwell Road. It had only a large room on the ground floor and a bedroom and attic above that. In tears, Mama was forced to let go of staff, including those who had been part of the family for years such as Dor-tze who would have trouble finding other work as the Chinese were superstitious about hunchbacks.

In the spring of 1935, Louise spotted an advertisement in the *North-China Daily News* for an opening at a new Chinese government publication.

When she arrived for the interview at 1283 Yuyuen Road, near where she once lived, she was surprised to find the office was in a residential block, quite far from the commercial district.

Her bewilderment increased when a servant opened the door and she could see behind him an apartment bare of furniture.

The surreal experience continued when a Chinese man in his mid-30s appeared, dressed in an English three-piece suit, cut from fine cloth. When he introduced himself, Wen Yuan-ning spoke with an educated British accent.

As the two faced each other across the desk, both Chinese, both speaking well-enunciated English, Wen said he would read a poem by A.E. Housman for her to transcribe.

She was by this time beyond astonishment and reached for her pen as he began reciting *A Shropshire Lad* in a shrill voice:

From Clee to heaven the beacon burns,
The shires have seen it plain,
From north and south the sign returns
And beacons burn again.
Look left, look right, the hills are bright,
The dales are light between,
Because 'tis fifty years to-night
That God has saved the Queen.

She didn't even try to decipher the meaning of what was being said, intent only on putting down the sounds correctly.

She waited while Wen read her typed notes. Looking over his spectacles, it was his turn to look amazed. She was, he said, the only candidate to produce a transcript without a single error.

He offered her a salary of 150 yuan a month. It was double what she was making at Reuters. Was this all a dream?

Back home, Mama asked: "Will Reuters take you back?" She fretted that her daughter was leaving an established agency for an untried magazine.

"What will happen if this doesn't succeed?" she asked.

But, for once, Louise made the decision for them both.

"Let's worry about that when the time comes," she replied. "Meanwhile, let's think about what we can do with the extra money."

13

Letter from Tsingtao

Frank Newman spent his last decade in a German-style bungalow with a red roof and walls of fading ochre. Its location in Tsingtao reveals immediately why he chose it. Frank spent his childhood in the 1870s and 1880s in front of Chefoo's number one beach. By the time he retired half a century later, Tsingtao, which had been developed by the Germans from the late 1890s, had eclipsed Chefoo as north China's most popular resort and had even acquired its mantle as the "Brighton of the Far East."

Frank resided at 4 Huei Ch'uan Road, overlooking Tsingtao's best bathing beach on Huiquan Bay. He was within strolling distance of the Strand Hotel, where he could drink Tsingtao beer, and the racecourse, another favourite haunt for British expatriates. It was a town with modern water and sewage systems and efficient hospitals and schools. It had everything he needed for a comfortable life, including a White Russian community for Nina.

After 35 years of serving the Chinese government as a Sinicized Briton, he had parted from his employer in a brutal manner. Nonetheless, a rueful Frank would have acknowledged that, though the foreigners had been useful in getting the customs and postal office started, the Chinese had always intended to manage their own affairs eventually. He had had a long and brilliant career, but now the era of foreign-dominated institutions, indeed of extraterritorial concessions, was nearing its end.

The question was: could Frank be happy in his own twilight years?

Meanwhile, down the coast, his daughter was starting her career in a golden era for Shanghai literati in which Chinese and foreign writers were cooperating in bold new enterprises.

It did not take Marylou long to persuade Mama that she had joined a reputable and well-financed group of Chinese intellectuals who were putting out a new type of magazine.

Wen was the chief editor of a monthly publication to be called *T'ien Hsia*, which translates as "Everything Under Heaven." It was to be a cultural magazine, written by Chinese and western scholars in a pioneering venture. While all the editors were Chinese, the content would be in English and the readership would be international.

It all sounded exciting and, importantly, the financing seemed assured. Although he rarely appeared, the publisher was Sun Fo, son of Sun Yat-sen, representing the Sun Yat-sen Institute for the Advancement of Culture and Learning.

Like many leading Chinese figures, Sun Fo had been educated in America, holding degrees from the University of California, Berkeley, and Columbia University, and after his return to China had been appointed Mayor of Canton (Guangzhou) where the Kuomintang government headed by his father was based. Sun Fo was President of the Legislative Yuan and, despite disagreements with his father's successor, Chiang Kai-shek, held key ministerial positions in the Nanking government.

T'ien Hsia was to be a cultural bridge between east and west – with the hidden aim of strengthening international opinion against Japan, which had occupied Manchuria in 1931 and was, according to seasoned observers, looking for a pretext to expand its presence in China.

Despite the magazine's strong links with the Nationalists, its content was to be cultural, not political, and it would employ well-known scholars from China and abroad.

Miss Newman was officially Wen's secretary but, in fact, he would increasingly saddle her with more responsibilities. "I soon discovered that I was a one-man show acting as the office manager, accountant, proofreader, telephone operator, typist – in fact, Girl Friday," she would tell historian Dauril Alden.

She had turned 19 when she learned the magazine would be launched in August 1935. She had to furnish the office, create a filing system, contact contributors and remind them about deadlines, help edit their articles, take them to Victor Arlington at the printer, Kelly & Walsh, and proofread the galleys.

Wen was a clever, multi-faceted man – and an avid Anglophile who dressed, talked and behaved like the upper-class Englishmen he admired. He started life as an overseas Chinese, son of an affluent Chinese family in the Dutch East Indies and the British colony of Singapore. He studied at Cambridge University where, as well as causing a stir by bringing his own manservant, he befriended scholars like A.E. Housman, who was the subject of his article in the first issue of *T'ien Hsia*.

Wen had excellent Chinese academic credentials as a professor of English language and literature at Peking University, but in the *T'ien Hsia* office he wore well-cut English three-piece suits and liked nothing better than hobnobbing with the diplomats at the British consulate and the intellectuals who visited Shanghai.

Wen so adored the English that he was also a snob – with a touch of the autocrat, as Marylou discovered soon after joining the staff.

Wen could turn on the charm but Marylou knew he would also shout at the Chinese servant for the slightest reason. One day, a cheque from the Sun Yat-sen Institute went missing, and Wen turned to Marylou and asked if she had seen it. Marylou replied that she had not, adding that it was T.K. Chuan who handled the finances. Wen raised his voice, insisting that he had given Marylou the cheque to pass to Chuan, who said he had not seen it. As Wen shouted with exasperation, Marylou retreated to the office library and locked herself in. Wen knocked on the door and asked her to come out, but Marylou told him she was not coming out until the cheque was found. She stayed put for two hours while Wen and others searched until Wen found the cheque tucked away in a book. He apologized, telling Marylou he had not realized she had a temper too. Miss Newman had shown she could stand up for herself and he never raised his voice to her again.

Despite looming political problems with the Japanese and the Communists, these were the best of times for China's intelligentsia.

The Republican era brought warlords, but it also ushered in a period of unprecedented cultural rapprochement between China and the West. Shanghai was the obvious wellspring for such interchange. Its foreign concessions had started as trading centres but had swiftly grown into hubs for the exchange of ideas and methods through universities, schools, libraries, bookshops and theatre groups, as well as numerous newspapers and periodicals. The warlords' takeover of Peking in 1926 had caused 50 university professors to leave for Shanghai, further boosting its stock of intellectuals.

During this *belle époque* many Chinese academics went abroad to study at universities in America and Europe, becoming well-versed in Western languages and culture before returning home. In fact, this was a time when Chinese of all classes travelled widely and English was spoken to a surprising degree, even in the countryside.

All the *T'ien Hsia* editors on the masthead were *hua chiao,* as overseas educated scholars were known. John C.H. Wu was a lawyer and philosopher who had studied under Justice Oliver Wendell Holmes at Michigan Law School and had maintained a friendship with the eminent Supreme Court judge. Back in China, Wu had become a judge as a young man and served in the Legislative Yuan, where Sun Fo had asked him to draft China's constitution in 1933.

Tall, with tapering fingers, Wu was a patriot who generally wore Chinese gowns and deliberately spoke English with a Ningpo accent. The son of a banker, Wu had once been a playboy and, when Marylou met him, he was in the process of converting to Catholicism. He became devout but cheerfully so, expressing his joy in God with enthusiasm and humour. Marylou was a Catholic, too, and Wu would become the godfather of the author.

Another distinguished editor was Lin Yutang, who was writing *My Country and My People* – which Marylou helped type up – a witty, philosophical work that turned him into an international best-selling author.

Older than the others and an established literary humorist, Lin was raised as a Christian by his minister father and educated at a mission school and Shanghai's St John's University. He went to Harvard for a doctoral degree but financial hardship forced him to drop out and he went to Europe to work with the Chinese Labour Corps in France during the Great War before finishing his doctoral degree at the University of Leipzig.

He was the most overtly political of the editors. With his puckish smile, Lin was a campaigner for women's rights and civil rights. Like other *hua chiao*, he wrestled with the dilemma of being influenced by Christianity and Western ideas while firmly keeping his Chinese identity.

Rounding off the editorial board was Chuan Tsen-kuo, an alumnus of Illinois University who was teaching Greek philosophy at Tsinghua University as well as looking after the office finances. A highly-strung bachelor who was devoted to his younger sister Mei-Mei and an Annamese cat, T.K. would burst into tears over trivial matters. He wrote in an esoteric style that some found hard to follow.

Unlike Reuters' humming newsroom, the pace at *T'ien Hsia* was often relaxed. Wen usually came in, but the others dropped by to bring in articles or to chat. Soon, the office became a gathering place for writers to gossip while sipping hot tea and chewing watermelon seeds.

One frequent visitor, a good friend of Lin, was the Chinese poet Zau Sinmay, a slender man with a beautiful oval face, deep brown eyes and pouting lips. From a wealthy family, Sinmay went to Cambridge before bursting onto Shanghai's literary scene at the age of 21 with his first collection of poems in 1927 that were regarded as brilliant and decadent. He had rapidly become a celebrity, as much for his debauched lifestyle as his literary endeavours, which included publishing.

To many, he symbolized Shanghai's rapid transformation into a city of scintillation and style, recklessness and excess. Wearing silk gowns with brightly coloured capes, Sinmay would bring friends such as the English poet William Empson, another contributor to the magazine. Empson was teaching at Chinese universities after being expelled from Cambridge for being caught *in flagrante delicto* with a female companion.

Marylou had reason to recall the occasion Wen brought along the British aesthete Harold Acton, an elegant cognoscente of Chinese language, traditional drama, and poetry. The staff took Acton out in a small car with Marylou sitting on Acton's knee at the back. She recalled thinking, "If only Dad could see me now."

The inaugural issue of *T'ien Hsia* appeared in August 1935. In an editorial, Sun Fo lamented that improved communications had not produced greater international amity. International goodwill could only be achieved by concentrating on the good points countries had in common rather than harping on their differences, he asserted, and *T'ien Hsia* was born of a conviction that the best way to do this was through cultural understanding.

In an article, Wen Yuan-ning argued that the Chinese expressed themselves intuitively rather than logically, and he compared the "synthetic" structure of Chinese with the "analytical" Indo-European languages. An early feminist, Lin Yutang described how Chinese women, as well as being denied equal treatment and educational opportunities, had to struggle against concubinage, foot binding, the encouragement of suicide in defence of chastity, and a ban on widows remarrying.

The "scoop" of the first issue was the "Unpublished Letters of D.H. Lawrence to Max Mohr." Lawrence's controversial book *Lady Chatterley's Lover* had created a literary storm in Shanghai and Max Mohr, a distinguished German dramatist and novelist as well as a physician, happened to be in town and brought his letters to the office. Seeing a copy of Lawrence's book, Marylou blushed as she read its graphic descriptions of sex. She had never read anything like it and this was one event she didn't mention to Mama.

Marylou raised her head from her desk to see a glamorous American woman, who looked as though she had stepped out of a fashion magazine. With short brown hair curled in the latest Shanghai style and a fox stole slung carelessly around her neck, Emily Hahn was proffering a book review.

"I discussed this with Wen and hope I'm not too late for your deadline," she drawled in a mid-western accent. In Mickey, as her friends called her, Marylou saw a warm and captivating personality and, although Mickey was 10 years her senior, they struck an immediate rapport.

"What brought you to Shanghai, Mickey?"

"I was taking a world cruise with my sister and we stopped off for a few days. That was weeks ago and I'm still here," said Mickey. In return, Mickey asked Marylou if she knew where to get a permanent wave.

The women laughed.

To Marylou's delight, the magazine's only woman writer became a frequent visitor. She wanted to know about everyone and everything and it was a tonic for Marylou to discuss personal problems with someone so empathetic and worldly. Mickey was always ready with sensible advice – and never failed to make her laugh.

Mickey was looking for help to type up a book she had finished, *Steps of the Sun*, and Marylou offered her services. Mickey, who soon realized Marylou was supporting her mother, paid generously.

A regular contributor to *The New Yorker*, Mickey worked as a journalist for the *North-China Daily News* but she became such a sought-after personality on the social circuit that she soon began appearing in its gossip columns as well.

Raised in Chicago of German-Jewish parents, Mickey had views ahead of her time and was not afraid of expressing them. She was quick, for example, to denounce the patronizing way the British treated Chinese and Eurasians and was outraged when she heard of a British family cutting off a son for marrying a Eurasian.

"They remind me of our American South," she said. "They call every Chinese 'boy' no matter how old he is, just as the whites call the blacks 'boy.' And they treat Eurasians the way that our Southerners do mulattos. Good for sleeping with, but nothing more."

In Shanghai's stifling moral climate, Mickey's opinions were a breeze of fresh air, but it was her behaviour that caused a tsunami of indignation. She smoked cigars in public and she arrived at parties with a pet gibbon perched on her shoulder. Her choice of escorts caused tongues to wag furiously. Mickey appeared as the companion of Sir Victor Sassoon, one of Shanghai's wealthy Baghdadi Jews, at his lavish parties in the Cathay Hotel and in his private box at the Shanghai Racecourse.

But her most scandalous action was becoming the lover of the opium-smoking playboy poet, Zau Sinmay. This raised an outcry of indignation which Mickey took in her stride. Through Sinmay and his large family, Mickey immersed herself in Chinese ways and penned articles for *The New Yorker* about a Mr Pan, modelled on her lover, which would help fan strong American interest in China,

"Mickey did whatever she pleased and didn't give a damn what anyone thought," said Marylou. "She was unlike anyone I had ever met, and she taught me more than anyone." Marylou's friendship with Mickey was to last a lifetime.

Marylou continued to see Lillian, who had managed to find a job working for an English solicitor. But one day she received a barely coherent call from her friend saying, between sobs, that something terrible had happened to Bunny. She didn't explain, but the newspapers soon trumpeted the details.

Bunny had been on duty when two Chinese police officers called in to request assistance with a beggar. He and a colleague, who had turned up late and somewhat drunk, left to deal with the matter. Finding a long-haired Chinese beggar on the ground, moaning and frothing at the mouth, Bunny and the other police officer placed the man over the mudguard of their car and directed the driver to a nearby creek. From this point, the story grew murky. According to the driver, the police officers threw the beggar into the water, but Bunny and his colleague claimed that they had lowered the man into a passing boat. Rescuers hauled the beggar from the creek, but he died of pneumonia in hospital.

Marylou could only shake her head, remembering the way Bunny had spoken of Chinese vagrants. Lillian poured out her distress to Marylou, but they never discussed whether Bunny was innocent or guilty. Lillian's boss agreed to represent Bunny.

The court case drew huge publicity in the British and Chinese press and touched a sensitive nerve. The argument against the police officers was strong, especially after an inspector admitted the men had tried out different stories before deciding which one might work best. However, guilt was a secondary issue in the foreign community, which expressed astonishment that two "clean-living" Englishmen should be on trial for their lives over a Chinese mendicant.

Although the judge indicated that he thought the men were guilty, a British jury returned a verdict of Not Guilty.

"Thank God it's over," said Lillian, and that was her only comment on the matter. Events moved quickly for Lillian and Bunny for the authorities decided it was best to send him home. Bunny proposed and Lillian quickly accepted him.

Soon after, Marylou was a bridesmaid at the wedding where Lillian looked lovely in white lace and floppy hat.

Marylou (second left) at Lillian and Bunny's wedding

In June 1936, Marylou bade goodbye before Lillian and Bunny sailed to England. She was happy to see Lillian's smiling face but she harboured misgivings about the relationship. As it turned out, Lillian did not find happiness for long. She would give birth in 1940 but die shortly afterwards at the age of 23. Bunny would remarry within months.

In early February 1937, Marylou arrived home to find Mama in tears. Mama handed her a telegram from the British consul in Tsingtao which informed them with regret that Frank Newman had died of heart failure on February 1, at the age of 64.

Then, a curious thing happened. A second envelope arrived from the consulate a week later. This included a note from the consul, explaining that he had found a letter that had been found in Frank's pocket and he was now enclosing it. He had addressed it to Marylou, so she read it aloud to Mama: "I have really wanted to come home for a long time, but circumstances have not made this possible. I beg of you to believe me and not to think too harshly of me."

The letter changed everything. Mama had been right after all. She had not kept his Ming vases in vain, even if he would never see them again. Mama wept once more – for love lost, restored, and gone forever.

The two women huddled together in their tiny home, unaware that their modest survival mode, carefully rebuilt after his departure, was about to be swept away, along with Shanghai's burgeoning literary resurgence.

14

Billie Lee, War Broadcaster

The second quarter of 1937 was relatively peaceful, but it was only a lull before the storm. On the national scene, there had been a major crisis the previous Christmas when a northern warlord kidnapped Chiang Kai-shek to force him to join forces with the Communists against the Japanese and, for several tense days, the leader's life – along with hopes for unity – hung in the balance. But after negotiations involving Madame Chiang and her foreign advisor, Australian W.H. Donald – both of whom Marylou would later work for – the Generalissimo emerged as a stubborn man seemingly without fear for his personal safety, an image that transformed him instantly into a nationally recognized hero.

T'ien Hsia was quickly gaining prestige and, after a few issues, Marylou was settling into a routine. She and Mama had earlier moved to the tiny house in nearby Lansing Terrace. Hongkew had developed as the Japanese quarter with its own restaurants, tea gardens, beer halls, cinemas, brothels and a fire station. Since acquiring the same "rights" in China as western nations, Japan had become the largest foreign investor in Shanghai, setting up hundreds of factories in Pudong across the Whangpoo River.

In the spring, ever looking for ways of increasing her income, Marylou answered a newspaper advertisement for a part-time English teacher. Within days, she received an invitation for an interview and was intrigued to find it was at the Japanese consulate. Marylou had mixed feelings. She shared the national outrage that Japan had been occupying Manchuria since 1931 and fought a mini-war in Shanghai in 1932, killing thousands of Chinese.

Yet the Japanese she encountered on a day-to-day basis were hard-working shopkeepers and white-painted girls in gay kimonos who served her sukiyaki as she sat cross-legged on a tatami mat.

At the Japanese consulate, Ishii Itaro, an urbane, slightly built man, showed no surprise when a Chinese girl turned up and he offered Marylou tea in an exquisitely painted cup. A bespectacled man in his 50s, the consul's English was quite good as he had previously been posted in Washington and London and he wanted to brush up his conversational skills.

They met three times a week and, over delicately flavoured tea, discussed topics of the day or editorials in *The Times* of London that he would read aloud. Politics they avoided for, even as they exchanged pleasantries about Shanghai, the Japanese were making threatening noises up north.

Marylou did not know that, as a veteran of the *Gaimusho* (Foreign Ministry), Iishii-san was, like his boss in Tokyo, firmly opposed to the militarists' aggressive policy in China – and, in fact, had clashed violently with them, even getting his face slapped on one occasion. Marylou could not guess that this courtly Japanese would soon extricate her from a highly inflammable situation.

In early July, she reached the magazine office to find Wen and T.K. in animated debate. Japanese and Chinese troops had exchanged fire on the Marco Polo Bridge near Peking and the incident had escalated, with the Japanese pouring troops into northern China.

"It's a classic trick," cried Wen. "The Japanese are claiming a 'provocation' and using this to start something."

Wen was correct and the Japanese went on to seize five provinces, including Peking, in what they called "a special undeclared war." Within weeks, it was clear the Japanese were going to extend their campaign to Tientsin and Shanghai.

As she rode the red double-decker bus to work, Marylou saw Japanese marines erecting sandbag barricades at street corners.

Her colleagues urged her to move to the safety of the International Settlement, but this was not easy as many had the same idea and rents were soaring. After a frantic search, Marylou grabbed the offer of a one-bedroom flat in Hardoon Road.

Japanese warships were anchoring off the Bund and Chinese troops were amassing around the city. When the Japanese claimed that a Chinese group had kidnapped one of their seamen, Marylou told Mama they had to leave immediately.

Marylou said their new place was so small they could take only what they needed and would come back later for the rest. Nonetheless, Mama insisted on taking Frank's lacquer vases.

They joined an unending procession of refugees on North Szechuan Road heading for Garden Bridge. Most were on foot, with families pushing handcarts piled high with mattresses, pots and pans, bundles of clothes.

Marylou was unpacking in their new home when she heard an unfamiliar thud in the distance. From the window, she could see smoke rising from the Bund and, shortly after, she heard on the radio that bombs had fallen around the Palace Hotel.

Marylou was stunned; the International Settlement was off-limits for any incursion. She heard later that the bombs had been dropped by Chinese pilots who had opened the hatches too early on their way to the Japanese warships off the Bund.

Later that day, more bombs fell on the crowded Great World amusement palace, killing hundreds. Dubbed Black Saturday, it was one of the earliest occasions that war claimed a large number of civilian casualties.

A few days later, Marylou went to Wing On to buy shirts for a friend who had been called up by the Shanghai Volunteers. With the parcel tucked under her arm, she boarded a bus near the junction of two major thoroughfares, where a Sikh police officer, with red turban and flowing black beard, was directing traffic. Moments later, she heard a blast and looked over her shoulder to see billowing flames and smoke. Only when she saw the newspaper pictures the next day did she realize that a bomb had landed by the bus stop where she was standing minutes earlier. It killed hundreds of shoppers and employees. The Sikh officer, pinned to his traffic island, had surely not stood a chance.

Fighting broke out all around the foreign concessions, but not within them. Marylou heard the whine of artillery shells and saw flares lighting up the night sky, but she was not directly threatened.

Nonetheless, foreigners in droves took their wives and children to the Bund and waved them off on steamers to Hong Kong.

At *T'ien Hsia*, Wen shelved plans for the next issue as it was uncertain where it would be printed, if at all.

Wen was anxious because, with his close links to the Chinese government, he was convinced he and the staff were on a "blacklist" compiled by the Japanese secret service. Mickey Hahn would write in a book that John Alexander of the British consulate "has a talent for sniffing out intrigue, I think inherited from his Italian ancestors, and he thought he was on the trail of a really dangerous plot against Wen and the magazine."

She was sceptical because, as she said, "*T'ien Hsia* could not be called anything but a cultural publication given to articles on oriental calligraphy, history and books."

But Mickey, despite her excellent sources, was wrong. She did not know that Wen was a member of the local Anti-enemy Committee, a group that set itself up to inform Shanghai's foreign residents about Chinese positions in the war. Other members included Xin Jinlin, president of the Anglo-Chinese Medhurst College and a member of the Legislative Yuan; Liu Zhanen (Herman Liu), president of Shanghai University; and H.J. Timperley, correspondent for *The Manchester Guardian*.

Chiang Kai-shek's information chief, Hollington Tong, was based in Nanking and turned to the committee for help in reaching Shanghai's foreign community. With government backing, Liu organised the Cosmopolitan Club in Shanghai where consular officials and bankers met to discuss how to deal with warfare in Shanghai. Wen also had ties with the strongly anti-Japanese publication the *Far Eastern Mirror*, another English-language monthly, and would secretly publish it after it moved from Wuhan to Hong Kong.

That Wen was in danger was not in any doubt. The Japanese army, after they took over Shanghai, assassinated anti-Japanese journalists and activists and on April 7, 1938, Liu Zhanen, Wen's fellow member on the Anti-enemy Committee, was shot dead while waiting for a bus with his young son. *T'ien Hsia* publisher, Sun Fo, would also be the target of an assassination attempt when the Japanese forced down and strafed a passenger airliner from Hong Kong, believing he was on it.

With work on *T'ien Hsia* suspended, Wen surprised Marylou by asking if she could help the Mayor of Shanghai, O.K. Yui (Yu Hung-chun).

"He asked for someone who spoke excellent English and I recommended you," said Wen.

Marylou agreed, without having a clue what might be involved.

The next day, a black car arrived to take Marylou to City Hall in Rue Cardinal Mercier, in the French Concession, where the mayor held office in an imposing grey stone building behind a large garden and a driveway.

She found Mayor Yui behind a desk, issuing rapid-fire instructions to several aides. Although the prospects of his city holding out against the Japanese were pretty much zero, he exuded geniality.

He sprang from his chair and pumped Marylou's hand.

"Wen says I can count on you. We're having a press conference in a few minutes. Please take down everything verbatim. Transcribe your notes and give them to Mr Chen. One copy will go to Chiang Kai-shek and another will be translated into Chinese for the media."

Chiang Kai-shek! Bowled over by the responsibility being thrust upon her so suddenly, Marylou could only nod as she took her place beside the mayor on a small dais in front of a couple of dozen correspondents from the world's press.

In the front row was the familiar figure of Spencer Moosa, who smiled and raised his eyebrows quizzically, as if to ask what she was doing there. She was wondering the same thing.

The mayor reported on the fighting, the casualties and the damage. The city's fire, water and health services were all under great strain, he said. When questions came from the floor, the mayor handled them candidly, even admitting it when he did not have an answer.

Chinese officials were generally cagey with the press, giving only vague answers but she learned that Mr Yui, who had only recently been appointed mayor, was a former newspaperman. This explained his ease with the cut-and-thrust of press conferences, especially with questions from a new contingent of foreign correspondents who had arrived to cover the war. He also had a lively sense of humour, telling jokes to relieve the serious business. Marylou could see the newspapermen liked him.

Marylou noticed two correspondents who asked a lot of questions: Pembroke Stephens from the *Daily Telegraph* in London, who had a long, thin face with intense eyes under curly unkempt hair, and next to him a burly Fleet Street colleague, Michael Killanin of the *Daily Mail* (who was also a lord).

As the battle for Shanghai intensified, the briefings became a daily event and Marylou chatted with the correspondents over *dim sum* and drinks that were served beforehand in the garden. One afternoon, a Japanese plane appeared out of nowhere, roaring over their heads. Without shelter, people dived under the tables. On her knees, trembling, Marylou felt a bump. It was Spencer Moosa, crawling around on all fours.

"Miss Newman, fancy you being frightened," he said, drily.

A few days later, just before the press conference was due to start, an aide approached the mayor on the platform and whispered into his ear. The mayor frowned, then turned to Marylou.

"We have a problem," he said. "Our broadcaster, T. K. Chang, is sick and cannot go on the air tonight. Can you broadcast in his place? We will give you a script and a car will take you to the studio."

Marylou stared at him blankly.

"I beg your pardon, Mr Mayor, but I'm not sure that I understand you correctly. Are you asking me to go on the radio and read the news?"

"Exactly," replied Mr Yui, with a broad grin.

"But, Mr Mayor, I have no experience at all of radio work." Her voice sounded like a squeak.

"Don't worry, Miss Newman. You have a nice, clear voice. Just speak slowly and I'm sure everything will be fine." Mayor Yui added, briskly, "Now let's begin our press conference."

Marylou focused on the proceedings with great difficulty.

Turning to her at the end of the briefing, the mayor said, "You cannot use your real name on air as the Japanese will be listening. You will have to adopt another name."

He added quickly, "How about Billie?"

An American actress called Billie Dove was the rave of Shanghai cinema audiences and Billie guessed this was why her name had popped into his head.

She nodded without comment.

"That's settled then. You will be Billie Lee."

In this casual manner did Billie acquire her most lasting nickname. Unlike her previous names, from Louise Mary to Marylou to Louise, 'Billie' would stick with her for the rest of her life.

An aide escorted her to a black Cadillac, where a chauffeur with a peaked cap handed her a heavily padded garment.

"What's this?" she asked.

"It's a bullet-proof vest," said the driver.

She peered into the car but could not see through its heavily tinted windows.

The driver told her the glass was bullet-proof as she sank into the deep leather seats.

Drawing up in front of an anonymous Chinese house – she had no idea where they were – Billie entered a small makeshift studio, padded to make it soundproof. A microphone dangled in front of her. "I can't believe this is happening," she told herself. "I haven't even had time to tell Mama so she can listen."

In those pre-television days, radio was king and broadcasters, almost all of them male, became celebrities.

As she stared at the microphone, the thought of thousands of listeners made Billie feel weak.

On the other side of a glass screen, a technician wearing earphones gave her the thumbs-up signal. Then he held up both hands and started showing fingers. This was the countdown. Six, five, four.... A red light came on and the man gestured for her to begin. Billie took a deep breath and said, "Good evening, this is Billie Lee of Station XGOY of the City Government of Greater Shanghai."

She was so nervous that she had no idea what she was reading, but she was alert enough to scan a few words ahead to check the script was grammatical and made sense. "Please God, don't give me any names I can't pronounce," she prayed.

By the end, her blouse was damp with sweat as she looked up at the technician. He was smiling with approval and, as she stepped out of the cubicle, he handed her a telephone. Mayor Yui was on the line.

"Congratulations, Billie Lee," he said. "You were fine. You must do it again tomorrow."

As it began to sink in, Billie was exhilarated and could hardly wait to break the news at home. Mama was incredulous and she worried what it might mean for her little girl. But she soon became Billie's biggest fan, though she did not fully understand the English-language bulletin.

Almost every evening for two months, Billie Lee went on air. The time of the broadcast stayed the same, but the studio location changed every few days to avoid detection by the Japanese. She was in the front line of a propaganda war in which the Japanese, who were broadcasting different accounts of the hostilities, wanted to silence the voice of "Free Shanghai."

Gaining confidence, she kept her eyes open for names and places in the news and checked on their pronunciation in case they cropped up in the bulletin. The material was always put together in a hurry and she sometimes changed a sentence to make it more grammatical or to sound better.

Her voice, with its Chinese name and English accent, became one of the best-known in Shanghai. Many listeners were curious about the woman with the cultured tones and some, mainly students, called to ask if they could meet her. Billie was light-headed when friends called to say they recognized her voice.

Billie was never busier. The evacuation of European women led to an acute shortage of English-speaking secretaries so when the British consulate's John Alexander asked Wen for help, he once again volunteered Billie's services.

Alexander and Wen were good friends and Billie had often liaised between them regarding distinguished British visitors and possible contributors to *T'ien Hsia*. It was Alexander who had forwarded to her the message about her father's death from Tsingtao.

Now, instead of reporting to *T'ien Hsia*, she began the day in the consulate's beautiful colonial building, with its large and immaculate lawn, near Garden Bridge. She would type up reports on the war that she had broadcast the night before. From there she would proceed to Mayor Yui's afternoon press briefings and the evening broadcast would close a demanding day.

The British consulate in Shanghai where Billie worked in the mornings

The work was exciting, but all the reports pointed depressingly in one direction. Through sheer force of firepower, Japan was assured of victory though Chinese troops put up unexpectedly strong resistance, yielding block by block in some areas. Japanese naval planes pounded the industrial areas, killing women and children who worked in the factories, but this indiscriminate bombing of civilian targets evoked little more than indignation in a world distracted by events in Europe.

The settlement turned entertainment places into emergency hospitals and society women and taxi dancers alike became nursing aides to tend the wounded. In the city of Nantao, south of the French Concession, a tall, gaunt Jesuit priest, Father Jacquinot, who had confirmed Billie in the Catholic faith, headed the International Red Cross and led an effort to create makeshift shelters from temporary sheds and old buildings, saving the lives of thousands.

When artillery fire landed in the settlement in late October, Pembroke Stephens raced in his yellow sports car to the *T'ien Hsia* office. British troops were stationed in nearby Jessfield Park, and Japanese shells had landed in the barracks, killing four British soldiers and five Chinese.

Hearing Stephens' voice, Billie ran to the tiny balcony overlooking Yuyuen Road. "The Japanese are only a few hundred yards away," shouted Stephens. "They're thinking of blowing up a bridge. You'd better get out of here." The *T'ien Hsia* office emptied quickly.

Yet the settlement was still a haven and people stood on the Bund's rooftops, cheering and groaning as they followed the aerial and ground action through binoculars.

One battle in particular became a topic of conversation. Just north of Garden Bridge, a few hundred Chinese soldiers, barricaded in two warehouses, held out for days under Japanese artillery and incendiary bombs. A Chinese flag fluttered atop the building, symbolizing their resistance. They evacuated only when the buildings were set ablaze and they still had to run a gauntlet of machine gun fire as they made for Garden Bridge.

Amid the fighting, the settlement's nightclubs thrived. The influx of soldiers and the "grass widowers" – those whose wives had been evacuated – created a roaring trade. "Let's make merry, for you never know what the morrow will bring" was the prevailing cry.

In early November, Stephens invited Billie and Edie, a pretty part-Russian friend of Billie, to join correspondents for dinner at the rooftop restaurant of the Arcadia Hotel.

It was a chance for the girls to dress up and for the men to relax. Apart from Stephens, the company included O'Dowd Gallagher of the *Daily Express,* Michael Killanin of the *Daily Mail* and Spencer Moosa.

That evening, as Gallagher flirted with Edie, Stephens was sporting a black eye – and some of the journalists ribbed him about it, pretending not to know what had happened.

"That's a nice shiner you have, Pembroke," said Gallagher. "Did you fall off a bar stool?" Gallagher and Stephens were friends, having covered wars together.

Billie and Edie with Pembroke Stephens (left) and O'Dowd Gallagher

Stephens had fought with some pranksters in the press corps who rigged the drawers in his room so that their contents spilled onto the floor when he opened them. It was not the first time this had happened and, exhausted from another trip to the front, an irate Stephens found the offenders at the Metropole Hotel and there was a scuffle.

With Shanghai's fall imminent, they solemnly raised their glasses to toast the doomed city.

Wen was now frantically making preparations to move the staff to Hong Kong.

On November 11, Billie stood near Mayor Yui as he announced that the day's briefing would be the last. It was a poignant farewell, as many of the journalists were sympathetic towards China.

Stephens was not present as he and other foreign observers were watching the fighting in Nantao. They were perched on a 50-foot-high water tower when a Japanese machine-gunner turned his fire on them. A bullet caught Stephens in the leg. He waved a white handkerchief as he pulled himself forward to get the Japanese to stop firing. But another bullet struck him above the left eye, killing him instantly. The firing continued for 15 minutes before a French soldier climbed up the tower and waved a flag. Three of the six men with Stephens were wounded. When Spencer Moosa called to tell Billie what had happened, she felt faint. Among the hundreds of casualties the war had claimed, Stephens was the only one she had known personally. He was only 34 years old and left a wife and two children in London.

After his death, Stephens became a victim of sickening propaganda. One Japanese newspaper, the *Nichi-Nichi*, claimed that Stephens had been killed as a result of wounds "received in a personal encounter with other British correspondents."

The *T'ien Hsia* staff had stayed as long as they could, but now they had to leave as soon as possible.

Billie had never been separated from Mama and she had the wrenching task of telling her she had to leave, but that it would not be long before they would be reunited. Jessie's in-laws, the Ellises, would keep an eye on her. Billie promised that, as soon as she was settled in Hong Kong, she would send for her.

Mama had never been without family and Billie could hardly bear to look at her before she left to join her colleagues and the throng of people at the Bund, all trying to leave before it was too late.

For security reasons, all the staff had been issued tickets under false names and Billie boarded the French ferry *Aramis* as Miss Feng. As a further precaution, they had second-class tickets to avoid looking conspicuous. Everyone was strained, having to leave China under such circumstances, but the journey was not without its amusing side.

Once at sea and feeling safe, Wen found the surroundings were not to up to his fastidious standard; he went to the purser and arranged to move up to first class. This prompted T.K. Chuan to ask a colleague if they should follow suit. After some discussion, they did – and the entire staff, including

Billie, transferred. They had left Shanghai as refugees, but they disembarked in a manner, as T.K. Chuan remarked, befitting the "prestige of *T'ien Hsia*." Billie watched with sadness as her beloved city, with fires raging in Chapei, faded from sight. She braced herself for the unknown but had no inkling that she was about to encounter the biggest shock of her life.

15

Mad Mission

Hong Kong Island was the same massive rock her grandmother had seen but the mountain backdrop was now green and dotted with white houses rather than bare and barren as it had been 70 years earlier. "It was so hilly and lush after the urban flatness of Shanghai," Billie said of her arrival in mid-November 1937.

As the *Aramis* nudged its way through the junks and big ships, she saw only one tall building and didn't realize that she and her *T'ien Hsia* colleagues would soon be working in it.

They stayed at the Kowloon Hotel in what was expected to be a temporary arrangement before they found their own accommodation. But there was one huge and immediate problem – they were latecomers among the thousands pouring in from Shanghai and rents were skyrocketing. Billie spent frustrating hours calling up newspaper advertisements, only to find nothing within her budget.

When they went out to eat and explore the night life, she found to her consternation that everything shut down, even the bars and nightspots, with a rendering of *God Save the King*. "I remembered a foreign correspondent in Shanghai called Hong Kong at night 'a lit-up cemetery'," she said. The bank, the courthouse and the Hong Kong Club formed a dignified cluster around a central square, but Hong Kong felt more like a village than the sprawling city she had left.

Just as she was starting to make plans for Mama to join her, Billie received a telegram from her brother-in-law Tom Ellis in Shanghai.

She opened it with a feeling of trepidation, and collapsed in a dead faint.

Billie opened her eyes to find her colleagues bending over her, with expressions of concern.

The telegram told her that Mama had suffered a heart attack on December 14 and had passed away.

Billie absolutely refused to believe it. "This has to be a mistake," she said. "Mama is only 49 and has never been ill in her life."

Her next thought was that it was a ruse by the Japanese to lure her back. Someone had told them she had not only worked for the subversive Wen but that she had been the Voice of Free Shanghai and they wanted to arrest her.

She told this to Wen, who commiserated but doubted that the Japanese would go to such lengths of deception. And, he added, none of the staff, including him, had received such a message. He told her they were booking her on the first available ship and gave her a blank cheque to cover Mama's funeral expenses.

Even as she disembarked in Shanghai, Billie clung to the hope that Mama would be waiting for her. Only when she saw Tom, his wife and their two children standing on the quay – all in black like crows, she thought – did dreadful reality begin to sink in.

Tom, who looked remarkably like his late brother Jimmy, told her gently, "Mama didn't suffer at all. She was having dinner with friends when she had her attack. They rushed across the road to fetch a doctor, but she had gone by the time he arrived."

Billie rebuked herself for leaving Mama. She was sure Mama had died of a broken heart after losing the last person she had loved. Billie had relied totally on Mama all her life and failed to notice how much Mama needed her, too.

At the funeral parlour, Billie was unprepared for the sight of Mama lying embalmed in the open coffin. She looked so serene and beautiful that Billie thought she was sleeping and would wake up at any moment.

Deeply comforted that Mama looked at peace, Billie lifted her mother's hand tenderly and placed her favourite rings on her fingers.

As it happened, Mama had been baptized shortly before her death and the Ellises had arranged for a priest, Fr S. Fitzgerald of the American Jesuit-run Gonzaga College, to officiate at the burial.

Mama was laid to rest in a grassy plot in the British cemetery at Hungjao Road. It is clear from the funeral notice Billie prepared that, despite what Wen had told her, she was terrified, even in grief, of being caught by the Japanese and was taking no chances. I suspect she had again travelled up on a fake name and she took care not to disclose her real name even in the obituary. She wrote that Mary Ann Newman had been survived by a daughter, "Lucy," who was in Hong Kong at the time of her death. Then she added that "a beautiful cross of flowers from Jessie, Dolly and Lulu was lowered onto the casket into the grave. Although "Lulu" might have been a contraction of Marylou, it was likely another obfuscation.

Mama's grave at Hungjao cemetery in 1937

She experienced a powerful sense of Mama's presence as the coffin was lowered and whispered, *"Au revoir*, Mama, but not *adieu,"* as she would talk to her mother during later crises when she needed to unburden her problems and seek advice.

She was pleased that Lillian and Bunny had arranged for a wreath even though they were in England. And she was delighted to see flowers from the Erin Villa Club. She also mentioned flowers from the wives of Wen and

T.K. Chuan as well as well-known Eurasian families like the Doodhas and Kellners.

Significant, too, was the absence of Mickey, who was still in Shanghai, having a hard time with the collapsing Shanghai dollar and Sinmay teetering on bankruptcy. If Billie wanted to keep a low profile, the last person she needed at the ceremony was a scandal-plagued American writer.

As Billie walked away from the cemetery, she gripped Tom's arm as she remembered something.

"Mama's last wish was to have her things around her. I have to go to Lansing Terrace and get her belongings that we left behind," she said.

Tom stiffened with alarm.

"I wouldn't advise that at all," he said. "The Japanese are now in charge and you'll have to go through checkpoints at Garden Bridge where their sentries are very nasty, making everyone bow and hitting them for any reason. They beat an old man to death there the other day."

Indeed, Japanese troops had arrived in Nanking the day before Mama's death and stories were already emerging that the Japanese were taking their aggression to a horrifying new level, with mass rape and butchery and other atrocities.

Tom and his wife warned things had become dangerous in Shanghai and they were all in a state of heightened uncertainty and fear with Japanese soldiers and gangsters of all stripes roaming around, killing with impunity.

But Billie was insistent.

"I must do this one last thing for Mama."

Remembering how distraught Mama had been when she could not take all her things, Billie became fixated on her mission, driven perhaps by the need to expiate an undeserved sense of guilt.

Outwardly calm, Billie hired a lorry with two Russian workers and took with her the lease agreement for the house. She did not take her passport, which would have revealed her identity.

When they arrived at Garden Bridge, as she had been alerted, two Japanese guards held up their rifles to stop the lorry and they examined

Billie's lease agreement. They seemed puzzled by the document but waved them through.

The streets of Hongkew were eerily deserted and many buildings were badly damaged. Smashed signboards littered the ground.

When they reached Lansing Terrace, Billie was relieved to find that their home had escaped destruction and that their furniture was intact.

The Russians loaded up the lorry and, two hours later, they were back at Garden Bridge. This time they had a different reception.

A new shift of guards waved their rifles belligerently and, after Billie handed over the tenancy agreement, one of them examined it, shook his head angrily, and shouted in Japanese.

Shaken, Billie realized he wanted identification. She tried to explain that she had left her ID at home on the other side of the bridge, but the guard would have none of it. He raised his weapon and waved her back.

Suddenly, she remembered her consul.

"Ishii-san! Ishii-san!" she cried, pointing behind her in the direction of the Japanese consulate, only a short distance away.

Using sign language, she told the guards she would go and find someone to help her at the consulate. After a tense exchange, they shrugged and let her go, but insisted the lorry remain.

By now thoroughly agitated, Billie ran to the consulate, praying hard the consul would be there. Fortunately, Ishii-san was, and he kept shaking his head incredulously as she stammered out her story. He sat down and wrote a letter of authorization.

After thanking him profusely, Billie rushed back to Garden Bridge. But one of the guards was still not satisfied. He read the letter but insisted she still needed to show some personal identification.

Through a fog of exhaustion, Billie explained that she was British and could obtain what they wanted at the British consulate, which happened to be just on the other side of the bridge.

It would mean revealing her identity, but Billie now had no choice. This was her last card, and she had no idea what she would do if it did not work.

The Russian workers were by now thoroughly fed up and the guards debated her proposal lengthily.

Finally, the guards agreed to allow her through, but again on condition that the lorry stayed. Billie ran unsteadily to the British consulate where, once again, she was lucky to find her friend John Alexander. He, too, was amazed at Billie's predicament, but hurriedly organised papers certifying her identity.

By the time she returned to the Japanese sentries, her legs were trembling, but they were finally satisfied and let her pass.

Billie asked the Russians to drive straight to the auctioneer, where, in her highly agitated state, she gave the simple instruction to sell everything.

So desperate was she to return to the Ellis home that she paid the Russians off and left before they had finished unloading at the auction house.

Wen had been sending cables, asking when she was coming back, and Billie, still in a semi-stupor, sailed for Hong Kong the next day.

It was some time before she wondered whether she had left a forwarding address with the auctioneer. She also searched her bag for a receipt for the goods but could find none. In her panic, she had omitted such vital details and would never receive a cent from Mama's belongings.

Still, her nightmare on Garden Bridge, which she formerly crossed without a second thought, jolted her into a realization that she could not return to Shanghai while impunity was rampant and that she was glad to be in Hong Kong. Yes, the Brits were snooty and staid, but they had a firm respect for law and order.

It was terrible what the Japanese were doing in China but at least she could somehow help from the safety of British territory. Little did she know the Japanese would in the not-too-distant future do the unthinkable – take on the British Empire by striking at her colonies in the Far East.

16

At the Front

There was a good reason Wen was cabling Billie urgently, asking when she was coming back from burying Mama. He, and she as his right-hand assistant, were about to become unexpectedly and frantically busy. The *T'ien Hsia* editors had arrived in Hong Kong as scholars with an erudite magazine, but they all quickly became part of China's front line in a propaganda war with Japan.

As the Chinese government retreated further and further westwards from the Japanese, first to Hankow (Wuhan) and then to Chungking, Hong Kong became its most important link with the outside world.

When the war started in July 1937, Chiang Kai-shek knew he could not defeat his far stronger enemy on the battlefield and that he needed to win support internationally, especially financial and material backing.

He had two key aides for this task: his official information chief, Hollington Tong, an American-educated journalist, and an unofficial advisor, W.H. Donald, a veteran Australian journalist who was a trusted intimate.

Donald quickly orchestrated a media campaign around Chiang's attractive and charismatic wife – Mei-ling Soong – portraying her as a symbol of defiance against the aggressor. Supported by American publisher Henry Luce, who was born and raised in China (and went to Chefoo School two decades after Frank Newman), Madame Chiang soon featured in *Life* magazine and made the cover of *Time* as its 1937 Person of the Year.

Billie did not know it yet, but she would soon be working for Donald whenever he came to Hong Kong and Hollington Tong would recommend her to an extraordinary position with the First Family.

With the Japanese occupying large parts of China, including its ports, Hong Kong was now massively important as both a voice for China and as the first stop of foreign correspondents on their way to cover the war.

Tong, who had relied on Wen's help in Shanghai, entrusted him with printing, in addition to *T'ien Hsia*, publications such as the anti-Japanese *Far Eastern Mirror* and *China at War* and distributing them through their other offices abroad.

This was a sensitive side of the operation as the Japanese pushed strongly to suppress such material and the British government in Hong Kong did not wish to antagonize Japan. Wen complained bitterly of reporting that buckled to Japanese pressure, although the tide began to change after the bombing of civilians and factories in Shanghai and the atrocities of Nanking. The Hongkong and Shanghai Bank, for example, changed its policy after 1937 from "active support for China" to "must be opposed to Japan."

Still grieving and trying to cope without Mama, Billie broke out in rashes, though they would mysteriously clear up as she approached the doctor's office.

Her immediate task as office manager was to organise their new premises. From a small apartment in a quiet residential quarter of Shanghai, *T'ien Hsia* moved into offices in the Hongkong and Shanghai Bank, the colony's grandest and tallest building – it had opened only in 1935 – in the heart of the city. Its Art Deco-style headquarters had views of the harbour and the distant hills behind Kowloon.

Despite its high-profile location, the office bore only the name of Wen Yuan-ning, as he sought to disguise the fact that *T'ien Hsia*'s expanding staff was doing more than producing scholarly articles.

Just as Billie thought she might have to stay at the Kowloon Hotel indefinitely, a Chinese teacher friend of T.K. Chuan came to the office to say goodbye and offered Billie her three-bedroom flat in Happy Valley at a reasonable rent. Billie moved into the ground floor flat at 111 Leighton Hill Road, a short bus ride from the office, and would share it with friends.

At work, because of her experience with media, she became involved in accrediting and assisting journalists to cover the war.

She already knew the agency men from Shanghai like Reuters' Bill O'Neill, AP's Spencer Moosa (who had changed jobs) and UPI's Jack Belden and she would meet China veterans as well as newcomers out to make their reputation. She met the gamut of journalists – Edgar Snow, whose 1937 book *Red Star over China* introduced Mao to the world; Agnes Smedley, a well-known American journalist and activist, of *Frankfurter Zeitung*, whose openly communist views made her a target of persecution by the Hong Kong authorities; James Bertram, a New Zealand Rhodes scholar who wrote for *The Times* of London; Teddy White, who was Henry Luce's star reporter until they fell out; and Carl Mydans and Shelley Smith, *Life's* photographer-reporter team.

Billie worked with a generation of pioneering women correspondents who had to contend with all kinds of prejudice from male colleagues, editors and officials, in addition to the occupational hazards of reporting on shifting battlelines in faraway locations.

She helped to organise the itinerary for war reporter Martha Gellhorn and her new husband Ernest Hemingway after they arrived, literally with a splash, in a Pan Am Clipper seaplane on the harbour. Having become lovers while covering the Spanish civil war, Gellhorn was now on assignment by *Collier's Weekly*, but it was Hemingway, rich and famous after the publication of his book *For Whom the Bell Tolls*, who received media attention.

Billie met Hemingway at a party thrown by Mickey Hahn before he and Gellhorn embarked on a long and complicated trip around China. It was meticulously organised by Tong and his team, but it did not go well. Though this was their first trip to Asia, Hemingway showed little interest and Gellhorn's enthusiasm waned after she was badly affected by "China rot" – the skin between her fingers began to decompose – and dysentery.

Unaware of the difficulties of arranging such a trip during wartime, Gellhorn wrote that she "fumed and fretted and complained of the delay" after deciding to do "a short aerial jump over the neighbouring mountains" near Chungking though later she admitted, "I now think it astounding that this trip ever got arranged; at the time, not knowing the practical obstacles."

The last straw was when the Hemingways sat across from the Chiangs in an all-important meeting, as far as Tong was concerned. Gellhorn asked Madame Chiang why China did not take care of its lepers, whom she had seen roaming the streets as beggars. Frostily, the First Lady replied that the Chinese were humane and civilized and, unlike Westerners, they would never lock lepers away. "China had a great culture when your ancestors were living in trees and painting themselves blue," she said.

The Hemingways quarrelled frequently during their trip and, after her husband, jealous of his wife's increasing recognition, tried to prevent her D-Day reporting assignment, Gellhorn left him for good.

Billie became friends with Annalee Whitmore, a Hollywood scriptwriter who tried to go to Chungking in 1940 as a correspondent but was told by the American war department that they weren't letting women journalists go to China.

Whitmore persisted and went as a representative of a humanitarian organisation. In Chungking, she and *Time*'s Mel Jacoby started a romantic relationship and they married in Manila in November 1941, the eve of the Pacific war. Months later, Jacoby was at an airfield in Darwin when a propeller blade detached itself from a plane and rolled into him, killing him. Whitmore continued with her career and she co-authored with Teddy White the book *Thunder Out of China* that exposed corruption and inefficiency in the Nationalist government.

One woman journalist with whom Billie became close was the New Zealand poet-journalist Iris Wilkinson, who wrote under the nom-de-plume of Robin Hyde, the name she had given to a son who had died shortly after birth.

Wilkinson was one of the first journalists to arrive at the office in March 1938, introduced by fellow New Zealander James Bertram.

The two had known each other slightly back home and Bertram was helping a compatriot whom he described as "very much the innocent Kiwi abroad, an unfashionable figure in a flapping coat and battered tricorn hat, limping along crowded streets and facing the world with a gaze as direct and trusting as Candide's."

Iris Wilkinson

When Billie met the mid-thirtyish Wilkinson, she was struck by her expressive eyes and her stiff right leg with a foot encased in a special boot.

Bertram was the younger man, still in his 20s, but had had a meteoric career, having won a Rhodes scholarship that propelled him from middle-class Auckland to Oxford University, where he obtained a first-class degree, became active in left-wing clubs and played rugby. He had parlayed this into a Rhodes fellowship that enabled him to visit Japan and China, meeting key political figures including Mao, and write for British publications including *The Times*.

The athletic Bertram was on a roll. A year earlier, he had been in Peking and, on hearing that Chiang Kai-shek had been seized by northern troops in Xi'an in December 1936, had made an arduous 11-day journey, including crossing the frozen Yellow River on foot, to capture a series of world radio scoops with Agnes Smedley from a city blockaded by the Kuomintang.

He had written a book about the Xi'an Incident and was collecting material for a second.

By contrast, Wilkinson, though she had a reputation as a campaigning journalist and a novelist and poet with a lyrical style, was a neophyte in Asia and was on her way to meet a publisher in England when she decided to make a detour to China.

She had been on a short trip to Shanghai where a fellow Kiwi, Rewi Alley, had taken her to see factories bombed by the Japanese and the effect this had had upon men, women and children whose livelihoods had been destroyed.

This had only whetted her appetite and now Wilkinson was in the office saying that she wanted to go to the front. Billie and Wen passed on her request to Hollington Tong in Hankow but it was met with alarm. Wilkinson was a woman on her own, a freelancer without the backing of a major news organisation, she could not speak Chinese, and she clearly had very limited funds. Tong, who was also responsible for the safety of journalists he sent to the front, wrote back about the difficulties facing women, such as a lack of suitable accommodation.

Wen took Wilkinson out for a meal and was charming, but evasive. As Wilkinson would write, "Dr Wen Yuan-ning, a slender youthful man who had graduated at Cambridge, in his office was ceaselessly, impossibly busy, and could not be talked to at all. When we went for lunch, he talked not of the war, but of modern poets … T.S. Eliot, Rilke, Walter de la Mare. I wanted to bring in the war, and Canton. But he was pleased at having received a letter from Walter de la Mare, and to interpolate seemed a little rude. As soon as dinner was over, he was ceaselessly, impossibly busy again, doing ten men's work, and for the time I did not see him any more."

Wen did, however, commission an article on early New Zealand literature and Wilkinson obliged with an essay, *The Singers of Loneliness*, which appeared in the August issue of *T'ien Hsia*.

Unable to talk further with Wen, Wilkinson found a sympathetic listener in Billie. Each recognized in the other a high degree of empathy as well as a sensitive disposition. "She told me she had dreamed of going to China since she was given a Chinese ginger jar as a child," said Billie. Wilkinson wanted to write about ordinary people caught up in the tumult of war and hoped that portraying the humanity of the Chinese might help soften New Zealand's anti-Asian immigration rules.

Billie warmed to Wilkinson's obvious compassion for the Chinese but she also had doubts that Wilkinson could handle a journey to the front.

An operation on her knee in her late teens had left her with a permanent limp.

After becoming pregnant, she had resigned from her job to go to Australia and have her baby in secret, but the infant had died almost as soon as he was born, and she had had a nervous breakdown. Later, she became pregnant to a married journalist, refused his offer of an abortion, and went into seclusion for six months to have her baby, losing her job as a result of rumours about her condition. She kept her son's existence from her family and, penniless, fostered him out with the intention of taking him back later.

Billie was astonished to hear that Wilkinson, undeterred by failing to get accreditation in Hong Kong, had made the long journey to Hankow where she saw Tong and pestered him for a pass to the front, which had moved to Hsuchowfu (Xuzhou) in Kiangsu Province.

Hsuchowfu was at the junction of two railway lines and the Japanese had to take it if they wanted to capture Hankow and the Chinese heartland. Tong told her, "What would be said about us if we sent a lady like you up there?" to which Wilkinson said she had never been so insulted. Some foreign correspondents, including a New Zealander, made it known that she would not be welcome to join them as she would be a heavy responsibility and would hinder their mobility. Wilkinson refused to give up and when, finally, Tong gave a pass, with misgivings, she was thrilled that she would be the first white woman to be allowed into Hsuchowfu.

In early May, Wilkinson took a train packed with Chinese soldiers to Hsuchowfu, where she found that the main press group had gone ahead without her. When she followed the day after, in a smaller group including two reporters and some soldiers, she waved to the truck of foreign pressmen returning from the front. That was the last the group saw of her before they left for Hankow. On May 10, the Japanese began bombing Hsuchowfu heavily and soon after they cut the rail lines out of the city.

No one seemed to know where Wilkinson was, or if she was still alive, and a frantic Tong cabled Chinese generals to look for her.

Over the next weeks, Billie and her colleagues were not only concerned about her safety but also sensitive to the publicity surrounding her disappearance. It was not until June 30 that a cable reached the outside world saying that Wilkinson was alive and with the British consulate in Tsingtao.

When Wilkinson reached Hong Kong nearly six weeks later, Billie went to meet her off the boat. "I could hardly recognize her," said Billie. "She was gaunt and had a terrible eye injury. She had been through a traumatic experience but, when she tried to talk about it, became hysterical and incoherent."

Billie took the writer back to her flat in Happy Valley which she was sharing with a Shanghai friend, Pilan Petigura, and Ena Corberley from Hankow. After a few days, realizing Wilkinson needed medical care, they took her to a hospital where she was diagnosed with sprue, an intestinal disorder, as well as a skin infection.

Between them, the three girls visited Wilkinson every day in hospital, though they found her still less than coherent about what had happened to her. Not surprisingly, a journalist who interviewed her in Hong Kong wrote an account that was muddled in its chronology.

However, the story attracted the attention of Madame Sun Yat-sen, who gave Wilkinson an interview that was likely arranged by Wen's office.

After a month in Hong Kong, Billie and friends saw Wilkinson off on a ship to England. "She was still unwell but at least she was in the care of a doctor," said Billie.

It wasn't until Wilkinson's book on her China adventure, *Dragon Ramparts*, came out in mid-1939 that Billie found out what had happened to her in China. She had reached the front after climbing a steep hill on a donkey and had observed Japanese and Chinese soldiers through binoculars before joining the Chinese fleeing towards town.

Her donkey tired and she fell behind. She arrived back at Hsuchowfu on May 6. The following Tuesday, the Japanese began bombing the city in earnest, in preparation for a major attack with ground forces. With the fall of the city imminent, the foreign correspondents and even the Chinese journalists were sent south to Hankow. For reasons that were unclear, Wilkinson chose to stay behind.

After the city fell, Wilkinson embarked on a long walk, following the railway line, through bandit country. Early on, a panicked Chinese woman pushed her down an embankment and into a thorn bush, where a spike pierced one of Wilkinson's eyes. Unable to see properly and in pain, she reached a railway station where she encountered a group of Japanese soldiers who claimed she was a spy. They did not rape her, but they beat her and stripped her, going through her belongings. Had she not been white, she would probably have been killed. As it was, the Japanese put her on a train to Tsingtao.

In England, sick and impoverished, Wilkinson lived in a caravan while writing her book with editing help from James Bertram. Billie noted that the book – described by Bertram as "fragmentary and chaotic, and not very easy to follow" – included an acknowledgement by Wilkinson: "And, for coming to see me every day in hospital, my friends, Billie, Ena, Pilan, and Lynne."

She had achieved her goal against great odds and now she talked of plans to retrieve her son and of returning to China. The New Zealand High Commissioner in London visited her to arrange her passage home. But her deep problems, physical and mental, persisted and on August 23, 1939, in a Notting Hill flat on the eve of World War II, Wilkinson died after overdosing on Benzedrine in a room smelling strongly of gas.

Billie mourned for her warm, brave friend. By coincidence, Wilkinson's loss of one child and delivery of another would presage events in Billie's future.

17

Beach Romance

It was handy as well as a source of pride to work at the Hongkong and Shanghai Bank headquarters. Though controversially modernist, and dubbed "Grayburn's Folly" by critics, 1 Queen's Road was the first fully air-conditioned building in the city and Billie's office could not be closer to people like David MacDougall, Wen's counterpart in Hong Kong's information services. The two became friends and Billie went up and down between the two offices, liaising between them.

Billie's capability so impressed MacDougall that he was almost certainly the person who offered to double her salary in 1940 but, as Wen would write, she "refused to accept it, and stuck instead to me through thick and thin, out of a sense of loyalty."

Billie was a dark-haired, slim 21-year-old with alert eyes, but if any of the bank's love-hungry young bankers had any interest in her, they would have been sharply reminded of the strict rules prohibiting any serious liaison with a Chinese or Eurasian woman, on pain of demotion or being sent home.

No less than the chief manager, Sir Vandeleur Grayburn, had written in 1937, the year he was knighted, that for a banker's wife to be "foreign, native, half caste are definitely taboo." His view was shared by many British *taipans*.

Social relationships were overly complicated in a city where, as one official observed, everyone seemed intent on looking down upon anyone who was different. It was not just that the British and the Chinese avoided mixing socially, but the British were snobbish about their own kind, with officials and merchants despising each other and both scorning the likes of police officers and soldiers.

Despite the broad racial divide, there were pockets of activity where British and Chinese worked together on the same level. One was government-media relations where each side depended on the other to produce news. Another was civil organisations where British and Chinese cooperated for a common goal, such as helping Chinese war victims.

The *T'ien Hsia* staff editors, mostly upper-class Chinese who spoke English well, operated in the first space while literature-loving Wen also managed to acquire friends among English persons with similar interests.

Needing suitable people who might share the flat and its expenses, Billie found the answer to her problems in a business club for women. The Hongkong International Women's Club in nearby Gloucester Building was started by a Eurasian woman to provide tiffin and tea for lowly-paid Eurasian and Portuguese secretaries at more affordable prices than the restaurants in Central District. By the time Billie arrived, the club was open to office girls of all nationalities, and it had 500 members with an average lunch attendance of 50-60. Left-wing English socialites, like Hilda Selwyn-Clarke, wife of the Director of Medical Services, or Elsie Fairfax-Cholmondeley, a squire's daughter turned socialist, sometimes made appearances to lend solidarity.

It was here that Billie recognized Pilan Petigura from Shanghai Public School. Pilan had escaped Shanghai with her mother and sisters but they were now returning while she was staying as she had a job with an Indian company. Billie also met Ena Corberley, a Eurasian secretary from Hankow, and the three of them decided to team up. "We were all in the same boat," said Billie. "We were new to Hong Kong, with nowhere to live and we didn't know how to speak Cantonese and we were a bit lost."

The girls moved into the Happy Valley flat and shared the cost of engaging a house *amah*. When Ena returned to Hankow, Pilan bumped into Mavis Ming, her Shanghai Public School classmate, and brought her home.

The SPG trio became close and would help each other, sometimes in unexpected ways.

The SPG girls in their white blouses and blue tunics. Pilan is second from left, middle row, and Mavis is on her right. Courtesy of Siaoman Yen and Richard Horsburgh

Through their mothers, Pilan and Billie knew each other as children, going to each other's birthday parties. Like the Doodhas, the Petiguras were Parsees. The family of Pilan's father, Ratan, had sent him from Bombay to Shanghai to expand the trade network. They wanted to arrange a bride from India for Ratan, but he did not want to marry someone he did not know. Instead, he married a Chinese girl, which shocked both sides of the family. He and his wife had five daughters and Pilan, the youngest, was only three when he died. After SPG, Pilan had studied at St John's University.

Tall and soft-spoken, Pilan had played hockey at SPG and took Billie to St Andrew's Club in Kowloon where she met many Eurasian members.

Mavis was a feisty and typically confident SPG girl. A Chinese Australian, daughter of a Chinese fruit and vegetable trader and an Englishwoman who had given him English lessons, Mavis spent her early years in Perth. When she was nine, her father took the family to Shanghai. After her mother died from smallpox, Mavis's father entered an arranged marriage with a 17-year-old daughter of a Cantonese merchant to look after his four young children.

Though barely older than Mavis, the new stepmother meshed well with the family while Mavis learned basic Cantonese and embraced life both in Shanghai and in the village to which they moved.

An eclectic education had included SPG, after which, in the mid-1930s, she had returned to Australia, where she took a keen interest in the League of Health and Beauty, a women's fitness movement aimed at improving physical and mental health and helping to ease the pains of childbirth.

In Sydney, Mavis trained under Thea Stanley Hughes, protégé of Mary Bagot Stack, founder of the league in England that had grown to 60,000 members. Mavis was convinced the movement would catch on in Hong Kong and she even had hopes of taking it to China.

Mavis's League of Health girls in action. Courtesy of Siaoman Yen and Richard Horsburgh

Caught up by Mavis's enthusiasm, Billie and Pilan became her first recruits. Smartly outfitted in white satin blouses and black shorts – rather daring for the time – the three would give demonstrations of stretching and swinging to music.

Billie was at the League's outdoor demonstration in early January 1940 when Hilda Selwyn-Clarke, wife of Hong Kong's Director of Medical

Services, gave the welcome address. Hilda was also secretary of the China Defence League, which helped the Chinese resistance and was chaired by Madame Sun Yat-sen.

Mavis placed an advertisement in the *South China Morning Post,* and over 50 women, most of them English, turned up for the first public meeting. Billie listened as an excited Mavis began her introductory lecture.

An Englishwoman in the front row put up her hand.

"Excuse me," she asked. "But are you in charge of the course?"

When Mavis nodded, the Englishwoman said the League of Health had been started by an English woman and she had been expecting an English instructor. Others in the audience nodded.

Mavis replied that she had qualified in Australia and had been sent to Hong Kong by the League in Sydney.

But the Englishwoman rose from her chair and made her way out of the hall, followed by half a dozen other Europeans.

The rest stayed to watch the pupils perform their routine and applauded politely. At the end of the session, however, the English women filed out without signing up for the course, and those who remained were mostly Eurasian.

Mavis was deflated, but undeterred. She continued to advertise; the meetings would draw dozens of women, but the outcome was the same – the British would leave without enrolling and would make comments such as, "My dear, you should have made it clear that this course is not for us."

After a month, Mavis had over 50 recruits, but the number was well below expectations and, though she drummed up interest among local schools, it was clear she would not be able to cover her expenses, especially since some of the Eurasian girls could not afford to complete the course. Mavis was giving them discounts to keep the numbers up.

She was bitterly disappointed, but failure opened another door.

To earn extra income she took a secretarial job with the international arm of the Chinese Industrial Cooperatives (CIC) which was encouraging cooperatives in China to provide employment to those who had lost their jobs with the bombing of factories. Started by New Zealander Rewi Alley and American journalist Edgar Snow and his wife Helen Foster Snow, it had the support of notables such as Madame Chiang and the Kungs.

Mavis met left-wing characters such as Snow, Alley, Ida Pruitt, Bishop Hall, Ted Herman, Elsie Fairfax-Cholmondeley, Dr Chen Han-seng and J.M. Tan who would inspire and shape her career. "Hong Kong is full of wartime organisations," she wrote to her sister. Billie also became friends with Elsie Fairfax-Cholmondeley, possibly through Mavis.

When Mickey Hahn stayed at the flat with Billie and Mavis in February 1940, she found the women painfully aware of how little they were paid for working very hard and they would passionately discuss the injustices and how one day these might be fixed.

Billie "did all the real work at *T'ien Hsia*" on a "ridiculous salary," Mickey would write in *China to Me*. "Billie kept in touch through her friends with all the downtown firms and all their private business, including the private business of the employees and employers. There were no secrets from me in Hong Kong. They were also in touch, through Mavis's job at the Co-op office, with the leftist element among the Europeans, and through Billie's job at Wen Yuan-ning's with all the visiting journalists."

Billie recalled how she spent her precious leisure time. "I enjoyed the wonderful outdoor life in the long tropical evenings. We had outings to Shek O, where one of my hockey friends had a home, and we spent most weekends at Repulse Bay, where friends had a temporary shed. We would start with curried tiffin, followed by an afternoon on the beach, dinner at the hotel and midnight swimming parties."

All that was missing was a boyfriend.

In early 1939, Billie and two teammates from St Andrew's Hockey Club, including a pretty girl called Ellie, were relaxing at Repulse Bay when two men strolled by, wearing baggy swimming trunks. One of them recognized Ellie, whom he had met at a dance, and the girls smiled when the men asked if they could join them.

They were off-duty warrant officers in the British Army. One of them – Billie guessed he was in his mid-thirties, though his receding hairline made him look older – spoke with a slight Irish accent. He introduced himself as Arthur but said everyone called him Paddy. Well built, and about five foot nine, he loved soccer and cricket.

Conversation was light and, after a while, the girls gathered up their things and said goodbye. It had been a pleasant exchange and Billie thought no more about it.

A few days later, walking down the steps of the Hongkong and Shanghai Bank, she saw a man leaning against one of the two bronze lions guarding the entrance. When he waved to her, she recognized the soldier from the beach.

Paddy, whose quarters at Wellington Barracks were only a short walk away, had remembered that Billie worked at the bank building and was waiting for her to emerge after work.

She was surprised but accepted his offer of a drink at a hotel. They soon hit it off.

"At first, we met only at weekends. Then Paddy used to take me for a dinner and dance at the Gripps, the cocktail lounge at the Hong Kong Hotel, and we would also go to the new Repulse Bay Lido and dance the foxtrot and the Charleston to a Filipino band in white tuxedos," she said.

"Paddy was Irish, loveable, sweet-looking, happy-go-lucky and full of blarney. I didn't know what blarney meant but I learned about it." Another quality that attracted Billie was Paddy's genuine curiosity when he asked about her work and her past.

Paddy had grown up in Dublin during the tumultuous conflict between the ruling British and Irish republicans who sought independence at any cost. Paddy was 10 during the Easter Uprising in 1916, which the British suppressed brutally, executing the leaders and jailing thousands. A few years later, Paddy was a teenager when civil war broke out in 1922.

After his mother died of pneumonia when he was 11, his three younger sisters took care of Paddy and their father, a frame-maker. Adept with numbers, Paddy joined a bank after school but soon found the work unsatisfying.

With a hunger to see the world but with no money, he followed the path of many young Irishmen. Soon after turning 21, he took the ferry across to Liverpool and on August 3, 1926, enlisted in the British Army at nearby Wrexham. He joined the Royal Army Ordnance Corps, which handled weapons and munitions. For 10 years, he served in various stations in England before getting his first overseas posting, to Hong Kong, in early 1937.

Soon after arriving, he made friends with an English family, the Redwoods, with three daughters in a flat opposite the barracks. The girls would go to whist drives and tombola (bingo) at the army base and Paddy would drop by their flat to play billiards.

One of the daughters, Barbara, had a crush on Paddy when she was 18, while he was going out with her beautiful older sister, Olive. "He liked to come over and be part of the family," said Barbara. "He wasn't conventionally handsome, but I thought he was charming and very attractive. He had wonderful, blueish eyes." Once Paddy met Billie, however, the Redwoods did not see him for months.

Paddy asked Billie to take him to the hole-in-the-wall restaurants and shops in Happy Valley which he had been reluctant to enter as he did not speak Chinese. Paddy would stop and watch a Chinese funeral procession or stare at the blackened chickens, smoked ducks and salted fish hanging in the stores.

He told her he had been teased for being Irish by the English "squaddies," but his affability and humour won them over and he liked being in the Army.

As a middle-class Chinese, Billie also had her prejudices and would confide in Mickey that her family didn't have a high regard for soldiers.

Billie was thrilled to see Mickey when she arrived from Shanghai in July 1939, but her friend's gaunt and sallow face shocked her. During 18 months under Japanese occupation, their blockade had driven many businesses, including Sinmay's magazines, to near-bankruptcy and Mickey had had to lend him money. Mickey loved Sinmay, but his opium habit – which she had acquired, too – and chaotic personal affairs were driving her crazy.

Mickey's big news was that she was starting a book on the Soong Sisters, three daughters of a printer who had married the most powerful men in China. Mei-ling, the youngest, was, of course, the wife of China's leader, Generalissimo Chiang. Big sister Ai-ling's husband, H.H. Kung, who could trace his ancestry to Confucius and had inherited enormous wealth, would become prime minister and finance minister through Chiang. Middle sister Ching-ling had married the much older Republican leader Sun Yat-sen and was called the "red sister." After she was widowed by Sun's death in 1925, Mei-ling's subsequent marriage to his successor caused a deep rift between the sisters as Ching-ling accused Chiang of betraying her husband's vision of unifying all political groupings with the Shanghai massacre of communists in 1927.

Billie sympathized with Mickey's daunting task as, apart from the feud between Mei-ling and Ching-ling, all three sisters were notoriously publicity-shy. Billie would soon meet two of the famous siblings.

With Mickey in town, T.K. Chuan decided to throw a party for his young sister Mei-Mei.

He hired a cabana at the Lido in Repulse Bay for the occasion. Billie invited her Irish soldier boyfriend to meet her *T'ien Hsia* family – and it would prove a turning point in their relationship.

Billie kept a photograph of the event which shows Chinese, Eurasians, a Parsee, an Irishman and an American relaxing together – typical for a *T'ien Hsia* gathering, but highly unusual in the context of Hong Kong's racial divisions.

In the photo, Billie is seated (second from right) beside Paddy, lending support as he meets Mickey, Sinmay and Wen for the first time. Wen is standing at the back in a white suit and open-necked shirt. He is not in swimwear, possibly because he is busy and cannot stay long. Sinmay is standing on the far right in black trunks and holding a glass. He is a little apart from the others, possibly because he is miserable in Hong Kong as, despite being an Oxford-educated Anglophile, he complains the British are patronizing him and excluding him in their invitations to Mickey.

Paddy had been pursuing Billie for a year, she told Mickey, and eventually she succumbed to his advances during "a romantic evening at the beach." This might well have been the occasion after all the guests had departed and they were alone long into the night.

Billie brought Paddy (seated fourth from right) to a T'ien Hsia party at Repulse Bay

Japan was now occupying neighbouring Canton and its militarists were talking openly about replacing western imperialism with a "Greater East Asia Co-Prosperity Sphere." Opinions among the *T'ien Hsia* group were divided, however, as to whether they would really take on the British Empire and, even if they did, would they be a match for the British?

Over the next weeks, Paddy was unable to see Billie as often as before and, when they were together, he seemed preoccupied.

One morning, Billie got out of bed, strangely nauseous. After feeling like this for a few mornings in a row, she went to see her physician, Dr Samy, who told her she was pregnant. Months earlier, she would have been sure Paddy would be thrilled, but now she had serious doubts.

18

Paddy's About Face

Billie could not understand it. Paddy had been so ardent for over a year and now he was cooling off, just as she had committed herself.

She had taken a long time before submitting to him, but there was much to consider, including the consequences to Wen and her colleagues who treated her as family.

The only thing she knew for certain is she wanted one day to settle down as a wife and mother – and that she wanted her offspring to have a proper education in England to avoid the stigma that mixed-race children faced in Hong Kong.

But, of late, Paddy had been calling far less frequently and their meetings were briefer and shorn of their earlier intensity. They both knew it was only a matter of time before he was sent away and she hoped this was why he seemed preoccupied.

The British in Hong Kong were far more focused on the war in Europe than the one across the border which was, in the words of one Briton, "between two natives."

She was apprehensive as she mustered the strength to tell Paddy of her condition. The frown that crossed his face confirmed that her news was far from welcome.

He recovered his composure and told her he would marry her, but he asked that they keep the marriage a secret.

They met at the Hong Kong Registry Office on January 31, 1940. Paddy was in uniform and Billie wore a blue taffeta dress and a gold wedding ring that had cost much of her savings.

At Paddy's request, Billie had asked Mildred Chan, a secretary at *T'ien Hsia*, and her Canadian-born Chinese husband, Lesley, to be witnesses. Paddy had met them at that fateful party at Repulse Bay.

None of Paddy's friends was present and, after a brief ceremony, the Chans took Billie and Paddy out for a Chinese lunch. They could not help but notice Paddy's lack of enthusiasm and, when he excused himself, saying he had to leave for army duties, Billie's humiliation was complete. There had been no talk of a honeymoon, nor was there any mention of their marriage in the local newspapers.

In late February, Billie opened her door to a new temporary occupant – her friend Mickey Hahn, who was flying in from Chungking, where she had not only been meeting Madame Chiang for her book but had endured months of heavy bombing from the Japanese and a lack of creature comforts.

Mickey astonished Billie by turning up with only a typewriter and a few personal items, explaining that Chungking had such severe shortages of everything that it was customary to give most of one's clothes and belongings to friends upon leaving.

Madame Chiang had resisted her book project, telling W.H. Donald she preferred to write her own book. She had come around only after Donald pointed out that it might be a long time before Madame got around to her memoirs and, besides, Mickey had agreed to cooperate, and her book was likely to be positive.

The reason Mickey was coming to Hong Kong at this time was that Donald had told her Madame was going to Hong Kong to have her sinuses treated and there was no point for Mickey to remain in Chungking.

Apart from being friends, staying with Billie would help them both financially. Pilan had left, so Mickey was taking her place and, with funds running low, would save money by not staying in a hotel. Besides, Mickey eagerly wanted the latest gossip on *T'ien Hsia*.

Meanwhile, she couldn't help noticing the thickening around Billie's waist.

Mickey wrote the following account of her conversation with Billie in her book, *China to Me*:

> I sat down on my bed. "Now tell me about you," I invited. "What is all this about getting married?"
>
> "Yes," said Billie, blushing. "You met him last summer at the beach, remember? Paddy Gill. He's a soldier." I remembered him. He was an Irishman, prematurely baldish. A sergeant or something, I recalled. "It's a good thing Mama died last year," said Billie. "It would have been an awful shock to her, me marrying a soldier. We don't think much of soldiers in our family. But after the war Paddy is going to get out of the Army, and he was going to be sent away soon, and he had been after me for more than a year, and I wouldn't have been happy marrying a Chinese. I'm too foreign in my ways. So, we were married secretly."

Though Billie did not realize it, the plan she revealed with those words was almost certainly the reason for Paddy's change of behaviour.

When Paddy assured Billie that he would leave the army after the war, he was talking to the woman he thought he would spend his life with.

In fact, he regretted those words almost as soon as they came out of his mouth – but could not bring himself to tell Billie, who pinned so much hope on them.

Billie did not understand that when Paddy joined the British Army, he was burning his bridges. The Republicans regarded Irish boys who joined the enemy as traitors and often took harsh reprisal measures if they returned. Moreover, Paddy knew he would also not be welcomed in England, where contempt for the Irish was widespread and it was not uncommon to see signs in the windows of boarding houses: "No Irish, blacks or dogs." Paddy knew the immense obstacles he faced if he wanted a civilian job.

In short, he had pinned his career on the Army, which would always feed and shelter him and put money in his pocket. The Army was more than family to Paddy – it was his life.

Mickey listened sympathetically, but she also envied Billie her pregnancy. She had been told by a doctor that she would never be able to conceive as she had a problem with her Fallopian tubes, a diagnosis that filled Mickey with a depressing sense of loss.

She had other problems on her mind, too. The Soong book was going well but she was low on funds and impatient to be done with it. Moreover, she had gone to Chungking to break off from Sinmay, but missed him in lonely moments.

In Europe, the German juggernaut had rolled over Poland and a British Expeditionary Force was in France to bolster the Allies' defences.

In early April, Paddy called Billie and asked her to meet him by the Star Ferry terminal. Paddy sounded strangely formal and she guessed he had received his marching orders. Surrounded by passengers getting on and off the snub-nosed green ferry, Paddy told her his regiment was leaving for England shortly and this was goodbye.

Billie had guessed she would be having her baby alone, but she was totally unprepared for what came next.

Paddy said she could contact him through his regiment, but she should not follow him to England. She thought he was telling her to stay put until the future was clearer but, when she asked what he meant, Paddy repeated, "Whatever you do, don't come to England. Don't follow me."

As the meaning of his words began to sink in, she could only stare disbelievingly as Paddy turned and strode off, suddenly a stiff-backed stranger.

He had given her no explanation for terminating the relationship and she struggled to find closure. "I realized the ceremony we went through was only a gesture to quieten Paddy's conscience," she wrote. "I died more than just a little. I was filled with grief and despair and helplessness."

Paddy's regiment would join the British Expeditionary Force in France and take part in the retreat and evacuation at Dunkirk.

A few weeks later, Billie's older sister Dolly arrived in Hong Kong after her long employment as a nanny for an American family in France had come to an end. Bandits had murdered the father of the children she was looking after, she said, and the family had given her a ticket to Hong Kong. Luckily for Dolly, Billie soon found her another job as a nanny with a family in May Road.

Within weeks, pretty and fair-skinned Dolly brought a tall, good-looking English soldier to Billie's flat and announced they were getting married.

Dolly had been sitting on a bench, looking after a child while watching soldiers play soccer in a park. "I was the only girl on the sideline," said Dolly, and as she stood up to leave, one of the players quit the field. "He came running after me and said he wanted to see me that night, but I had to go home with the child. He followed and climbed through a window to see me having dinner in the dining room."

Though in her 30s, Dolly's smooth skin made her look younger and a whirlwind courtship followed with Bill Rogers, a 20-year-old sapper with the Royal Engineers.

"We would meet in a canteen with other soldiers and their wives or sweethearts and we would go out for a beer," Dolly said. "Bill was a wonderful and gentle man."

On June 22, 1940, Dorothy Newman and William Rogers married in a civil ceremony at the Supreme Court. A photograph appeared in a local paper showing Rogers looking dashing in his uniform while Dolly is simply dressed, with a white beret tilted to one side.

Dolly said Billie, who was heavily pregnant, did not attend because she was unwell. No doubt, Billie was shaking her head in wonderment. Men vastly outnumbered women in the colony and many fair-skinned girls came out from England in search of a husband. The media described them as a "fishing fleet" and they often had their pick of suitors.

Dolly's good fortune continued when, on June 29, the Hong Kong Government issued orders that British women and children were to be evacuated immediately to evade a possible Japanese invasion.

The order, which applied to all British women and children under 18 "of European race," caused an uproar. Many British wives did not want to leave their husbands while Eurasians who sought to join were blocked by Australia's "whites only" immigration policy.

Dolly, with her new British passport as the wife of a British serviceman, was among the 3,500 women and children – over 40% of the colony's British population – who set sail for Manila around July 1, with the aim of proceeding to Australia later. Dolly and Bill had been married for less than 10 days. Mavis wrote to her sister Helen in Sydney asking her to help Dolly.

Wen applied for Billie to be exempted from the evacuation as she was an essential worker. Billie had no interest in leaving, anyway, and had more pressing concerns.

On July 31, Billie was entering the cinema with a Chinese nursing friend when she gripped her stomach. Even at this stage, Billie knew little about childbirth, but her friend realized what was happening and took her by taxi to St Paul's Hospital, where she was examined by Dr Samy. He pronounced that labour had begun, and then headed for the door. When an alarmed Billie asked where he was going, he reassured her he would be back.

The labour lasted several hours, during which Billie implored the nurse to kill her. The moment she held her baby in her arms, however, a flood of tenderness overwhelmed her.

"Fortunately, I had a marvellous baby *amah*, Ah Chun, who took complete charge of Brian," as she called the baby, "from the moment we got home from the hospital." A fiftyish woman with a kind, patient face, Ah Chun wore the standard *amah*'s attire of white blouse and black pants and tied her hair back in a knot. She quickly became part of the family and Brian proved a calm baby, rarely crying, with large brown eyes. Billie wrote to Paddy about the birth, and of the christening that took place at St Margaret's church on September 11, but she received no reply.

Paddy had been re-assigned to India since June, and was embroiled in the horrific Burma campaign for the rest of the war.

Mickey returned from another trip to Chungking. She had finished her book but, at 35, had few belongings and little money; she had finally severed her relationship with Sinmay and was disconsolately thinking that she had little option but to return to America.

For the moment, however, despite her precarious finances, she decided to stay at the Gloucester Hotel and splurge on new clothes and a hairdo.

She had survived near-disasters in Chungking. She had slipped on its steep steps and only the swift action of a coolie in grabbing her saved Mickey from a precipitous and likely fatal fall. Her house had been bombed and her draft book was buried under a heap of rubble. Fortunately, her suitcase was found a week later with the manuscript intact.

Mickey Hahn, with her gibbon, reunited with Billie in Hong Kong

Soon after her return, she had dinner with Major Charles Boxer and one of his friends. She had met Boxer occasionally over the previous few years.

Billie had been in the new *T'ien Hsia* office in 1938 when Boxer arrived to submit a book review. As well as being a senior intelligence officer, Boxer was an authority on Japan as well as the Portuguese and Dutch empires in the Far East.

In the *T'ien Hsia* office, he had made an unusual request. "He read Mickey's book reviews and wanted to meet her," said Billie. "He was interested in her mind and asked for an introduction." Wen told him that Mickey was living in Shanghai, adding that she was madly in love with a Chinese poet.

This had not stopped Boxer from calling on Mickey during a visit to Shanghai. He found her sharing a flat in the red-light district with a beautiful Australian prostitute and a gibbon in a bright red fez. He watched for a while as Sinmay and his Chinese friends visited, and he left believing that Mickey and her friends were quite mad.

Now, over dinner, she was drawn to Boxer although she knew he was unhappily married to a beautiful Englishwoman.

A few days later, Billie was with Mickey and Charles at another dinner when the major overheard Mickey telling a woman that she couldn't have children.

In her book, *China to Me*, Mickey described what happened next:

"What is this nonsense?" [Charles] demanded in the taxi, after we had sent the guests off to the ferry. "Is that why you carry on so about children, weeping at Wu Teh-chen's and keeping gibbons and all that?"

"Oh no. I don't want children. I never did."

"All women want children," said Charles with amusing certainty. "But see here; do you really want a child? If so, I'll let you have one."

"Huh?"

"Let's have one," he said. "I'll take care of it. It can be my heir. Just to make things all right, if I can get a divorce and if it all works out, we might even get married. If we want to, that is, and after a long time for considering."

"Do you mean it?" I asked after a pause. I knew already, though, that he did. He was being flippant, but that is the way Charles is; he just is flippant. It didn't alter the fact that he meant it.

"I never heard such nonsense," said Charles indignantly. "Can't have children?"

"All right," I said, "let's try."

"And you can turn in your steamship ticket," he said. "You had better do that tomorrow."

And so began one of Hong Kong's great love scandals.

Billie was also with Mickey at the Gloucester Hotel when a journalist, George Giffen, arrived, hoping to get a story out of Mickey's stay in Chungking.

Giffen, a good-looking man with thick dark hair, was an editor-reporter with the *Hongkong Telegraph*.

The meeting did not go well. Mickey was suffering from dysentery and she backed away as Giffen approached her. As Giffen would later describe it, "I went to interview her and she thought I was going to rape her or something. She told me, 'Don't come any nearer, I'm defenceless,' even though Billie was around."

Billie recalled George, whom she was meeting for the first time, as "the most self-effacing man I had ever met."

No one in the room could possibly foresee that, a few years later, behind barbed wire, Billie and George would conceive Ian (the author).

19

Donald and the Mei Hwa

Billie looked up from her desk to see a tall, broad-shouldered man standing over her, smiling through dark-rimmed glasses, balanced over a large, beak-like nose.

"I'm Donald," he said, holding out his hand. "You must be Billie. Holly told me about you."

The handshake marked the start of Billie's working relationship with the straight-shooting, unpretentious man they called China's "Number One White Man."

W.H. Donald was the Chiangs' closest foreign advisor, so trusted that he lived in their compound and ate with them in Chungking. He called them Generalissimo and M'issimo and they called him Don.

Though based in Chungking, Donald would make the long and sometimes hazardous flight to Hong Kong with increasing frequency in 1940.

He needed a secretary, one who was discreet as well as efficient, and Wen recommended Billie.

Initially, Billie worked with Donald in his room at the Gloucester Hotel. But when people learned that Donald was in town, a stream of visitors – journalists, businessmen and officials – would knock on the door, arriving unannounced.

He decided they would work in a place where they could not be disturbed – on the waters of Hong Kong aboard his 40-foot yacht, the *Mei Hwa*. A passionate sailor, the vessel was his pride and joy, named after China's national flower, the plum blossom. He would show off the compass that was a gift from Madame Chiang, but he especially liked to point to a highly polished teak desk and say, "That is where I will write my memoirs as I sail around the Pacific."

Before his visits, Donald would send a telegram to Billie with the message: "Fill *Mei Hwa* up with honeydew melons." This was her signal to tell the crew to stock up on provisions, including her favourite fruit. Billie was the one to liaise with the crew as Donald spoke no Chinese despite his decades in China.

The *Mei Hwa* would cruise around Hong Kong Island while they worked. "As the advisor the Chiangs relied on, most of the paperwork fell on him," said Billie. "His briefcase always bulged with urgent papers on China's policy matters, highly sensitive and explosive political intrigues, and letters from people all over the world who had notions of being able to cure China of her ills."

Donald was in his mid-60s and tired from years of travelling around China, but he was a vigorous and fluent

Billie on the Mei Hwa

talker, dictating detailed memos and letters to world leaders as the dark blue waves rippled around them. Around midday, Billie would take a dip in the South China Sea and have a light lunch.

In the tiny kitchen, a cook would prepare meals that were always western; Donald said Chinese food upset his stomach. Neither did the supplies include alcohol as he was that rarity among journalists, a teetotaller. Donald had come to Hong Kong after one desperate editor, fed up with his heavy-drinking staff, offered Donald a job from Sydney after hearing he never touched liquor. Donald was also a Christian and a member of the YMCA.

Billie, 26, was awestruck by the great man, but he soon put her at ease. "When we relaxed in between the hours of work, I enjoyed his remarkable conversation, his sense of humour and his great knowledge and wisdom in all matters," she wrote. "He was comfortable to be with and he would let me bring Pilan and Mavis on board."

Donald was known for his rapid style of talking, peppered with detail – though one British ambassador called him "a garrulous old man" – and he had an endless fund of stories.

He was enthusiastic when he arrived in Hong Kong to take up a sub-editor's job with *The China Mail* in 1901, but found the British pretentious and petty and was appalled that they were far more interested in English cricket scores than in China, the giant across the border. After years of being at odds with the establishment, he resigned and moved to Shanghai in 1911, the year of the revolution. He made friends with Charlie Soong, a printer of revolutionary materials, and watched Soong's six children grow up to play prominent roles in history.

The pragmatic Donald also became an unlikely friend of Sun Yat-sen, whom he considered a dreamer with grandiose plans. Nonetheless, Donald helped him draft Sun's manifesto which was published on him taking up the position of president in 1912 and, despite their differences, remained loyal to Sun.

With Chiang, Sun's successor, Donald had a shaky start, disapproving of his early attempts to foster Chinese nationalism by stirring up anti-foreign feelings. But, by the end of 1933, he decided that, despite his many faults, including aloofness and arrogance, Chiang was China's most viable hope. After one lengthy meeting with the Chiangs, during which Donald aired his views with customary frankness, Madame Chiang, whom he had known since she was a little girl, said to him: "You were wonderful. We needed that. Why don't you come and work for us?"

Donald's bluntness initially shocked the Chiangs, but they came to appreciate his honesty and pragmatic approach.

Donald had a scathing attitude towards Chinese "face," which he considered the cause of many of its problems and which brought him into frequent conflict with the bureaucrats. He once said, "I am the only man in China with no 'face' because I carry my own bags and do my own chores." Yet Donald also believed that being an outsider allowed him to say things no Chinese would dare say.

Donald had personally known the main players in the extraordinary, multi-sided drama of the Xi'an Incident in 1936 when northern warlords, alarmed at Japan's incursions in Manchuria, kidnapped the Generalissimo to make him halt his fight with the Communists and join forces against the Japanese. Apart from being with Mei-ling – who was so terrified she gave Donald a revolver and asked him to shoot her if soldiers threatened her – Donald was friends with the northern ruler, Chang Hsüeh-liang (Zhang Xueliang), whom he had once helped to conquer an opium addiction; Ching-ling Soong, Mei-ling's younger sister, who held sway with the Communists; and the pro-Japanese elements in Nanking who wanted to bomb Xi'an. While China, and much of the world, held its breath during the month-long crisis, Donald played a central role in steering it to a negotiated settlement.

Donald was one among others who provided Billie with a ringside seat in the theatre of Chinese politics.

The elder Soong sister, Ai-ling, had an interest in *T'ien Hsia* – she and her financier husband H.H. Kung would pressure banks to advertise in its pages – and she invited the staff to parties at her home in Deep Water Bay.

In February, 1940, Billie attended a dinner hosted by Madame Kung that was memorable for several reasons. "I sat at the same table as Madame Kung while white-gloved waiters brought one exotic dish after another, each representing a different province," said Billie.

"I was surprised that Madame Kung was almost as diminutive as me and she had her hair piled up to add height. She had tiny, dainty hands and would laugh girlishly, covering her face with a fan. She must have heard that I liked to dance but, when the dance music began after dinner, she took me completely by surprise by asking if I knew how to lead.

"I nodded and took her by the hand to the floor. I was so happy that I had spent $80, a small fortune, on an aquamarine Georgette ball gown for the occasion. The waltz was the Blue Danube and, as I glided along the marble floor with one of China's most powerful women on my arm, I felt I was in a trance."

That night, Billie replayed the scene in her mind, looking occasionally at the ball gown hanging outside her wardrobe to air.

But, waking the next morning, she was aghast. "The gown was gone. I leapt from my bed and searched everywhere. Soon, I realised a thief had hooked the gown with a long bamboo pole through the window of our ground-floor flat in Happy Valley. Such thefts were common in a city crammed with desperate refugees. Knowing that stolen articles often turned up in a nearby flea market, I searched for that dress for weeks, but never found it."

A few weeks later, Wen and Billie were organising a radio appeal by Madame Chiang in Hong Kong. The speech, a plea for China's war orphans, was for an American audience.

At midnight on the day of the broadcast, Wen received a telegram saying the programme had to be advanced by six hours due to some technical hitch in New York. "This caused a flap as it meant Madame Chiang had to go on air very early the next morning," said Billie. "And this also meant informing the Governor of Hong Kong, at the risk of waking him up."

Wen sent Billie with the telegram to the local broadcaster, ZBW, in the Gloucester Building. She saw two men through the glass pane of the door and knocked. They glanced up, but ignored her. She could imagine what was running through their minds: "Who is this Chinese girl and what on earth could she want at this hour?" But Billie persisted and, finally, one of the men opened the door with an exasperated air.

When she explained her mission and handed over the telegram, they were sceptical and kept examining the paper as if it was a hoax. Finally, one said, in a shocked tone, "Do you realize that this means waking up the Governor?"

Billie replied, "I'm afraid you will have to. The First Lady of China is waiting for an answer in Chungking."

The phone call was made and everyone was alerted to expect Madame Chiang at dawn.

The *T'ien Hsia* staff turned out in full when Madame Chiang arrived, her black hair swept back, showing her finely accented features. "She was beautiful and stunning in a simple red, embroidered satin gown," said Billie.

The First Lady delivered her live message in ringing tones. Afterwards, the staff lined up to meet her and, when Wen presented Billie, Madame Chiang said, "I've heard all about you. May I call you Billie?" Billie suspected that Donald had mentioned her.

Not long afterwards, Donald found the limits to his frankness with the Chiangs. He told Mei-ling that the Kungs were enriching themselves in the foreign exchange market while millions of their compatriots were starving, and something needed to be done. Mei-ling told him angrily that he was free to criticize many people, but not her sister or her husband.

Donald also made his view known on another sensitive issue. A faction of the Nationalists was arguing that, since substantive help was still not forthcoming from the western democracies, they might instead align with Germany and Italy. When a Mei-ling broadcast to America included the phrase "inimical totalitarians" (referring to the Axis powers), Chiang told Donald to take out the phrase. When he refused, Chiang called him a traitor who would sacrifice the Chinese to British interests. In May 1940, Chiang sent Donald a note: "I am not at war with Germany," to which Donald replied, "I am." He said goodbye to Mei-ling and left for Hong Kong to embark on his dream of sailing around the Pacific.

Mickey needed to move out of the Gloucester Hotel but she sprained her ankle while repelling advances from an amorous captain at a party, and Billie did the legwork to find her an apartment at Tregunter Mansions next to the building where Charles Boxer lived.

Billie saw a lot of Mickey and Charles at dinners and parties at the flat. Charles, with his languages, would invite Chinese, French and Dutch guests and Mickey had her Chungking journalist friends over, including Agnes Smedley, "a large woman with a square head," who made a pass at Charles, which Mickey, who was one of Smedley's friends, seemed not to mind at all.

Mickey and Charles had started their impregnation project and, as news of their relationship spread, some of Mickey's friends dropped her while other women ignored her in the street.

Mickey was unfazed by the fall-out, but she still believed she couldn't get pregnant and Charles was too busy to see her more than two days a week. With time to brood, Mickey, who had kicked her opium habit after a nightmare week in treatment, would occasionally relapse and ask Billie to accompany her.

Billie described one visit to an opium den in Cat Street. "After following Mickey up rickety stairs into a large, darkened room, a sweet-sickly smell hit my nostrils. The pipe smokers, lying on couches, were lost in a world of their own. I was uneasy as I watched Mickey take a pipe and bend over to warm a pellet over a flame. I would stay silent during Mickey's reverie and then I would help her groggily down the stairs and into a taxi back to Tregunter Mansions."

In early 1941, Mickey discovered she was pregnant. Soon after, Charles went on a mission to Singapore and stayed with his wife, Ursula. When he returned, he told Mickey that Ursula now wanted to reconcile and have a baby. Mickey, no doubt thinking of Billie, said she didn't want to be deserted with a baby. When she asked what would happen if Ursula became pregnant, Charles replied that he could afford to have two children. But he realized how caddish that sounded, told Mickey he loved her more than his wife, and wrote to Ursula that he was not returning to her.

They tried to keep Mickey's pregnancy a secret – Billie did not know and neither did Vera Armstrong, whose husband Jack was arranging Charles's will to make provision for the baby.

*Above: the author at the grave of James Warner, St Matthias, Malvern Link;
Below: the P&O headquarters on the Praya (now Des Voeux Road) in
19th-century Hong Kong*

CHEFOO   East Beach

Above: The Family Hotel in Chefoo, rebuilt by the author's great-grandparents, postcard courtesy of Lin Wei-bin; Below: The Newman family – Frank (far left), Annie (third from right) and Ellen (second from right), courtesy of Graeme Clark

Above: Emily 'Mickey' Hahn, her daughter Carola, Ian and Billie at Conygar;
Below left: Reuniting with lifelong confidante Mickey in 1994;
Below right: Charles Boxer – Billie was fond of him but found him an enigma

Above: At Oddenino's in Regent Street, London, in 1955 with Jimmy Noonan;
Below left: Paddy Gill – he married Billie before the war;
Below right: George Giffen

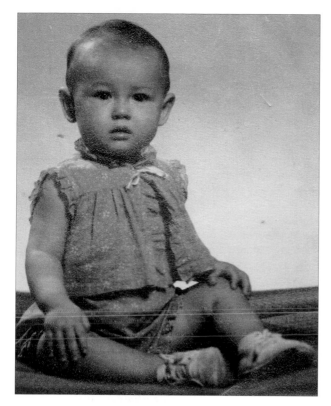

Left:
Brian Patrick Gill

Below:
Billie at Brian's grave in Stanley Military Cemetery during a remembrance service in 1995

Above left: Mavis Ming, W.H. Donald, Billie and Pilan Petigura on the Mei Hwa in Hong Kong before the war. Right: Dorothy Newman, Frank's second daughter, with her son Peter; Below: Billie was reunited with her Bungalow B room-mates Joan Witham (later Gordon-Thompson) and Freda Howkins (later Ingham) in 1985

Above: In 1993 Billie returned to Shanghai's Garden Bridge, scene of her traumatic encounter; Below left: With Margaret Lin behind her home off Yuyuan Road; Below right: Their once-grand three-storey home in Rue Lafayette

Above: Billie received her MBE from the Queen at Buckingham Palace in 1977; Below: Meeting her grandchildren Brian (right) and Sabrina for the first time, in 1999

In mid-1941 Billie and Mickey were walking through the Gloucester Arcade when a shopkeeper greeted them. Glancing at Mickey, the man said, "It's funny, but I thought for a moment you were pregnant." Realizing her condition would soon be impossible to conceal, Mickey replied, "As a matter of fact, I am," amazing Billie, who was hearing the news for the first time. Mickey told her a doctor had performed minor surgery which had been successful.

While some women called for the "shameless hussy" to leave town, an unperturbed Mickey asked every mother she met about childbirth. "It's easy as anything," Billie told her. "Look at me, small as I am, and the doctor said he'd never pull me through, but it wasn't bad at all." Mickey gave birth to Carola on October 17, 1941.

Her book on the Soong Sisters was published that year and it divided her friends, with Agnes Smedley denouncing it as Nationalist propaganda.

Around that time, Billie received a call from an army colleague of Paddy, Cromar Mitchell, who was trying to find dinner speakers for his regiment and asked if she could help him.

When they met to discuss this, Cromar asked if she would go out with him. He did not hide the fact that his wife and young son had been evacuated to Australia in June and that he was lonely. Billie, who had not heard a word from Paddy in the 18 months since he left, welcomed the idea of an evening out. During their first dinner, Cromar said his marriage was in name only.

Though Japanese forces were massing across the border, the British partied as hard as ever, believing that their threats were empty and, even if they did attack, they were said to have poor eyesight and would not match up to British soldiers. Commander Arthur Grasett, the Canadian in charge of the Hong Kong garrison, announced that the presence of British troops in the colony would deter the Japanese.

Cromar, who "had auburn hair and cut a dashing figure in uniform," took Billie out again and told her he was falling in love with her.

"We were both young and lonely," Billie recalled, without going into much detail. "Cromar's passion and sincerity struck a chord and, after a few dates, I responded to his advances."

In mid-November, two regiments of Canadian soldiers, the Royal Rifles of Canada and the Winnipeg Grenadiers, arrived to bolster Hong Kong's defences.

On December 3, 1941, General Christopher Maltby, who had replaced Grasett, toured the border and expressed confidence his six battalions could ward off any enemy offensive.

On December 5, Charles Boxer, as head of British intelligence, went to a Japanese dinner party and had a nagging sense that his hosts were more cordial and jovial than usual.

On Saturday, December 6, Billie went to Kai-tak airport to take delivery of two pandas that Madame Chiang was giving to the Bronx Zoo as a gift to the American people. Billie escorted them across town to a zoo representative and they departed on one of the last flights out of Hong Kong.

That evening, Billie and Mavis took part in a fund-raising pageant on Caroline Hill. Sponsored by the CIC, the programme included a burlesque football match and performances by comedians and singers. Mavis put on a callisthenics exhibition that ended with the schoolgirls forming a V-for-Victory formation.

The highlight of the evening was a fashion show with traditional Chinese costumes on the theme 'Through the Ages'. Billie, before thousands of clapping people, minced onstage as a T'ang dynasty concubine.

The next day, Sunday, Billie and Cromar were watching a film at the Queen's Theatre when a notice flashed onto the screen, ordering military personnel to report to their bases immediately. Cromar kissed Billie and said he would call later. It would be 40 years before they saw each other again.

20

Into Battle

Charles Boxer heard the news in Japanese at 4.45am on Monday, December 8. He was on shift in the Battle Box, the underground headquarters of the military in Central District. A fluent Japanese speaker, he was listening to Radio Tokyo when he heard a voice interrupt to say Japanese units were attacking British and American forces in the Pacific.

He called Mickey, who was feeding baby Carola and feeling relieved because Charles's wife had agreed to a divorce, and she could expect to marry Charles within a few months.

At 8am, Billie was on the tram, jangling its way to Central, thinking about Cromar as well as the pile of work that awaited her at the office. She heard faint thudding noises, but thought they were part of an A.R.P. (Air Raid Precautions) exercise that had been part of daily life for months.

When she saw the crowd outside the bank headquarters, she realized something was amiss. She saw Reuters' Bill O'Neill waving to her over several Chinese heads and he was shouting: "The balloon's gone up. The Japanese are here already."

As usual, Billie was one of the first to arrive at the office as the *T'ien Hsia* editors lived in Kowloon on the other side of the harbour and tended to arrive later.

She called Wen and could hear his voice rising. The sounds she had heard were bombs the Japanese had dropped on Kai-tak airport, not far from where Wen lived. He said he would contact the others and come in later. As Hollington Tong's man in Hong Kong, Wen feared for his life if the Japanese caught him – in fact, none of the staff would be safe.

Billie knew this was going to be different from Shanghai. Japan was launching an attack on a British colony, so there was no International Settlement in which to hide. Everyone would be in the line of fire.

Her 18-month-old son Brian was at home in Happy Valley with Ah Chun. She needed to be with him as well as in the office waiting for Wen and the others to arrive.

She went to see David MacDougall, of the Hong Kong government information service, who arranged for her to receive a billet and a tin hat. The billet, stamped by the Auxiliary Quartering Corps of the Royal Army Ordnance Corps – Paddy's regiment – instructed her to go to Peak Mansions, flat no. 2. MacDougall advised her to contact Colonel Rose of the Hong Kong Volunteer Defence Corps, saying he was certain she could be useful to him.

Billie went home to Brian and Ah Chun. When she or her flatmate Mavis switched on the radio, they heard a reassuring voice say that the attack on Kai-tak airport was no cause for alarm. Yet they looked up and saw Japanese planes flying without opposition, indicating that the small local air force had been wiped out.

From that first day, they frequently heard air raid sirens and the thudding of bombs and saw smoke billowing in the skies.

The authorities had assured the public that the Gin Drinkers' Line, a string of pill boxes, bunkers, trenches and an underground fortress (the Shing Mun Redoubt) strung out across 10½ miles of the New Territories – Hong Kong's Maginot Line – would keep the Japanese at bay for weeks. Early official communiques supported this, but it was not long before calls to panic-stricken friends in Kowloon made it clear the Japanese had broken through and that British forces were in retreat, sparking riots and looting around Kowloon's Nathan Road.

The rampaging of local gangs of Chinese triads and Fifth Columnists – Japanese dressed as Chinese – posed a more immediate threat than the Japanese to the women huddled around the radio in Happy Valley. This was not Shanghai, where patriotic Chinese troops put up a fight against overwhelming odds. The Chinese in Hong Kong had little reason to be loyal to the British. Although making up 98% of the population, they had always been left to fend for themselves, had no say in the running of the colony and had been excluded from whites-only areas and clubs.

With violence and rape lying in wait outside the door, the sleepless women decided they could not stay. Mavis headed for the International Women's Club in the Gloucester Building, where she joined her Eurasian friend Anna Matthews, the club's secretary and treasurer.

On December 11, the date stamped on her billet card, Billie and Ah Chun, carrying Brian and wicker baskets containing Cow & Gate powdered milk, diapers, Mama's wedding jacket and skirt, and the family Bible, emerged from the top of the Peak tramway and walked for a few minutes to reach Peak Mansions. The six-storey block of flats, with a small dome at the top, had been allocated to dependants of British soldiers.

Built as luxury flats in 1928, they were spacious, with three bedrooms, living room, dining room, hallway, servants' quarters, storage rooms and several fireplaces.

At their flat number 2, Billie found eight people already in occupation. The bedrooms were taken, so she and Ah Chun settled in the large living room and used the sofa as a bed.

The other occupants, women, children and an elderly man, were walking around in a daze. A small Mexican woman with two children clinging to her slacks complained loudly that she had brought only bedroom slippers. At her husband's insistence, they had run out of their Kowloon home to catch one of the last ferries to Hong Kong and he had told her she would be able to buy shoes on the island. One grey-haired woman asked Billie if she knew what had happened to her son, who had driven off to join the Hong Kong Volunteers and not returned.

Standing in line for food in a garage converted into a food depot, Billie saw that the wives included Eurasians, Chinese and Russians.

A spate of British soldiers had married their girlfriends of different nationalities in the months before the war. Many of the wives had never looked down upon the city from this height as the Peak was off-limits to non-whites unless they were invited or making deliveries.

China Command.
R. A. O. C.

G. R.

BILLETING

HONG KONG DEFENCE REGULATION No. 60.

This card authorizes the wife and dependents of

Mr. GILL ARTHUR ROBERT HIRST

an Essential Service Worker to take up residence in a portion of

.... 9 MAGAZINE Gab Rd. a 2 Peak Mansions
Flat No 2

provided that they arrive at the house within 48 hours of the
date chopped on this card. If they do not arrive within this
time, the space will be regarded as free for allotment to others.
The names of the persons so authorized are:—

GILL LOUISE MARY .... | WIFE
GILL BRIAN PATRICK ... HIRST. SON

IMPORTANT.

    This card must not be given to anyone else, and is only valid
for the persons named hereon.

    This card must be retained by the wife or senior dependent
of the above named Essential Service Worker and must be
produced to the Billeting Officer's and Food Controller's officers
whenever required. Failure to produce the card may result in
your being moved out of the billet.

J. RING,
Billeting Officer.

Billie Gill's billet card, December 1941

Billie asked Ah Chun to see if she could retrieve more things from home
but, a few hours later, she returned with the news that looters had already
ransacked the flat, taking anything that could be consumed or sold. Among

the objects she brought back were a wooden Buddha head and a ceramic Japanese bowl with a crack in it, mementos still with the family today.

Had Billie visited the office a day later, she would have reunited with John Wu, one of her favourite *T'ien Hsia* editors. Wu was staying with his large family in Kowloon but on December 12 his son dragged him to the last Star Ferry to cross the harbour as he could not afford to fall into Japanese hands. Wu wrote, "I went to the *T'ien Hsia* office and found all our friends there. Some of them wanted to go back to Kowloon to see their families, but the communications were already cut. All of us were mad with grief. I remained grimly silent like a convict waiting for the execution. The most pathetic scene was when philosopher Chuan Tseng-ku suddenly burst into a fit of wailing. He said, through his sobs, 'Who is going to feed my cat?'" That evening, John Wu and Francis Yeh went to St John's Cathedral and stayed there with thousands of refugees for the duration of the fighting.

In the *South China Morning Post* offices in Wyndham Street, George Giffen, whom Billie had bumped into a few times since meeting him through Mickey, was sleeping on a camp bed near his desk. He was fortunate – he was in the Hong Kong Volunteer Defence Corps but had been re-assigned from the combatant group as he was considered of essential service on the newspaper.

His editor, Stewart Gray, had sailed on leave for Australia the weekend before the war, leaving him in charge. Since then, he and his colleagues were facing unusual challenges. When the electricity went out, they had to hand-crank the linotype machines. More problematic was finding out what was going on outside as their younger reporters were on combat duty and the government's official communiques verged on the fictional.

David MacDougall set up an information office in the Gloucester Building and it was from here that a story went out about Chinese forces advancing on the Japanese rear – which was nonsense.

Restricted in their movements, reporters took to observing events through binoculars from the rooftop of the Gloucester Building. On December 13, journalists espied a small launch with a white flag coming across the water from Kowloon. It was a peace mission sent by Lieutenant-

General Sakai, with a letter demanding unconditional surrender. Major Charles Boxer met them at the quayside, exchanged salutes, and carried the document to Governor Sir Mark Young. On orders from Whitehall, the demand was rejected, with Young stating, "Not only is this colony strong enough to resist all attempts at invasion but it has the backing of the British Empire, the United States of America and the Republic of China… there will never be any surrender to the Japanese."

The *South China Morning Post* was still exuding a Blitz-like false cheerfulness, running advertisements for Christmas and New Year hampers from Dodwell while editor Henry Ching joked in his 'A Bird's Eye View' column, "Only one casualty so far. Night editor sprained his wrist digging for reprint" and "Then there was the jittery lad who went to buy milk and returned with a bottle of butter."

But the hard news trickling in from the outside world was shocking. Few had expected the Japanese, still bogged down in China after four years, to take on the British Empire and America, the most powerful economy in the world. But the Japanese were making headway after coordinated surprise attacks on Honolulu and in Malaya, the Dutch East Indies and the Philippines.

The attack on America seemed an act of madness that would rebound badly for Japan but then an ashen-faced man came into Billie's flat to announce that two British battleships, the *Prince of Wales* and the *Repulse*, had been sunk off the east coast of Malaya on December 10. Japan's use of long-range torpedo bombers signalled a new kind of war – as at Pearl Harbor, it showed that even the heaviest of ships could be destroyed by specially equipped planes. Britannia had ruled the waves, but this news smashed the image of imperial might and ended any hope of Hong Kong being relieved by the Singapore fleet.

Billie wished she could see Mickey, who was also on the Peak, staying with Selwyn Selwyn-Clarke, Hong Kong's director of medical services, and his wife Hilda. Charles had insisted she move in with them in the event of war. Hilda was called Red Hilda because of the colour of her hair and because she was a socialist and secretary of the China Defence League, headed by Madame Sun Yat-sen. Hilda was one of the few among Hong Kong's society elite who had not frowned on Mickey's affair, calling marriage a "bourgeois nicety." Hilda would irritate Mickey with her self-importance but recruited her into her network engaged in dangerous efforts to get food and vital supplies to prisoners of war.

Peak Mansions was an easy target for the Japanese artillery guns mounted on the rooftops of Kowloon. On hearing the early whine of a shell, Billie would freeze, remaining in suspense as the sound grew louder or softer, depending on its trajectory. Only after the blast indicated it had found its mark elsewhere would she exhale. She thought she might get used to this awful lottery, but the opposite was true – she felt the odds of cheating death grew shorter each time.

Although some had said the island could hold off an invasion for months, it proved a bluff. The military side of Churchill knew even before the war that the garrison was doomed, but the political Churchill needed to show the Americans and the Chinese that Hong Kong would not go down without a fight.

On December 14, the Hong Kong Volunteer Defence Corps moved its headquarters from Lower Albert Road to Peak Mansions. Billie met Colonel Rose, an old-school type. He had been loath to take charge of the HKVDC, a motley group of non-professional soldiers that included businessmen, bank officials, civil servants, clerks and engineers, many in their 60s or older. But its five batteries and seven rifle companies would acquit themselves admirably.

The Volunteers were spread out across the island and Colonel Rose assigned Billie to one of the phones to receive reports from the field and pass them on to the officer in charge. For Billie, it was a welcome chance to do something useful.

On December 17, the Japanese sent another peace mission over the water, which was again met by Charles Boxer. He had already met Othsu-san, one of the delegates, who told him that hostilities would be suspended until 4pm and that, in the event of a refusal, future bombardments would be indiscriminate. In reply, the Governor declined to enter negotiations and said, moreover, he would not receive any more communication on the subject.

After this rejection of their offer, the Japanese began, on the evening of December 18, sending three infantry regiments across the harbour in landing boats, using an amplified gramophone to play tunes such as *Home Sweet Home*. Unopposed, they reached the beaches at Sai Wan, Lyemun and North Point.

Contrary to rumours that they were poor fighters in the dark, their battle-hardened troops advanced across the north-east of Hong Kong Island to reach Wong Nai Chung Gap, the junction in the centre of the island and key to controlling the battle. Once they captured the Gap, they split the British defences, leaving the Stanley Peninsula as the last British bastion. Nonetheless, the Japanese sustained heavy casualties and the slopes of Leighton Hill, near Billie's flat, were covered with their dead.

Though Billie would not learn of it for years, Dolly's husband, engineer Bill Rogers, was thought to have been with one of the searchlight units on the north shore that were overrun. On December 19, Rogers was reported as a 'casualty return', meaning he was missing, presumed dead.

At Peak Mansions, Billie was finding the telephone reports increasingly incoherent as men in the field had little idea what was going on. As Lieutenant Drummond Hunter, of the Royal Scots, related at a later prisoner-of-war reunion, "It was total confusion all the time. We didn't even know whether the Japanese had landed or not. Just suddenly, we heard these shouts in Japanese."

On the morning of December 20, Major Charles Boxer, of the Lincolnshire regiment, and his friend and fellow trooper with a luxuriant moustache, Alf Bennett, drove to the Repulse Bay Hotel to see what was going on. They found a leaderless Punjabi regiment in retreat, so Charles joined them with the intent of leading them out of a gully. Bennett later described to the author what happened next: "I was standing here and Charles was standing three feet away and he was hit in the arm by a sniper. He had to be whizzed to hospital, but I don't know how we got back or anything about what happened afterwards." The bullet pierced Charles's chest and he lay in a field for hours, delirious and losing blood. When found, he was rushed to hospital where he was considered in such poor shape that he was placed in the morgue.

At Peak Mansions, the electricity went off with the Japanese capture of North Point power station after a 24-hour battle with white-haired Volunteers known as the "Hughesiliers," who had an average age of 65 and fought until they ran out of ammunition.

The roads around the Peak were near-impassable, strangling transport and supplies.

Artillery fire rained and, on December 20, Billie's worst fears were realized when a shell landed on their building. Billie heard no warning whine, but the explosion knocked her off her feet. Scrambling to get up, covered in plaster, she found Brian, also coated in white, but unharmed.

The explosion claimed the lives of three women, Mrs Nina Goldin, Mrs Valentine Horowitz and Mrs Barbara Veronkin. Two died instantly and the third on the way to hospital.

The following day, an official proposed moving the older children to a safer place and Billie volunteered to escort them. She climbed into the truck beside the driver with half a dozen chattering children behind her. All fell silent when they saw the boulders and burnt-out vehicles strewn over the road. The truck weaved between them and at every corner, Billie feared they would find the way blocked. She was relieved to reach Matilda Hospital, where she handed the children to a nurse.

When Hilda told Mickey about Charles being wounded, Mickey set off, against all advice, on a trek of several hours, dodging bombs and Japanese troops, before reaching Queen Mary Hospital where Charles told her she wasn't supposed to be there. Mickey insisted on staying, provoking harsh exchanges with the already over-burdened staff.

At Peak Mansions, they were spending evenings in candlelight when the water supply stopped after the Japanese captured the reservoirs.

On Christmas Eve, the Japanese shelling lasted through the night, making sleep impossible. On Christmas Day, the cacophony stopped. At around four in the afternoon, someone noticed that the Union Jack at Government House had been replaced by a white flag.

"We've surrendered," said an official, wearily. "Merry Christmas."

George Giffen

At Wyndham Street, George Giffen was bent over his typewriter, working on the biggest story of his life – a lengthy account of the war, finally unencumbered by official communiques. He was writing not only for his paper but also the *Daily Telegraph* in London and the *Toronto Star* in Canada.

But, as he finished, two Japanese officials walked in to announce they were taking over the office and the plant. They found George's article, and gave it to their news agency, Domei, which sent it to Tokyo.

To his mortification, they ran a much-sanitized propaganda piece under George's byline in the Japanese-run *Hongkong News* three weeks later under the heading: "British Journalist Praises Conduct and Valour of Japanese."

21

Rathole

The abrupt cessation of war did not mean the end of danger. An officially sanctioned orgy of looting began immediately after the surrender as the Japanese allowed the triads three days of plunder as a reward for their disruptive activities against the British.

Billie set off to see Mickey for what she expected to be a short walk to May Road.

She and Ah Chun, with Brian in a pushchair, picked their way through the rubble and had walked only a few minutes when they stopped. Less than 50 yards away, they saw half a dozen Chinese looters forming a human chain outside a large house. Some were pushing silverware and carpets out of a window which were passed along for others to carry away.

The looters had sticks and knives. Billie could have turned back but she was frozen, staring at the wanton gutting of someone's home.

Once the looters finished their work, Billie resumed walking, trembling as she led the way down a footpath that was a short cut. They had not gone 30 yards before a large boulder blocked the way. Just as Billie was trying to work out how to best manoeuvre the pushchair past the rock, she looked up and saw a column of Japanese soldiers marching up towards them.

As a young Chinese girl, Billie knew instantly that she was in grave danger. She knew about the massive scale of rape in Nanking. Only a few days earlier, near her home in Happy Valley, Japanese soldiers had raped Chinese and British nurses at a hospital at the racecourse – and would soon rape several thousand Chinese women in Wanchai.

As the Japanese patrol approached, Billie could not go forward and it was too late to turn back. She stood, petrified.

*Brian in his pushchair
– Japanese soldiers lifted
them over a boulder*

Suddenly, an image of "Auntie" Ayano, Lois's Japanese mother, flashed across her mind. With the khaki-clad soldiers only feet away, she pasted a smile on her lips and bowed deeply and slowly, from the waist. "*Ohayo, ohayo*," she said. She lifted her head, half-expecting to find a sword poised above her. Instead, the officer leading the group put up his hand for his men to halt and he barked an order.

Two soldiers strode purposefully towards Billie. The last time she had encountered a Japanese soldier in Shanghai, it had not gone well and, when the soldiers bent towards Brian, Billie stepped forward protectively.

The men lifted the pushchair over the boulder and lowered it on the other side. The officer signalled for Billie and Ah Chun to pass. As she brushed past the soldiers, Billie could smell their pungent body odour, but she bowed repeatedly, saying "*Arigato*" and "*Sayonara.*"

When the last soldier had disappeared, Billie felt giddy. She had no idea why she had been spared, though it helped that it was morning, the men were not drunk, and were bent on a mission.

Delayed shock hit her and she walked faster in case other troops were around. She was in a state of near hysteria by the time she reached Mickey's flat at Tregunter Mansions. She knocked repeatedly, but no one answered the door. Billie could not bear the prospect of going back.

Finally, she heard a familiar voice calling her name. It was Vera Armstrong, who was peering from her flat. Vera, one of Mickey's closest friends, let Billie inside her home where the windows were boarded up to deter looters.

Her children, Bridget, 10, and John, 7, were with her, but her husband Jack, Charles's astute lawyer, had gone out to find out what was happening.

In her mid-thirties, Vera knew the Japanese well – she had grown up in Yokohama with her French and English parents and spoke the language fluently. She had the unusual feature of having different coloured irises, one brown and the other blue.

Speaking with her customary rapidity, Vera told Billie that Mickey was staying at Queen Mary Hospital where Charles was being treated and would be there for several days.

Billie was shocked when Jack returned. A big, broad-shouldered man who exuded self-assurance, his frame drooped with fatigue and he seemed to have shrunk. Not a talkative man like his wife, Jack's brief observation was nonetheless alarming: "The Japanese are celebrating by getting drunk and things could get ugly."

That evening, they sat in the dark – the power was still out – eating canned food, heated over a kerosene stove. They could hear Japanese officers carousing and laughing in a nearby flat they had taken over. They knew that when the soldiers got drunk, they could burst into their flat and do whatever they wished. The tension in the Armstrong flat continued into the night until the noise of partying grew fainter, followed by silence.

During this period of limbo, they did not know that Japanese army officers were in fact imposing discipline on their troops with regard to the treatment of Europeans, no doubt to avoid the kind of publicity that Nanking had generated and turned much of the world against them.

Such restraint did not extend to locals, however. On December 28, following the Japanese victory parade, when commander Takashi Sakai led a two-mile military procession through the town, the soldiers, mostly country boys who had been brutalized by their superiors, would, as tradition allowed, go on a three-day rampage of looting and rape. Historians estimate the Japanese raped 10,000 Chinese women during the "sack" of Hong Kong.

Once their pact with the triads expired, the Japanese cracked down on Chinese looters, shooting some on the street and throwing others into the sea. One evening, Jack reported that he had seen looters strung up from lamp posts by the lower Peak tram station.

After placing the enemy's armed forces into prison camps in Kowloon, the Japanese now pondered what to do with the civilians. Japan's victory had brought prestige and a strategic asset in its port, but otherwise the colony had none of the natural resources – oil, tin and rubber – that they needed and they found themselves ruling 1.6 million Chinese whom they had no wish to feed.

On January 4, 1942, Jack brought home a poster that instructed European nationals – British, American, Dutch and Belgian residents – to assemble at Murray Parade Ground the following day, with the threat of severe punishment for those who did not turn up.

Jack thought they would be registered and allowed to return home, but Vera decided it would be prudent to take clothing and other essentials.

By the time Billie arrived with Ah Chun and Brian at the parade ground, several hundred people had already gathered, including many Chinese and Eurasian wives and children. The Japanese clearly did not expect so many people and registration was slow. Billie showed her British passport but registered as a secretary with a Dutch bank, Nederlandsche Ind Handelsbank, to hide her links with the Nationalist government.

The Japanese shouted orders and grew angry when they were not understood. It rained, adding to the general misery and making it difficult for officials to write things down. After several hours, they began moving people off in batches.

Japanese cameramen recorded the occasion to show the world how Asia looked once freed of the yoke of white imperialism. If they wanted to capture images of liberated Chinese, however, they were disappointed. A few of the Chinese onlookers may have smirked at seeing the British humiliated, but most looked on in sullen silence.

The batch of people including Billie trudged along Des Voeux Road, with its shops and department stores boarded up and only hawkers on the streets, charging exorbitantly for their wares. They stopped outside a row of dingy waterfront hotels used by Chinese prostitutes and their seafaring clients and Billie was directed to the Nam Ping Hotel.

As she climbed the rickety stairs, she could see on each landing a row of cubicles, divided by thin partitions and with curtains drawn across the entrance. Reaching the top floor, Billie and Ah Chun entered cubicle 413 which they would share with three adults and a child.

The cubicle contained a single bed and a washstand with a grimy, chipped basin. Attached to the room was a veranda, big enough for two rattan chairs. Each floor had only one toilet.

Billie's companions were an American Baptist missionary couple, Cecil and Margaret Ward, and a Chinese woman with a child. Both women were pregnant. No food was provided that day and, when they settled down for the night, Ward insisted that the four women and two children sleep crosswise on the bed, while he lay on the floor. Billie rested her protruding feet on a chair.

After a while, she began to itch and, as others began to scratch, she realized they had bed bugs for company. Then she heard rats running along the floorboards. One of her friends in the Nam Ping, Fr Bernard Tolhill, would recall: "We were three in a bed and the first morning at 4am I woke up and there was a big rat kissing my nose and after that I woke up at 4 every morning and could not sleep."

The following morning, the guards allowed Chinese hawkers to bring in food and Billie bought *congee* and tinned milk. Cecil Ward, who spoke some Cantonese, bargained with hawkers through the door grille and returned holding up dried milk, telling Billie they would be happy to share whatever they had. Their kindness and selflessness would sustain Billie through those nightmare days.

During the day, the Chinese woman and her child stayed on the veranda. Billie took Brian to the rooftop and looked down to see an unending stream of Chinese with their belongings. She did not know it, but Mavis, realizing that the Japanese were not interested in detaining Eurasians, had talked her way out of the Kai Toon Hotel and contacted a friend who took her to a flat in Kowloon. The intrepid Mavis would make two attempts to escape Hong Kong and would succeed in walking to the mainland.

A scream woke Billie in the night, and she heard someone shouting, "Fire! fire!" Scrambling with others to the rooftop, she saw a hotel in flames a few buildings away. She stayed, fearful the wind would blow the conflagration in their direction, until the fire was extinguished.

While the POWs were cooped up, the Japanese and British debated over where to accommodate them. The Chief Justice, Sir Atholl MacGregor, requested that they be kept on the Peak but the Japanese were insulted by the idea of captives looking down on them. Dr Selwyn-Clarke, who was respected by the Japanese, recommended Stanley, a peninsula on the southeastern tip of the island. Its open spaces and fresh air, he argued, would help prevent diphtheria and typhoid. The Japanese, who feared epidemics, agreed.

Billie was glad to hear they were going to Stanley and, on January 22, she emerged from the Nam Ping, blinking at the sunlight after three weeks of gloom.

The ferry ride took them past Repulse Bay and, as they approached Stanley jetty, she looked at the green hills with anticipation.

When they disembarked, Billie expected to find people to tell them where to go. But there were no arrangements, and she realized it was everyone for himself.

People rushed around, staking claims like a gold rush. Once a person or group found a room, they would fend off others who sought to enter. If they left their space for a moment, strangers would rush in to fill it. Arguments broke out. That first day set a tone of aggressive selfishness that left its mark.

Billie trudged up a hill until she saw some large buildings that had been part of a school. However, as she approached, someone told her it was mainly for men. She turned and saw a red-roofed bungalow with a lawn, glinting with broken glass.

Inside, people were milling around. The rooms had been stripped bare by looters, the door and the windows were broken, and the sole toilet was blocked.

A man she recognized, Philip Witham, approached her and asked how many were in her group. When she said she was with her son and his *amah*, Witham told her he and his wife also had a boy the same age as Brian and suggested they share one of the bedrooms. It was the first gesture of help that she received.

In the room, she met Witham's wife, Joan, their little boy, Anthony, and two other men. There were no beds or mattresses and they sat on the concrete floor. No food was available that evening.

An exhausted Billie watched Ah Chun tending to Brian, who adored her. For the umpteenth time, she told herself how thankful she was that Ah Chun had stayed with them when so many *amahs*, along with servants and drivers, had fled from the onset of war.

Billie would shortly find out the real reason Witham had invited them to share the room – and she would lose Ah Chun.

22

Cheek by Jowl

The six of them were sharing a square bedroom measuring 13 feet by 13 feet.

The bedroom had an attached closet which, though small, had the advantage of privacy and even had its own window. Two men had occupied the dressing area for a few days but, when they left, the Russian wife of a British soldier in another camp moved in. Sophie Lowe, in her mid-40s, had to go through the bedroom any time she wanted to leave or return to her closet.

Outside their room was a large hallway with two bedrooms on the other side and, to the right, an annex with a kitchen, servants' quarters and a toilet.

"What an assortment we were," wrote Billie of the early days, which she recalled with clarity as the experience was joltingly new. "We were 48 men, women and children, ranging from the old to infants, in our bungalow and the garage next door and, in the following days, the race for life began."

Thrown together higgledy-piggledy were civil servants and merchants, secretaries and stenographers, police officers and housewives, and a ship's purser. As well as Caucasian, the British subjects were ethnically Chinese, Eurasians, Portuguese, Russians and Czech.

The congestion and lack of privacy would inevitably cause friction but, in this microcosm of Hong Kong's highly stratified society, a strange thing began to happen. Knowing they were all in the same boat, and that they had to get along to survive their abruptly changed circumstances, people were forced to look at each other with new eyes.

The enforced physical proximity had the unexpected result of lowering the barriers of Hong Kong's unofficial segregation.

"There was no room for snobbery. We were down to basics and everyone's personality, whatever was inside them, came out," said Billie. "You couldn't hide anything from anybody and there were all sorts of surprises. People we thought were nice didn't behave well at all, while there was unexpected kindness from others."

Some changes came quickly. On January 24, the British, by far the largest group among Stanley's 2,800 POWs, met to elect committees to organise urgent matters like food and housing. A public meeting exploded with anger at the government, not only for misleading them and mishandling the war but also over a government corruption scandal that had blown up before hostilities. The result was that not a single public official was voted in, a severe blow for once-hallowed civil servants.

It did not help that the new Colonial Secretary, Franklin Gimson, who had arrived in Hong Kong from Ceylon (Sri Lanka) to take up his position only on the eve of war, was not present and, when he did enter Stanley later, faced a rebellious constituency.

Leaders were chosen from the business sector, including Philip Witham. Billie knew him because he had an office in the Hongkong and Shanghai Bank building as a tea expert who worked with both the Hong Kong and Chinese governments. In his 40s, a big man who could fill the door-frame, Witham was a former Army officer and tea planter in Assam and had an authoritative air.

He had bagged the best room in Bungalow B, which was not only one of the bigger bedrooms but also had direct access to a tiled veranda and a garden. A walk of 40 yards to neighbouring Bungalow A, one of the highest points of the camp, offered a wide view of the camp, including the Japanese headquarters, the white concrete roofs of the new Stanley prison, and the dark blue South China Sea. Though adjacent to the camp, the prison was a separate facility used for imprisoning criminals, as well as Allied internees accused of serious offences.

Witham was elected bungalow representative after showing initiative and organising skills on the first day of captivity when he lugged two pails of rations up the hill and told people to form a queue to receive them.

A famished Billie looked down at her small helping of rice with a few spoonfuls of whatever the Japanese had managed to put together in the way of meat, fish or vegetables on the day. Twice a day since then, at around 11am and 5pm, they lined up for this watery gruel, which tasted foul and was never enough. Billie was revolted to see the grains of rice move – and she tried to pick out the weevils and maggots until a man pointed out that bugs had nutritional value.

The bungalow had been a scene of battle and a pressing problem was its filthy state, broken windows and a non-functioning and putrid toilet. With women, children and elderly making up two thirds of the occupants, the dirty work was left to the able-bodied men.

These included half a dozen police officers. Before the war, the British scorned their "seedy expatriate policemen who came from the wrong sort of background and were to be found drinking *samshu*, a Chinese rice spirit, in Upper and Lower Lascar Rows," wrote historian Philip Snow. But these fit young men with Cockney, Geordie and Glasgow accents – there were about 100 in Stanley – bore the brunt of cleaning latrines and drains and digging outside refuse pits to make conditions habitable and stave off cholera and typhoid. They earned the gratitude of others by carrying buckets of rations and foraging for firewood.

Lorries delivered food to a garage on the other side of the camp, from where it was distributed to the various kitchens. The police often took charge of Bungalow B's kitchen.

The first time Billie was assigned to cooking duties, she was paired with Harry Tyler, a young man who had arrived in Hong Kong just before the war from London's Metropolitan Police. Billie was too embarrassed to admit her complete lack of culinary experience but thought she could mask it by following Harry's instructions.

That afternoon, a rare consignment of fish arrived, leading to a ripple of excitement and jokes like, "Fish and chips tonight."

Billie was so small that she had to stand on a crate to join Harry at the scullery and she watched him empty a pail of fish onto a concrete slab. Repelled by the fishes' glassy eyes and slimy skin, Billie suppressed an urge to throw up as she imitated Harry in removing their scales. With the fish degutted, Harry told her to lay them side by side, add peanut oil, and place them in the oven.

"All we do now is wait," said Harry. Billie was surprised when Harry left for an errand but he assured her he would be back. He had not told her how long it took to bake the fish and, as the minutes passed, she grew restless. When Harry returned and saw the fish were still in the oven, he gave a strangled cry.

When they opened the oven, all that was left were blackened remains. As they learned that their dinner had vanished, the internees were not shy about expressing their disappointment and Billie ran to her room. In fact, she was not the only woman in Stanley who lacked kitchen skills, as many of the British ladies had relied on servants for years, but that was of no comfort to her. "I was never as miserable as I was that evening," she said.

Harry stood up for her and remained a friend. He would make Billie a pair of wooden clogs that she wore until they were so paper thin "you could place them on the palm of your hand and blow them away," she said.

Billie never forgot his kindness and she was able to thank him and his wife Cynthia, another Stanley internee, over a lunch many years after the war.

It wasn't only the physically strong who drew new respect in Stanley.

Sitting on the veranda, Billie watched a man going through his daily workout of callisthenics. As the first cases of beriberi and pellagra (both Vitamin B complex deficiencies) started to appear because of malnutrition, Gray Dalziel, in his early 30s, was the only resident to maintain a lean and muscled body. "He would eat an egg a day," Billie recalled. In fact, Dalziel could have as many eggs as he wanted.

Dalziel had come into Stanley with his wife but had soon left her in Bungalow C, a short walk away, and moved into Bungalow B. From the start, he kept his distance from the others and even slept outside, stringing a hammock between branches of a tree. Gray stayed outside because that is where he did his nocturnal business with traders who sneaked in from outside.

Before the war, Dalziel was managing director of the Dairy Farm Company and brought money into camp as well as strong connections in the local food industry. He had also been rowing captain of the Royal Hong Kong Yacht Club and was determined to keep fit. Although he kept a low profile, he would become one of the most powerful men in Stanley as a black-market king.

Most of Bungalow B's occupants were neither strong nor rich.

A list of its residents after an evacuation had thinned its number to 32 makes a distinction between "eight able-bodied men" and the others, who comprised "ten sick or elderly men and women, seven women and seven children."

When Billie had to answer a call of nature, she would find a queue outside the sole toilet. As often as not, she would see Mrs Renee Levi, in her late 50s, hopping from one foot to the other, pleading, "I can't wait, I can't wait." Some people made way for her in the beginning but, after a while, many ignored her.

Meal times saw little conversation as internees were bent on devouring their tiny servings. One occasion stuck out in Billie's memory. "It was normal for the sounds of scraping on tins and enamel to come from all corners of the bungalow as people consumed their rations," she said. "But there was one old man who used to go on scraping in his tin long after he had eaten every scrap. His scraping went on and on, day in and day out, until one day, his younger friend, Gray Dalziel, couldn't stand it any more and exploded. 'For heaven's sake, stop that bloody scraping, you stupid old fool,' he yelled. The old man had tears in his eyes. Close friends fell out for the slightest reason."

Mrs Lowe, the Russian who lived in the closet, faced a showdown with Philip Witham who, as bungalow representative, told her that, under new rules, her space was categorized as a room as it had a window, and she would have to share it.

Their loud and protracted feud played out in front of the whole bungalow before Philip was forced to give in to common sense. The small dressing area could hardly fit more than one person, so Mrs Lowe remained alone.

One middle-aged couple, George Fish, a civil servant, and his wife Alexandra, showed enterprise in obtaining some yeast and mixing it with flour rations to make bread. They were doing this in their large bed in a curtained-off area in the hall, with Mrs Fish making the bread rise by keeping it in a warm but unspecified area. Billie thought this was fine, but others criticized the practice as unhygienic, which hurt Mrs Fish's feelings.

Billie was a single Chinese woman with a small infant, who had only ever lived with her family or Eurasian friends. She had no brawn, and little money. Moreover, in a new hierarchy where practicality ranked high, she could not boil an egg and she had not a clue how to change Brian's diapers.

With the lowering of social barriers, an ability to get along with others became more important than the hue of one's skin.

Forced to live cheek by jowl, a white civil servant would discover that he had more in common – such as an English education and a middle-class background – with a Eurasian saleswoman at Lane Crawford or a Portuguese cashier in Treasury than he had imagined.

Barbara Redwood, the naïve young civil service secretary who had fallen in love with Paddy before he met Billie, told the author, "I had never had Chinese or Eurasian friends before the war and it was only in camp that I realized they were just like us." Barbara and her sister Olive became friendly with Billie.

Vivienne Blackburn, secretary to the *taipan* at Jardine, also became a friend and told the author, "Everybody liked Billie. She was such a bouncy little thing."

Billie said, "In pre-war Hong Kong, the Chinese were looked down upon, but in camp I was not made to feel I was different from anybody else."

No one was more useful and underrated than Ah Chun.

Billie heard Philip Witham talking to Ah Chun in Cantonese and saw Ah Chun shake her head several times and finally blurt out in pidgin English, "If one boy run this way and other boy run that way, which boy I catchee?" She realized that Witham was going behind her back to try and enlist Ah Chun's services.

"Philip had brought a lot of money into camp so he was prepared to pay my *amah* to look after Anthony but, with wonderful Chinese logic, she refused to look after him," said Billie.

Billie and Ah Chun could communicate only in pidgin and Billie always regretted she knew virtually nothing about the woman who had remained loyal and had become indispensable.

On February 14, 1942, around mid-morning, the Japanese announced a roll call.

Everyone stopped whatever they were doing and assembled at a football field in front of the jail. At first unperturbed, as there had been line-ups before, Billie soon sensed this might be different. A rumour spread that the Japanese wanted prisoners out of their billets so they could search their quarters. As the internees gathered, Japanese and Indian guards inspected them and told them to form groups by nationalities.

This was new and Billie wondered if it had anything to do with calls to reduce the number of internees so there would be more food and space to go around. Some resented the presence of women and children, arguing they should have left in the earlier evacuation, while others sought the removal of the Chinese and Eurasian women even if they had British husbands.

Billie and Ah Chun joined the ragged British ranks. The roll call took a long time and it began to rain. When an official stood before Billie, she showed her British passport. When he moved on to Ah Chun, his request for papers met a blank stare. Billie told the official that Ah Chun was part of her family and was looking after Brian, a British subject. But the guard insisted that, without the required ID, Ah Chun had to leave.

Brian started crying as Ah Chun handed him over to Billie. "Ah Chun pulled out a little purse which she had hidden somewhere around the top of her trousers," said Billie. "It contained her life savings. She was terrified the Japanese would find the money when they searched her, so she asked me to keep the money until the end of the war."

Billie could only watch as the guard led Ah Chun away and she wondered how the *amah* could survive, as she had never heard her talk about family. "I was truly lost when they took her away," said Billie. "She took care of Brian from the moment we left the hospital after he was born. She did everything for him."

Billie never forgot Ah Chun and even 30 years after the war, when visiting Hong Kong, she kept searching the crowds in the hope of recognizing her. She even enlisted the help of a local newspaper, the *Hong Kong Standard*, in trying to find her. In camp, her problems mounted as soon as Ah Chun left. "I had to take over looking after Brian and my first problem was a dirty diaper," said Billie. "I didn't know what to do about it. I couldn't face washing it and I was so afraid of touching it I rushed out into the garden and buried it."

Later, she asked Joan Witham what she did with Anthony's nappies. "I wash them, of course," was the astonished response. "I'd soon run out if I didn't."

When Billie admitted what she had done, Joan stared at her for a long moment before bursting out in laughter. "Now I've heard it all," she exclaimed, but said she would show her other points of childcare.

Ah Chun's departure forced Billie "to buckle down and learn many things" – and also had an unexpected consequence. To take her place, Witham brought in a young English girl who had just arrived with a group of nurses from the hospitals – and would change Billie's life.

23

Offer of Escape

When Witham introduced Freda Howkins to Billie, the newcomer immediately recognized her name. Freda was a secretary with the British consulate in Shanghai and had come to Hong Kong with her boss to take part in currency stabilization talks to prevent China's depreciating currency from collapse.

"How extraordinary!" she told Billie. "I was told to get in touch with you if there was any trouble because you were with the Chinese government and could get us out of Hong Kong."

Freda and her boss were unable to leave after the bombing of Kai-tak airport on December 8.

Finding herself trapped in a war, Freda had sought to make herself useful. She did what she could to help with the wounded and dying at the Gripps, which turned into a makeshift hospital to handle overflow cases from the British Military Hospital at Bowen Road.

A slim girl with blue eyes and short, nut-brown hair, Freda grew up in Shanghai where her father worked for the Shanghai Power Company, and she had attended the British-only Cathedral School and later Cheltenham Ladies' College in England.

Along with others from the hospitals, Freda had had more time to prepare for internment and brought a camphor wood box and a suitcase. Billie, wearing a halter-top and shorts, gasped when Freda took out two silk dressing gowns, which already seemed from another planet.

Without waiting to be asked, Freda pitched in with the bungalow chores and helped Billie and Joan Witham heat water in a *chatti* pot over a charcoal fire and bathe their boys together in a large Cow & Gate tin Joan had brought into camp.

When Joan had to spend a few days in hospital, Freda took charge of Anthony and called him her 'first baby'.

Philip was happy as he had an extra pair of hands while Billie had a new best friend. In a camp that included a significant proportion of people who were uncooperative, the selfless and uncomplaining Freda was a godsend.

Some evenings, they would join others around a Ouija board, reaching out to fingertip an upturned tumbler in the middle of the table. Those taking part never tired of asking questions like: "Are we going to be released?" and "Is so-and-so's husband still alive?" More often than not, said Billie, the tumbler would move to the letter "Y."

They decided to learn bridge and went to see Henry Kew, an Australian Eurasian who taught the game and had devised his own system. Billie took to bridge immediately, finding it relatively easy after playing mahjong with 144 tiles to memorize 52 playing cards. Billie and Freda played in the cemetery using the flat gravestones as tables. They shared two packs of cards with other enthusiasts and soon found the pips so faded it was hard to distinguish hearts from diamonds or spades from clubs.

Brian was standing in the garden one day when he began screaming for no apparent reason. Thinking he might have been bitten by an insect, Billie examined his arms and legs. Freda came out to cradle Brian, but he continued yelling. As Billie became desperate, Freda took Brian inside and placed him on top of her trunk. With Brian on his back, Freda pointed to the soles of his feet, which were an angry red. He had been standing on a manhole that had been heated by the sun. A trip to the hospital treated him for minor burns.

Billie knew her friend's 21st birthday was on March 13 and that she would mark her coming of age without her parents, who were in Shanghai. For a week, Billie scoured the footpaths for cigarette butts and, when she had collected enough, arranged through George Giffen to swap them for 21 soda crackers as a birthday gift for Freda.

George, the journalist whom Billie had met through Mickey, was living at St Stephen's College in a large room with his colleagues and had become a regular visitor.

He was always welcome as he would bring a few twigs for the *chatti* fire, or a biscuit, and he usually had a story that he told in his wry style.

"Happy birthday, Freda!" George greeted Freda.

"What's going on in your neck of the woods, George?" asked Freda.

"We had a spot of bother last night," said George. "I'm in charge of checking the building at night and a couple of burly chaps started throwing their weight around. One of them was a bailiff and it took a while for me to calm him down."

The women chuckled at the thought of George dealing with troublemakers, as he was such a gentle-natured person. Freda had taken to teasing Billie about George.

"I think he's got a twinkle in his eye for you," she said.

"Oh, I don't think so," protested Billie, reddening. "He's married, you know. His wife was evacuated to Canada before the war. George just finds our company a change from all those men."

Freda had quickly made friends and one of the police officers in the garage baked her a small cake with a white candle while another internee brought pancakes with raisins; such gifts reflected a remarkable sacrifice in their straitened circumstances.

One friend who was almost certainly present was Elsie Fairfax-Cholmondeley. Billie knew Elsie well and Freda had met her at least twice, once at the currency stabilization talks, where Elsie had shocked a British representative by siding with the Chinese and Americans, and again at the "Gripps hospital" in the Hong Kong Hotel where Elsie also helped out as a volunteer nurse.

Elsie took Billie aside and asked to meet in the cemetery as she needed to discuss something confidential.

Billie was curious as she joined Elsie for a stroll among the old gravestones, some dating back to the settler days, and the casuarina trees that provided shade for those who wanted to rest.

They made an unusual couple as Elsie was exceptionally tall, towering over many men, and Billie did not reach her shoulders. In her early 30s, Elsie arrived in Hong Kong in 1939 and soon became known as a radical. Many of the elite thought she was betraying her pedigree; Elsie's father was squire of a large Yorkshire estate that had been in the family since the 16th century. In fact, Elsie took after her father, an Oxford-educated man who espoused reformist social ideas.

During the fighting, Elsie visited the offices of the CIC where, undoubtedly helped by Mavis Ming, she destroyed papers to prevent their falling into Japanese hands. Elsie told Billie that she and Mavis had tried to escape from the island just before she came to Stanley. With others, including another volunteer nurse, Gwen Priestwood, they had walked to a local village to meet a boatman who had been paid to take them to Macau. They waited all night, but the boatman did not show up, no doubt deciding that the risk of being shot by Japanese patrol boats was not worth the money.

Elsie was worried that the Japanese would find out about her anti-Japanese activities and she knew Billie also had reason to fear the Japanese. In short, she asked Billie if she would join her in an escape attempt from Stanley. They would be joined by another mutual friend, Israel Epstein. Billie knew Epstein, who had covered the Japanese invasion for United Press International and later joined the China Defence League to enlist international support for the Chinese. He had famously faked his own death to avoid arrest by the Japanese and had registered in Stanley under an assumed name.

Billie stopped and stared at Elsie's intense blue eyes as she realized what her friend was proposing. It was virtually impossible to flee from Stanley – the Japanese had chosen this promontory precisely because it jutted into the sea between sharp cliffs overlooking rocky beaches. It was a natural fortress.

Elsie said she and her friends had spotted a boat on the beach below Stanley Prison. From a distance, it was impossible to tell whether or not it had holes in its bottom but, if it was serviceable, they planned to use it to try and reach Macao and, after that, China.

She emphasized that they needed to make the break very soon as security was still fairly lax but would only get tighter.

It was a tempting offer. Talk of repatriation had fizzled out and hopes of any rescue by British forces had been crushed when the Japanese put on a film show at St Stephen's showing the fall of Singapore in mid-February. Billie was constantly hungry and the thought that Brian might succumb to malnutrition was too awful to dwell upon.

"Why are you asking me?" she said, to which Elsie replied, "It would be very useful to have someone who speaks Chinese."

Seeing her uncertainty, Elsie told her they could discuss it again very shortly. That night, Billie tossed and turned, unable to discuss the plan with Freda. The thought of freedom was intoxicating, yet to try and escape by sea in a boat of uncertain condition was extremely risky and they all knew the penalty for failure – one prisoner who had escaped from the military camp of Shamshuipo had been caught and executed.

The deciding factor was, of course, Brian. Mothers had to make life-and-death decisions with their children foremost in their minds.

Vera Armstrong, whom the Japanese had offered a job as interpreter, persuaded her captors to let her out of Stanley to sell her watch and buy food for her children. She spent a night at the home of the Selwyn-Clarkes where Mickey told her she thought her baby Carola's chances of survival were better on the outside. Vera admitted she sometimes regretted her decision not to accept the Japanese job offer, mainly because she might have been able to better feed her children.

Elsie was a single woman and wanted to escape to join the fight to free China but, since Mama had died, Billie had no compelling reason to return to China, especially with Shanghai in Japanese hands.

Regretfully, Billie told Elsie that she would not accept her offer.

Brian was a calm child but anything might upset him and a wail at the wrong moment could blow up the enterprise for all of them. If she stayed, no matter how awful camp was, there was always a hope that things might improve.

Only a couple of days later, the Japanese threw the camp in turmoil when ordering an impromptu roll call. The guards rushed around, pointing and counting and recounting the internees.

"What's going on?" Billie asked the man standing beside her.

"Some people have made a breakout and they want to know how many."

To the unconcealed glee of the prisoners, Elsie and her friends were missing. Another group, which included Gwen Priestwood, also could not be found. It seemed that both groups had independently made their bid for freedom on the moonless night of March 18/19.

The Japanese were furious. They instituted two roll calls a day and imposed an 8pm curfew as well as bringing in more guards and expanding the barbed wire around the camp.

While talking about the escape with another of her friends, Morris "Two-Gun" Cohen, Billie confided that Elsie had approached her. "No kidding!" said Morris, saying he had also been made an offer. "Israel asked me because I once helped him before the war," he said. "But the Japs had already done me over once (Morris had been beaten up by the *Kempetei*, or military police, soon after internment) and I don't think I could have taken it again if they had caught me."

Years later, Epstein described the escape in a book: "After dark, our group – myself, Elsie, Van Ness, O'Neill, and Wright – made our way to a ridge overgrown with shrubs and trees alongside the road that ran around the camp's perimeter. Below the road was the forbidden beach surrounded by barbed wire, and below that the sea. Along the road the Japanese patrol of twenty or so men would tramp on its regular circuit.

"We sat in the bushes waiting for them, then, as they passed, we waited as they went forward another couple of hundred paces before we stole quietly across the road and down to the beach. There we lay prone beside the barbed wire before cutting it with a pair of wire cutters we had taken. We uncovered our goods in the sand where Van had bravely hidden them, placed them in the boat, then heaved and dragged the boat into the water.

"While still close to shore, we sighted a promontory where a Japanese patrol craft was anchored and occasionally swung its searchlight. If caught on the beach, we would almost certainly have been beaten senseless at the very least. If spotted in the water, we would have been machine-gunned on the spot."

Billie had probably made the right decision.

Hoisting a blanket as a sail, Elsie's group covered over 15 miles to the island of Lantau, travelled by junk to Macao and, after many adventures, reached Chungking. Their escape had another happy ending when Elsie married Israel.

The second group, which included Gwen Priestwood and a police superintendent who spoke fluent Cantonese and some Hakka, made it to Chaiwan, where they persuaded boatmen to row them to a bay where they linked up with Chinese guerrillas, who took them to China. Priestwood's breakout was important for all of them as she took with her, on thin paper wrapped around a toilet roll, the names of the British internees, so that many families in the outside world would know their loved ones were still alive.

As a result of tighter Japanese security, however, there were no more successful escapes. A month later, another friend of Billie, Brian Fay, a young, athletic police cadet, and three others did manage to slip past the guards by climbing over rocks on the beach. But after two days on the run, they sought shelter in a hut, only to find it occupied by Japanese soldiers. The captured men were paraded in the streets of Hong Kong, badly beaten and sentenced to two years' solitary confinement at Stanley jail. Fay would emerge in dreadful shape and Billie would be among those involved in trying to rehabilitate him through conversations.

Meanwhile, Billie resumed her bridge games in the cemetery while keeping an eye on her son as he played among the stones. He was safe for now, but she would be powerless to save him from a tragic accident.

24

Sail Away

It was the best news in the world for the 350 Americans in camp, but heart-breaking for everyone else.

On May 6, 1942, a camp bulletin listed the ships that might carry the Americans home in exchange for Japanese prisoners. This would be the first batch of POWs to be freed after being incarcerated only for being in the wrong place at the wrong time.

The British and the Americans in Stanley had regarded each other with a mix of admiration and resentment. Under the leadership of Bill Hunt, a wealthy and ruthless shipping magnate, the Americans were well-organised long before the disparate and divided British. The Americans arrived in Stanley early enough to claim the best quarters and once, while the Japanese allowed a Chinese merchant to operate a canteen, bought its entire stock, leaving nothing for the others. Generally, however, they pulled together with the British for the common good.

Billie's first reaction on learning the Americans were going home was fear that Mickey would be among them. At great personal risk, Mickey had been sending her food parcels – often a five-pound sack containing up to five articles – and, if these stopped, Billie did not know how she and Brian would manage. She had no money to pay the exorbitant prices charged by the canteen, which was run by an exploitative Chinese, or the black market.

She also developed close ties with the American Maryknoll missionaries, led by Fr Barney Meyer. On Sundays, Billie walked down the footpath to the old prison officers' quarters where Fr Meyer said Mass for hundreds of Catholics. She was particularly indebted to the Catholic Action Group which provided nurses to give single mothers a break from looking after their children 24 hours a day.

As the British looked on enviously, bags of food started arriving at the American quarters. The Japanese wanted to fatten them up so the world could see how well they treated their POWs.

"We hung around the American quarters, waiting hopefully for anything they could not carry or take away," said Billie. "We loaded them with names and addresses of relatives and families in England to tell them we were still alive."

During these unsettling developments, the camp was suddenly united in uproar by a strange and terrifying incident near Bungalow B.

Billie was not long asleep when a piercing scream caused her to sit bolt upright. She could swear that a woman was shouting, "Lau-foo! Lau-foo!" which did not make sense as that was the Chinese word for tiger.

Billie saw others were running around, asking, "What's happening? What the hell's going on?" By the light of a full moon, Billie saw through a window Hugh Goldie, a Scottish police officer, scampering up a tree. She knew Goldie slept in a hammock between two trees. Then an Irishman rushed into the bungalow and started talking almost incoherently. He had also been sleeping outside, on wooden boards which he was clutching under his arm.

He said that Gray Dalziel was bargaining with Chinese traders in the garden when he saw a tiger. Then a Chinese woman hawker had come face to face with the tiger on the footpath to the garden. Her shrieks had woken Billie and the others. Goldie rushed in and said, "I swear to God, I saw a tiger leap over the bushes." Soon, others had a story about a tiger sighting.

Yet, despite a search, no trace of a tiger was found. The next day, guards scouted around the garden and the surrounding hills, looking for footprints, but found none. Meanwhile, Goldie and Dalziel transferred their bedding inside and Lucille and Margaret, two girls who slept on the veranda, moved to the rooftop. During the day, people walked around in groups. The Japanese placed gongs around the camp to be sounded if anybody saw or heard the tiger.

Not long after, a party of Japanese, Chinese and Indian police shot a tiger at the back of Stanley Village near the camp, an event trumpeted by the *Hongkong News*, the newspaper run by the Japanese, under the headline, "Fierce Tiger Shot in Stanley Woods." A photograph of the tiger strung up by a pole showed a fine specimen six feet long weighing 240 pounds. According to the newspaper, its skin was sent to Japanese Emperor Hirohito as a gift, although to this day there is a skin hanging in the Tin Hau temple in Stanley which is claimed to be this one.

The best guess was that during the fighting the tiger had escaped from a circus that was visiting Hong Kong. Some internees wondered whether the tiger might end up in the camp kitchens. In fact, the Japanese did make a feast of it and even invited a few internees who were officials of the Royal Hong Kong Jockey Club.

Meanwhile, as plans for the US repatriation proceeded, it was evident that the Japanese were going to make use of it for propaganda.

At the end of May, a team from Domei, the Japanese news agency, arrived to interview American journalists, as a result of which articles appeared describing Stanley as "probably the most comfortable (internment camp) in the world."

It was untrue, as the Japanese were on orders from Tokyo to secure all Hong Kong's food supplies, including Red Cross parcels, for their own purposes while providing the POWs with only the minimum to stay alive.

If Billie thought Mickey was better off on the outside, she was wrong. To avoid internment, Mickey claimed she was the wife of a Chinese, Sinmay, and that this entitled her to neutral status. Though this argument was far from convincing, it was accepted by the Japanese consul, Takio Oda, a friend and admirer of Charles Boxer before the war; but she knew his support might not save her from the *Kempetei*, who were terrorizing the local populace at will.

Mickey was sharing her Tregunter Mansions flat with a motley group of refugees and, though technically free, was trapped in a desperate cycle of survival. With Charles in a military prison camp with a disabled arm and her daughter losing weight, Mickey had sold her jewellery but was running out of cash. Her hair was falling out and her teeth were rotting. In town, food was becoming so scarce that coolies were dying on the streets and human flesh was being sold in the market.

The Japanese were losing the initiative they had gained from their lightning strike at Pearl Harbor. The Americans, fuelled by their industrial might, were fast recovering and, in early June, inflicted heavy losses in the battle of Midway, a turning point in the war at sea.

The Stanley repatriation did run into problems. The American men expected to go home with their wives but their spouses included British, Australian, Russian and Chinese women. After lengthy debate, the Japanese posted a notice proclaiming that wives would be included, unless they were Chinese. This disgusted, but did not surprise, Billie. She had long known that the Japanese, for all their claims of liberating Asians from western imperialists, disdained the Chinese.

After many delays and false alarms, a large ship sailed into view off Stanley's coast. It was the *Asama Maru*, its black hull painted with white crosses to indicate it was carrying POWs.

Billie was among those who gathered in the cemetery on June 29 and watched, in silence, the Americans preparing to board the small craft to take them to the ocean liner. Amid tearful goodbyes, some Americans handed over most of their possessions to friends while others went on board pulling heavy suitcases crammed with tins.

Billie spotted her missionary friends from the Nam Ping Hotel, Margaret and Cecil Ward. Margaret, still pregnant, would give birth to a baby boy on board.

The *Asama Maru* sailed the next day without Mickey. She had declined repatriation, choosing to stay and keep Charles alive with precious food parcels he always shared with his fellow prisoners.

Another American who declined to board the vessel was Fr Meyer, who stayed behind to look after his flock.

One benefit of the American departure was that it freed up space in camp. The Withams were among those who left Bungalow B for the former American quarters.

Taking their place were Barbara Parkin and her young son, Leslie, who were the same ages as Billie and Brian. Barbara, who was of striking appearance with expressive eyes and thick dark hair, was a Czech who grew up in Harbin and had left for Shanghai to stay with her sister.

In Shanghai, she had a relationship with a British submarine officer, as a result of which she gave birth to Leslie in May, 1940. Tragically, three months later, Leslie's father went down with his submarine in the Mediterranean.

Barbara moved to Hong Kong where she met and married a British soldier, Sergeant William Parkin, only two months before war broke out.

Barbara Parkin shared a room with Billie at one time

She had lost contact with her husband during the fighting and was frantic to find out what had happened to him and if he was still alive. She had been asking people the same question every day in the six months she had been in Stanley.

Billie was sympathetic but she could not help much. Barbara, already struggling outside her language and culture, would be tortured by uncertainty for two more years before she received an official letter, in July 1944, confirming that that her husband had been shot during a massacre at St Stephen's College, only yards from Bungalow B, on the last day of the battle.

Billie and Freda partnered each other at bridge, they listened to concerts put on by the popular camp pianist and singer, Betty Drown, and they watched plays staged by internees with great ingenuity under the circumstances.

Barbara Redwood wrote in her diary on August 1, 1942 that her sister Olive visited Billie at Bungalow B and invited her and Freda back 10 days later for tea made from pine needles. Barbara wrote, "Brian looks mostly like his mother, but he has Paddy's mouth and teeth. Very big and talkative for his age. So sweet."

Billie saw relationships change between her friends. Vera Armstrong began visiting Bungalow B more and more frequently, not to see Billie but Gray Dalziel. With his trading activity and her Japanese, they made natural business partners but their relationship developed into more than that. Dalziel became the first person to get a divorce in Stanley, from his wife Freddie, and married Vera after the war. Vera's husband Jack Armstrong did not mind too much – he would start a relationship in Stanley with 'Dinnie' Dodwell, of the Dodwells business family.

George Giffen watched his Australian colleague Dick Cloake, who shared his room, court Betty Drown, whose husband was in another camp. George took German lessons with Betty and came to know her well. "Dick was a Puritan sort of chap who neither saw nor did evil. He was too good to be true. He sang and played bridge with Betty and was in love with her, but it was unrequited," he said.

George said Betty "was remarkable in an ephemeral way. She was graceful, lighter than air. Men adored her, but she was virginal and unapproachable and, because of this, hardly aroused any envy among the women. Betty wasn't in love with anybody."

That might have been true, but Betty did care for George. Betty was a few years older than both the men. She told the author after the war, "Dick was quite the opposite of George. They didn't get on at all. Dick was a devout Roman Catholic and George was anything but. George had a very good sense of humour and he was extremely cynical, but he was very kind-hearted, would help anybody, and go without himself to help. I've still got his poems. I was very fond of George, but my husband was unhappy that I was pally with Dick and George."

Like the other internees, Billie was thrilled when a series of Allied air raids rocked Hong Kong in October and November and many wondered if the end of the war was near. From the other side of the world came news that the Allies were driving the Germans out of North Africa and landing in Italy.

Then, in mid-November came alarming news. The Japanese announced that, because of the air raids and security concerns, all unmarried men between the ages of 18 and 35 (or 40 in the case of police officers) were to report in front of Stanley prison with their bedding. This caused consternation among the men, as well as the women, as everyone knew of the torture and beatings that took place behind the thick walls.

Billie related what happened next: "Each man found he had a clean cell to himself and only the outer doors were locked, so they could mingle. Soon, they were making the most out of the absence of women with crude jokes and bawdy songs.

"When they were let out the next day, some men were grinning like schoolboys. The pattern of being locked up at night and released by day was repeated for several nights.

"The Japanese had organised the nightly lock-up to prevent a mass breakout but had not expected the men to organise revues, lectures and debates and someone even proposed asking for roller-skates to race in the corridors. Soon, males outside the age limits tried to join them. After the prison gates closed one evening, one man sprinted up and banged on them, pleading, 'Let me in, let me in!'"

Soon after this, the nightly confinement was discontinued. Billie loved to tell the story of British humour that helped keep up their morale.

By then, Billie knew that Freda would soon be leaving them. A group of 50 Shanghai-based POWs were evacuated in August and another was planned.

Evacuations stirred passion and one internee had written a song called
Sail Away, with the words, *"We're going to sail away, sail away... We know
internment here will end one day; we want to go; we've got to go, for we're
longing to see the land that we love so."*

Billie had come to depend heavily on Freda and tried to fight
despondency. Freda duly appeared on the list to be evacuated before
Christmas. On December 21, 1942, the Shanghai POWs were vaccinated
but the discovery of a case of diphtheria caused panic; their departure was
postponed and even a concert by Betty Drown was cancelled.

But on Christmas Eve, Freda left with some 30 internees. She would
be met by her parents and live with them until the British were interned
in Shanghai in 1943.

That evening, Betty Drown's choir sang carols at the prison officers'
club.

George knew how Billie was feeling during her first Christmas in Stanley
without her best friend. He arrived at Bungalow B on Christmas Day with
a toy for Brian, a crude but clearly distinguishable toy motor car, fashioned
from a butter tin. Brian was delighted with it, even though he was not sure
what a car was.

25

Shirt off His Back

In February 1943 the Japanese announced that the internees were to receive a financial windfall as a result of a British government contribution through the Red Cross.

"This generated enormous excitement and it became a favourite pastime among us to dream of how we would spend the money," said Billie. "When I learned I would receive 75 military yen, a substantial amount, I carefully weighed one commodity against another, discussing with friends the relative merits of milk powder, flour, peanut oil against an egg or a tin of bully beef or sardines."

A delay in the distribution of funds served only to prolong the tantalizing decision process and caused frequent changes of mind.

Billie discussed the handout with her friend Morris "Two Gun" Cohen, whom she knew well as a former bodyguard and aide to Sun Yat-sen and who was close to many prominent Nationalists.

Morris had been chubby when Billie had seen him – and had the occasional dance with him – in the Gripps lounge in the Hong Kong Hotel where he was a fixture, known for his generosity in buying drinks and for telling colourful stories about his exploits.

Morris was in his mid-50s when he was interned and, within days, the *Kempetei* had found out who he was and hauled him off for questioning about his ties to the Chinese.

When Billie saw him after his return to the camp, Morris's cheeks sagged and his frame had shrunk. He told her the Japanese had punched and kicked him until he wished he was dead. At one point they dragged him out of his cell and one officer held out a samurai sword and told Morris to kneel before him.

"I thought I was a goner, but the bastard just laughed and kicked me in the ribs," Morris told Billie. "Those Japs are lower than whale manure."

Despite his ordeal, Morris, with his pugilist's crooked nose and an outgoing nature, was soon his former self, cracking jokes and ready to share the latest gossip.

While Billie was in a dilemma over items to buy from the canteen, Morris had no trouble at all in making his decision.

"I'm going to blow the lot on *wong tong* (Chinese brown sugar) and give it to the kids," he said. He was as good as his word and, when they finally received their funds, Billie saw dozens of children crowded around "Uncle Morris" holding out their hands as he gave out the "sweets".

Some of the British looked down on Morris as a pushy Jew with a dodgy past and a penchant for tall stories. It was true that Morris, the son of Polish Jews who had fled a pogrom to London, grew up in the rough-and-tumble of Cheapside markets, where he learned to pick pockets. After he ran afoul of the law one too many times, his parents packed their incorrigible son off to Canada.

There were stories that Morris had become a card shark, con man and slippery real estate dealer in Edmonton, but he always had a soft spot for the underdog and became a friend of the Chinese community, then scorned and persecuted as an alien group with a heathen religion.

Everything changed after Morris sailed to Shanghai in 1921 with a contractor to discuss a railway project with none other than Sun Yat-sen, who dreamed of unifying China with trains. Down-to-earth and big-hearted, Morris won over Sun and his young wife Ching-ling and was hired as a bodyguard, acquiring his "Two Gun" nickname by carrying a pair of Smith and Wesson pistols. He progressed to aide-de-camp, military general (non-acting) and arms dealer, building extensive political and military connections and impressing Chinese and westerners with his inside knowledge.

When Billie met him in Hong Kong, Morris was living off a Chinese government pension. On the eve of the Japanese invasion, he took Ching-ling and her sister Madame Kung to Kai-tak airport and put them on a plane to Chungking, while he opted to remain.

Around February 20, at the time Billie was debating her food choices, Dr Harry Talbot – known to Billie as the doctor Madame Chiang saw when she flew in from Chungking for her chronic sinus problem – was arrested while trying to smuggle 4,000 military yen under his bandages into Stanley, after being treated for a kidney infection outside by Dr Selwyn-Clarke.

Though Dr Talbot did not reveal the source of the money, Sir Vandeleur Grayburn, head of the Hongkong and Shanghai Bank, knowing Talbot was likely being tortured, told Takio Oda, Mickey's friend at the Foreign Ministry, that he had provided the funds. When Oda told the *Kempetei*, this ignited a series of events that affected a large number of people, including Mickey, who had borrowed money from Grayburn and feared this would be discovered and investigated.

Not long after her chat with Morris, Billie was in the kitchen on cook duty for the 5pm meal when she suddenly felt nauseous and told an assistant who went to get help.

When Dr John Loan, a medical missionary, arrived, he found she had a fever and diagnosed acute appendicitis. Even in normal times, this was a situation that required urgent treatment before the appendix burst. In Stanley, they faced a shortage of medical supplies and, almost as bad, no electricity.

Additionally, they encountered a bureaucratic hurdle: they needed permission from the Japanese, so Billie's friend Vivienne Blackburn went on a frantic search for Vera Armstrong, who then ran up the hill to the Japanese headquarters. By the time approval arrived, Billie was semi-delirious as friends carried her by stretcher to Tweed Bay Hospital. Because of the curfew, the surgeon who would perform the operation, Dr Gustav Canaval, had to be fetched under escort from the Dutch block. As there was no power, Billie's friends ran around collecting rations of peanut oil, which they poured into the lids of cigarette tins. They threaded shoestring through corks which, floating on the oil, created lamps for the operating theatre.

The hospital had, fortunately, sufficient anaesthetic for the procedure. When Billie came to, she was lying on a proper mattress with clean linen, heavenly after her bug-infested camp bed. She also ate better food than the usual rations and was attended by dedicated nurses in smart uniforms.

"The nurses were simply wonderful, bringing cheer and comfort in place of medicine, which was lacking," Billie wrote. "They spared nothing to make a patient comfortable."

Despite operating in far from ideal conditions, Dr Canaval left Billie with a neat scar as testimony to his skill.

In fact, the entire hospital, a three-storey building converted from Indian warders' quarters, was a tribute to the ingenuity and dedication of internees and those working from outside to help them.

As she was recovering, she looked up to see Morris.

"Hi, kid! You look swell."

For Billie, it was a tonic just to hear Morris's voice.

But big-hearted Morris was not there just to offer his good wishes.

"What do you need to get you back on your feet?"

Billie smiled but said nothing, taking the offer as rhetorical under their threadbare circumstances.

But Morris was persistent.

"Come on, kid. Whaddya want? Just name it. Anything, and I'll get it!"

Billie could not help giggling. Morris was an amateur magician as well as a card shark but even he could not conjure up anything she wanted.

Seeing his earnest expression, she pretended to take him seriously.

"More out of devilment than fancy, I told Morris I would love a pineapple," she said. "It was like wishing for the moon and I never gave it another thought."

Morris clasped her hand before leaving.

A few days later, Billie heard a commotion outside the ward. The door opened and in burst Morris. Billie was surprised to see clumps of white hair on his chest as he arrived bare-chested.

"He stood by my bedside, shirtless, waving something, and I thought he had taken leave of his senses," said Billie.

Then Morris plopped a tin of pineapples on her bed.

Billie tried to ask how he had managed to get it, but each time she opened her mouth, tears rolled down her cheeks.

Embarrassed, Morris stood up. "Don't you say nothing," he said gruffly. "You just enjoy the pineapple and I'll see you when you're up and about."

When Morris had gone, a nurse came over to Billie's bed.

"I've never seen matron so taken aback," she said. "She told that man he could not possibly come into the women's ward without being decently dressed, but he was very insistent. 'Goddammit, lady, this *is* my shirt,' he had said, holding up the tin of pineapples for which he had traded his shirt. Matron was speechless as he brushed past her."

Billie told the nurse, "I can now truly say that Morris is one man who has given me the shirt off his back."

The Japanese had kept Grayburn and other bankers in a low-class hotel while they liquidated bank assets and transferred them to Japanese hands, but in March the *Kempetei* arrested Grayburn and, a few weeks later, detained Selwyn-Clarke.

The Japanese crackdown would involve the arrest and brutal interrogation of dozens of people suspected of smuggling money, messages and vital supplies into Stanley and the military camps.

They would uncover messages between the bankers and POWs and the British Army Aid Group (BAAG), an underground resistance group started by an early Shamshuipo escapee, Lindsay Ride, with the aim of helping POWs escape.

What especially alarmed the Japanese were BAAG's plans for a mass breakout by internees, despite their weakened condition. Rations were so poor for the military POWs that some thought it was worth trying to escape rather than die by starvation. As well as clamping down on written messages – and their bearers, such as the ration truck drivers – the Japanese also feared POWs learning the truth about the war – that the Allies were taking back the Pacific, island by island – through short-wave radio and instigated searches for hidden radios in the camps.

The arrests of Grayburn and Selwyn-Clarke terrified Mickey as the bank chief had extended her a 2,000-yen loan and she had helped the Selwyn-Clarkes with illicit deliveries to the camps.

To make matters worse, her friendly Japanese contact, Oda, had left in April 1943 to take up a position as consul in Nanking. Treachery was everywhere and one man was trying to blackmail Mickey over the loan.

Oda's successor at Foreign Affairs, Tsuneo Hattori, was, like Oda, also 'old school' and proved friendly towards Mickey, but he warned her the *Kempetei* were watching her and, if she ran into trouble, he might not be able to rescue her.

Hattori told Mickey another Japanese-American prisoner exchange was being arranged and that she should go on the ship.

In Stanley, Billie heard all kinds of rumours as the *Kempetei* began, from late June, arresting people, subjecting them to interrogation by torture, and charging them with espionage.

Grayburn and Talbot were convicted by a military court and sentenced to three months' labour in Stanley prison. It was a relatively lenient sentence but Grayburn, a man of great vitality at 62, would deteriorate under execrable conditions in jail.

Harry Talbot saw Grayburn on August 21 and found him in a hopeless condition, with no medicines to cure him. That evening, Grayburn died. The cause of death was officially avitaminosis (vitamin deficiency), but malnutrition, sepsis and medical neglect were contributing factors.

News of the death of Hong Kong's most powerful civilian in such a manner cast a deep pall over the camp. "We were terribly, terribly cut up," recalled Vivienne Blackburn. "If they could treat Grayburn like that, no one was safe."

Hattori told Mickey he saw Charles Boxer in the Argyle Street camp and asked him what he thought Mickey should do. Charles's answer had been blunt: Mickey and daughter Carola should leave. Realizing it was time to go, Mickey wrote to camp commandant Tokunaga to ask if she could see Charles at Argyle Street to say goodbye. It was such an effective letter that Tokunaga cried as the interpreter read it to him. So, Mickey met Charles, who was dirty, tired and gaunt but clearly happy to see her, and a guard turned his back as they exchanged a goodbye kiss.

On September 22, the *Teia Maru*, with a large white cross painted on both sides of its hull, anchored off Repulse Bay. Ironically, this was the same ship that Billie had taken when fleeing Shanghai six years earlier. It was then called the *Aramis*, but was seized by the Japanese in April 1942 and was now taking away her friends.

From the cemetery, Billie looked down and saw the evacuees at Stanley jetty, waiting to be ferried out to the *Teia Maru*.

"I was standing on the wall with Brian and recognized Mickey in the distance and she, too, recognized me," she said. "We waved goodbye and cried. Her departure also meant the end of parcels for me from town."

Morris Cohen, claiming Canadian citizenship, was also on the jetty. He weighed eighty pounds less than before internment and was simply glad to be alive.

In her cabin, Mickey wrote later, she wept. She was 38, a single mother, and all her possessions were with her. Most terrifying of all was that she might never see Charles again.

What she didn't know was that, only the day before, the *Kempetei* and Japanese troops had gone to Charles's Argyle Street camp and, after a lengthy search, found a radio receiver in a four-gallon can buried in the camp garden.

Charles not only knew about it but was using it as a source for his camp's news service. The Japanese arrested four people and, six days later, came back for Charles. They grilled him extensively but did not torture him.

A month later, Charles and others arrived at Stanley jail after signing a document summarizing the result of their interrogations.

On the afternoon of October 29, 1943, Billie was at Bungalow B when Ron Murray, 11, rushed in with some news. He had been outside the prison, waiting for a guard to escort them to the beach, when he saw a van coming out of the gates. As it passed him, he heard people shouting "goodbye, goodbye," from inside.

A short time later, the internees heard shots from the jetty area as people were forced to kneel beside trenches before being executed. A few days later the Japanese posted the names of those who had been killed. Charles was not among them but expected his turn would come.

The executions for what many considered a minor offence of listening to outside news sent a wave of fear and uncertainty around the camp.

More trials and executions followed. Charles's guards in Stanley prison took him from his cell to an outside site and told him he would soon be executed. Five days later, on December 23, Charles and three others had their own trial and were provisionally sentenced to 15 years' labour, later reduced to five years.

In his cell, Charles knew the war was going against Japan and believed that the Allies would prevail. What he did not know was whether he could survive solitary confinement – which included being forced to sit in front of a wall for several hours each day – and starvation rations long enough to see that day.

26

Tragedy at Tweed Bay

Vivienne Blackburn's quarters were across camp, but she came over frequently to Bungalow B with pine needle tea in an old thermos she had brought into camp. She and Billie would take Brian to the cemetery and sit in the shade while Brian, who was approaching four years old, scampered among the gravestones.

The women were amazed they had not met before the war as they had both played hockey – Vivienne had represented Hong Kong Ladies – and had many friends in common. Vivienne and her friends would rush from hockey to watch their boyfriends play rugby; then they would all head to the Gripps for the Saturday night dinner and dance.

Three years older than Billie, tall, fair-haired Vivienne was born and raised in Hong Kong – her father was manager of a gas works in Kowloon and had extensive dealings with the Chinese. Vivienne's Cantonese was fluent and she would joke that she was more Chinese than British. She was secretary to David Newbigging of Jardine, one of the colony's biggest trading companies, who was also in Stanley. She shared a room in a three-bedroom flat next to the Kadoories of China Light and Power, with their two children and Chinese *amah*.

She had been delivered by Dr George Black – "he was an institution before the war" – who was in charge of the temporary hospital at St Stephen's and who was among the first to be bayoneted in the Christmas Day massacre. She had had a lucky escape during hostilities. As an auxiliary nurse, Vivienne was originally posted to the Happy Valley hospital where the Japanese raped several nurses, but she had asked to be transferred to join a friend at Hong Kong University.

Vivienne was active in the theatre productions staged by the internees, including the ballets *Esther* and *Genghis Khan*, which were composed in the camp and which Billie – and the Japanese – would enjoy.

Vivienne was fond of Billie. "There was so little to go around in Stanley and you certainly found out who your friends were. Billie was a dear friend. We'd go for a walk and talk about what we'd do after the war," she recalled. "We joked that we didn't need manicures or pedicures or even visits to the hairdresser as our nails and hair grew very slowly with our meagre diets."

The women sometimes took Brian to Tweed Bay beach, below the jail. The Japanese had opened the beach during the summer months, always with a guard present. They enjoyed swimming while others would dive in search of sea urchins to supplement their diet.

To get to the beach, the walk was down a long and steep path which, by 1943, became more difficult for the captives to climb in their starved and weakened state.

On May 9, 1944, a bright day, Vivienne thought about a swim. "I was a regular swimmer but that day decided against going. It was uphill coming back and, if you weren't feeling well, it was quite a drag," she said.

Billie woke up that morning anticipating a game of bridge with friends in Bungalow C, a short walk away.

Bridge had become more than a way of passing time. She had a real knack for cards and quickly became so adept that people sought her out as a partner. It also made her happy as a young Chinese woman to sit around a table with people to whom the red and black colours of the suits were more important than the shade of one's skin.

Brian was quite a handful as he wandered around the garden and beyond, and she was grateful when two nurses, Nina Quin and Patti Mace, arrived to take Brian to Tweed Bay for a few hours.

Nina, the same age as Billie, was a secretary with Asiatic Petroleum before the war. "Nina and I played in the same hockey team before the war," said Vivienne. "She was a nice girl, a bit hard, of Russian extraction."

Her friend Patti was a few years older, married, and warm-hearted. They became inseparable in camp.

At the beach, the women let Brian play with a friend in a shallow wading pool, which was used by swimmers to rinse off after a swim. It was built of stone cemented together to act as a dam for water coming down the mountain.

As Billie settled down at the bridge table, Edith Hamson, whom she knew well from Bungalow A, was on the beach watching men trying to fish. "The atmosphere was always one of serenity at Tweed Bay and gave me a brief respite from the realities of war," she said in a book.

"All of a sudden, I heard a commotion coming from the children's wading pool. I will never forget the awful screams. I jumped to my feet and everyone else on the beach did the same."

At Bungalow C, Billie looked up from the table to see Stephen Balfour, a tall lecturer and magistrate who taught Russian in camp, standing in the doorway. Balfour was pale, and breathing heavily.

"Billie," he said. "Please come with me."

She sensed immediately that something was not right.

"What is it, Stephen? Is it Brian?" she cried. Balfour could only repeat, "Please come with me."

It was quite a walk to Tweed Bay and, as she struggled to keep up with Balfour's long strides, Billie prayed harder than she had ever done in her life.

On the beach, a small crowd had gathered around the freshwater pool and, according to an account by Barbara Redwood, a Japanese guard had pulled a boy out and was breathing into his mouth to try and revive him.

When Billie arrived, the gathering parted to make way for her. She saw Brian in a woman's arms and thought he might be sleeping.

No-one knew exactly what had happened. Nina later recalled, "Patti and I were chatting and Brian was with this other boy and, when we turned around, he was lying face down and the other boy had this odd expression on his face."

Whatever happened had clearly been a dreadful accident.

Witnesses said Billie cried out Brian's name before she fainted. Redwood saw Brian's "pathetic little body brought to the hospital on a stretcher," accompanied by his mother.

When Vivienne heard the news, she said, "I was absolutely stunned. The pool among the rocks was deeper than usual, perhaps it rained the day before. I rushed to Billie's room and removed all of Brian's things. Then I went with Sister Bill Williamson to the mortuary place off the hospital and we dressed Brian in a little pair of trousers and shirt Billie gave me. Billie couldn't help us. She was in a state."

Billie had little recall of the events. "Brian wasn't gone from me for more than an hour when Stephen Balfour came up to the bungalow," she said. "I still don't know how I survived the shock that was to numb and cripple me. Those days are blacked out and I don't know how I lived, day after day, with grief that knew no bounds."

The next morning, on May 10, young Ron Murray, who lived in the garage at Bungalow B, saw Nina and Patti walk past to visit Billie. "I saw them come out and one was crying as the other held her shoulder," he said.

The funeral was held the same day. Wood was so scarce that the same coffin was generally used for all burials. The box had an adjustable base so, after a body was lowered into the grave, it could be used again.

According to Barbara Redwood, Fr Barney Meyer made a special coffin out of a drawer from a chest-of-drawers and lined it with bunched-up white satin.

The death of a child was unusual and the camp was in shock, with the children among the most affected.

Dressed in white sheets as angels, the young ones formed a procession and sang the hymn, *Heaven is the Prize*. It was, said Redwood, "unforgettable."

Fr Meyer, the American priest who had turned down repatriation, conducted the service.

George Giffen stayed close to Billie during the ceremony. "She couldn't walk very well," he said. "She was fainting and I tried to catch her."

During the next few days, George thought his friend was having a breakdown and visited her often.

He also wrote a poem about Brian. It was an extraordinary piece of writing for, though George was cynical about religion, he knew Billie was a Catholic and he supported her belief without compromising his own. Six days after the tragedy, he gave the poem to Billie.

My dear, no human heart can swell,
So much as mine, no tongue can tell,
The words that are themselves too weak,
To touch the chords where grief may wreak,
Her muted anguish for a loss like yours,
Such sorrow where recompense implores,
The babe that from your womb,
Has gone, too young, to mortal tomb,
Bore all the marks of happiness and joy,
The promise of a man was in that boy.

The gentle earth has opened, dark and mild,
To give protection to another child;
Some heaven, somewhere, I know has gained,
The soul from eager lust unchained.

The oft-anticipated peace of all is his
Before he tasted early woes or bliss.
The mind that never learned to scheme
At living, has attained life's dream.

Unworried and at rest, untouched by sin
He opened wide his arms and entered in.
Sleep, child, sleep. Your story lives in leaves,
And stones, and streams where nature weaves

Her slow, unbounding and unending way
And see, the Spring is here, the sky is gay.

His words caught Billie unawares. She knew George was reserved by nature but this was the first time she realized that, beneath his jokes and stories, he concealed a deep sensitivity.

On June 14, her birthday, Billie said, "Vivienne never smoked but, as soon as the all-clear was given in the morning, there she was, beside me, the first to say Happy Birthday, with a cigarette lit in the ashes of the communal kitchen on her way to me."

On June 20, a friend of Billie, Brian Fay, was released from Stanley jail after a lengthy imprisonment for a failed escape attempt in the early months of internment. A fellow POW said Fay's "once powerfully built frame was emaciated and his limbs like sticks" and he was taken straight to the hospital. "Billie was a friend of Fay, one of four police officers who broke out but only got as far as Shaukiwan before they were caught," said Vivienne. "Billie would ask me to go along to visit Fay. We used to take a friend and have tea and a chat to try to rehabilitate the poor man." The "therapy" worked and Fay recovered to lead an active life.

In the first week of July, Billie was roused from her grief by another incident. When Edna Mae Sando, a married secretary in her thirties, moved into her room, Billie marched off to see no less than Franklin Gimson, head of the British community, to complain about the arrangement.

Billie never mentioned the contretemps, but the Colonial Secretary detailed it in his diary entry for July 5, 1944: "Mrs Gill saw me in the morning on the subject of Mrs Sando's transfer to the former's room. The former appeared very annoyed and kept accusing me of a grave injustice though I really fail to see it. At any rate, I said I had no objection to Mrs Sando going to another room in the bungalow provided an amicable arrangement could be made between all the parties concerned. Mrs Gill immediately dashed to Roberts and said I agreed to Mrs Sando's further transfer without mentioning in any way the proviso that I had added.

Roberts luckily thought there might be some mistake and asked me about it and I was able to inform him of the correct position though I expect Mrs Gill will immediately accuse me of going back on my word." With a note of exasperation, he added, "This is a habit the camp has."

The two sides of the story are not known but nearly a year later, on May 19, 1945, Gimson would write of another incident, this time involving Sando and someone in the bungalow next door. He wrote, "(Harold) Priestley (the urbane bungalow organiser who had a tiny room to himself in Bungalow A) saw me about some trouble he is having in the bungalow with Mrs Sando. The latter is rather an aggressive personality and the clash between the two is likely to cause considerable trouble which will be sure to cause procrastination from time to time."

One week after confronting Gimson, Billie walked across camp to do something else that was unusual. She went to visit Joseph Beten, a Belgian man in his 70s, to have her fortune told – a very Chinese practice – and would almost certainly have paid him. It might have been Vivienne who told Billie about Beten as he was a senior engineer for her neighbours, the Kadoories.

China Light and Power apparently required that Beten reside on company premises, presumably to be on hand to deal with emergencies such as power failures at night. He had also developed an interest in astrology and, in camp, would draw up horoscopes for internees.

For Billie, Beten produced a three-page report, dated July 13, 1944, that included an assessment of her character as well as a prophecy that would prove uncannily correct.

Of her personality, Beten wrote: "You have ready wit and facility of thought. You are 'Peter Pan-ish' (sic), bright, talkative, active, you are perhaps lacking in concentration and tenacity. Speech and writing come easily to you, and you have keen perceptions, full of the joy of life. You are fond of children and very likely children and young people will enter much in your life.

"You make friends easily and get on well with all sorts of people. You are mentally very highly strung. You live on your nerves, and crave changes and excitement. You are quick in thought and decisions, and impulsive in your actions. You detest any plodding kind of work and you will naturally drift in all methods of making money quickly. You have a keen sense for inventions and new ideas, and generally are willing to take risks in all that you undertake.

"You have the most wonderful elasticity of character; you rebound quickly from the heaviest blow; nothing seems to affect you for very long."

On love, Beten, continued: "You need love as much you do food. You are capable of deep affection and make an excellent partner. You must guard against marrying someone of a station beneath you, because you lack just the toleration for making such a union successful."

The horoscope concluded with a prediction: "Your destiny is to be associated with combinations of people or nations."

News was filtering in from Europe that the Allies had launched a seaborne attack on the beaches of Normandy while, in Asia, the Americans were slowly retaking territory against a dogged enemy.

Billie was 28 and alone after losing everyone she had ever loved. Her prime years were passing swiftly, with no end to a captivity that was taking an increasing toll on her body and mind. In desperation, she had turned to a part-time astrologer for a glimmer of hope. Was she clutching at straws?

27

A Yearning

Billie went to see her vibrant friend Dorothy Jenner, whom she had known before the war as a war correspondent applying for accreditation to go to Chungking. "She was entertaining and attractive, full of stories," said Billie. "Dorothy had a great sense of humour in camp, too, and wore flour bags as pants with the words, 'Australia's Finest' on her buttocks."

"She had been given an egg, which was worth its weight in gold, and was excited. She was standing over an open fire and using a makeshift frying pan. She cracked the egg, but she lost her grip and the pan tilted and the egg dropped into the ash. Dorothy broke down in hysterics. I tried to soothe her and retrieve some of the yolk, but I couldn't do much," said Billie.

The incident showed how nerves were worn ragged and how easy it was for even resilient people to crack.

The near-starvation diet was taking its toll on Billie, too. Another of her walking companions was Mary Smalley, daughter of Billie's medic in camp, Dr James Smalley. A civil service stenographer, Mary had a rapid stride and an acid tongue, and loved to complain about anything and everything. But when she noticed Billie's clogs were wearing thin, she made a pair of rope sandals for her, using a sardine tin opener as a needle, blistering her hands.

But by then, walking, Billie's only escape from her room companions, was becoming an effort and she had to stop and rest more often. Sitting or lying down in the same position for long was also uncomfortable as she had lost the fleshy padding on her haunches. She felt chilly on balmy evenings.

With the lack of vitamin B, her eyesight deteriorated and she could read for only short spells. Her teeth were decaying from calcium deficiency. More frightening was mental lassitude. Her memory was slipping and she took a frustratingly long time to make the smallest decision.

One of her biggest worries, however, was that she had stopped menstruating. In fact, this was a common enough condition, caused by malnutrition. Stanley women had a name for it – they would say they were "malnutrited." Billie could not bear the thought that she might not have another child.

Then, in mid-September 1944, as the war was going against them, the Japanese allowed into camp a batch of Red Cross parcels which had been in storage.

Each internee received three boxes, including butter, powdered milk, cheese, corned beef, chocolate and sardines. Since they contained more carbohydrates than vitamin B-1, they weren't particularly effective against beriberi, but they raised morale and were beneficial in other ways, too. They weren't enough to put back the pounds Billie had lost but, after a while, her menstrual cycle resumed.

George told Billie the parcels had come too late for his golfing pal, Frank "One Arm" Sutton. One of Stanley's most daring and inventive characters, Sutton had been lobbing grenades at the Turks at Gallipoli in World War I when one with a short fuse blew up and took part of his arm. This had not prevented him from leading a full life. He became a businessman who made and lost three fortunes, and an engineer who built railways in Argentina, Canada and Mexico and mined in Siberia and Korea. In China, he became a major general for the Manchurian warlord Zhang Zuolin. Despite his physical handicap, he was an excellent golfer, as George remembered. "My wife was secretary to him briefly, so I got to know him. Sutton must have been between patrons because he was so broke that I used to pay for his games. He was crazy about golf and would say, 'I'm going to make this bloody ball disappear' and he would take this tremendous swing, let off a terrific fart, and would lose the ball."

Sutton was so optimistic he had brought his golf clubs into Stanley and took the occasional swing. But he was a big man for whom the camp rations were grossly inadequate. He took to eating grass stews and, as the Red Cross parcels began to arrive, he was admitted to Tweed Bay hospital suffering from beriberi and a lacerated stomach. He was only 60 when he shocked his friends by suddenly appearing to lose the will to live, going into rapid decline before he died of dysentery on October 22.

George and Billie had become close since Brian's death. He rarely spoke about his past but once told her he had met his mother only once or twice. Before he had left for Hong Kong, she came down by train from Cambridge to meet him. They sat across from each other in a tea-house near Euston Square, where he was in cheap accommodation. She had dressed up, looking like a maiden aunt, but she was careworn after decades of labouring as a domestic servant. He waited to hear something about his father but she did not mention him. George thought he must have been a "cad," who had abandoned her with child, condemning her to stigma and hardship as an unwed mother.

Despite such a start, George was almost entirely self-taught. In his first village school, he had borrowed *Beowulf*, not the easiest book to read, from his headmaster four times. In Stanley, he was studying Russian and trying to read Anton Chekhov in the original.

That Christmas, he arranged with Beryl Church, another good friend of Billie who lived in adjoining Bungalow A with her civil servant husband Basil, to surprise Billie with a special gift.

Beryl had once given her what Billie described as the "best birthday cake I ever tasted." Beryl had saved a portion of her rice ration for weeks. "The final product, iced with ground soybean flour, and topped with a Mercurochrome rose and the inscription 'Billie' in triple dye, was truly magnificent," said Billie. "When I learned what had gone into its preparation, I cried and could hardly bring myself to eat it."

Now George gave Beryl his precious woollen blanket and asked her to turn it into a lavender-and-cream housecoat for Billie.

"It was the most beautiful gift," said Billie. "It kept me warm on the chilly winter nights, but I slept in the coat on summer nights, too, because it reminded me of George's tenderness."

On Christmas Day, George gave her a poem:

Not in the old prosaic way
I love you dear
The immemorial holly gay,
Old-fashioned cheer,
The cries and smiles
Of happy juveniles;
Grandfather's knowing looks
Fire-shine on treasured books
Are there no more,
In a new way but still my own
I call you dear, my life, my home.

Youth's gay alarms,
Old charms still born
In memory's fond arms
Familiarly worn
Like flowers rust
To dross and dust.
Old seasons portents new will bring
From distant hills strange peals ring,
Sweet souvenirs
Are not the substance of our dreams,
In a new way love works our schemes
From George, with love, X

Tenderness? My life, my home? It appears their friendship had moved to another level.

Long after the war, Billie described her feelings at the time: "When I lost Brian, it was a terrible, terrible tragedy," she said. "I couldn't live with myself. I wanted another child. George knew my situation. He knew if I didn't have you, I'd go out of my mind."

On January 15, 1945, internees heard a droning sound and looked up to see a swarm of American planes heading for various parts of the island. There had been air raids before, but nothing on this scale.

Billie yearned to replace her loss

"We knew the sounds of the American planes and we danced with excitement," recalled Billie. "I hadn't seen so many planes at the same time, not even during the battle for Hong Kong."

"At last," said George. "We are not forgotten." From the first air raid alarm at 9am, the guards ordered internees to stay indoors.

The following day, the planes were back, once more in large numbers. The Japanese in Stanley fired at the planes with machine-guns mounted on the roofs and some guards fired at them with rifles. Late in the afternoon, two bombers roared directly over Stanley and one of them dropped a bomb over Bungalow C.

According to one account, it fell into a small compound surrounded by the bungalow, the garage and servants' quarters. The blast killed 14 internees, most of them instantly, who were found sprawled in the garden, unscathed, and looking as if they were asleep.

"Four were playing bridge in the garage and they were still sitting there, cards in their hands, dead from the blast," said Vivienne. "One chap was sitting with his leg out. His trousers were taken off in the blast, but a pillar saved his life."

George was among those who rushed to help. "I helped put Stephen Balfour on a stretcher but, as we carried him out, we were so clumsy – we weren't trained, you know – that we dropped him off the stretcher and had to pick him up again. I don't know whether he was already dead at the time."

Among those killed were "three very good friends," said Billie. "We lived in the shadow of this disaster for a long time."

Victims of the Bungalow C bombing included Billie's bridge friends

Some thought victory might be imminent and scoured the skies each day for another wave of American planes, but they were disappointed.

With this brutal reminder that life could be snuffed out at any moment, even while holding a hand of cards, Billie and George sought their moments of privacy.

There was a path, with shrubbery on both sides, leading from St Stephen's College to the cemetery. Billie, taking the author around Stanley 30 years after the war, pointed out a grassy area which, she said, "resembled our alcove."

Billie was aware that what she sought so ardently involved great risk to her life. Her priest, Fr Barney Meyer, was so alarmed by the precipitous drop in the blood count for pregnant women by that time that he came up with a remedy called "Father Meyer's Powdered Egg Yolk," a concoction that became a joke in camp.

But the situation was so serious that doctors were advocating abortions to save the lives of pregnant women. They argued that, already weakened by malnutrition, most pregnant women suffered from iron deficiency, raising the spectre of complications during and after pregnancy – and they lacked the drugs to deal with such a crisis.

As Stanley's Dr Kenneth Uttley noted in his diary on May 27, 1945, "Thirteen out of the last 15 deaths in camp were due to beriberi and all the pregnant women have macrocytic anaemia. Some may blame them for getting pregnant under these conditions, and goodness knows they have had enough warnings; it is very distressing to watch them slowly dying for their foolishness in getting pregnant, but they have only themselves to blame. We have had to perform abortions on several to save their lives. There are also a number of illegitimate pregnancies, six or eight at the moment."

The incendiary issues of pregnancy and abortion had led to a fierce debate between clergy and doctors, with Franklin Gimson sometimes stuck unwillingly in the middle. It had also been inflamed by a scandal concerning a *taipan* who had impregnated a young secretary and had pressured her into having an abortion that she had not wanted and which was not warranted on medical grounds. The outrage reached a new pitch when the woman subsequently had a breakdown.

So the arguments raged, with British doctors concerned about the effects of pregnancy on the health of mothers and the clergy troubled by the moral aspects of both abortion and whether, by performing abortions, the doctors were encouraging promiscuity.

The Japanese added their own take on the situation. At one point, they tried to discourage sexual activity with an edict against "immorality" on the roofs of buildings though they exempted "married couples and good friends." They also stated that if a woman did not declare the name of her child's father, she would be classified a prostitute.

It says much of Billie's need and determination that she overrode all such dangers and criticisms.

Indeed, when she started missing periods, she feared it might be a recurrence of amenorrhoea, or being "malnutrited" again.

On Friday, March 23, she went to see Dr Smalley who, in his early 60s, was also Hong Kong's deputy director of medical services and a surgeon of long experience. With a serious demeanour, he confirmed she was pregnant and could expect to have her baby around November. He also added a grave warning – if she chose to see the baby to term, she would need a Caesarean, a difficult procedure at the best of times but now hugely complicated by the lack of proper equipment and dearth of medical supplies.

In response, Billie grinned from ear to ear. "I was overjoyed," she said, simply.

War had robbed her of everything, but now it had re-affirmed her womanhood and given her a lifeline to the future. She could not wait to tell George.

28

Desperate Race

From the moment Dr Smalley confirmed her pregnancy, Billie said, "We were the happiest couple in Stanley."

When she broke the news to George, he shared her joy but, after he had time to think about it, echoed some of Dr Smalley's concerns.

News of Billie's condition spread quickly – she certainly was not going to hide it – and the reception was mixed, with congratulations from her friends and predictable tongue-wagging from others.

The Americans kept up their sporadic air raids and sea blockade of Hong Kong and there was news that, in the Philippines, they were slowly recapturing the country, including liberating the Santo Tomas civilian camp in Manila where W.H. Donald was imprisoned but had somehow managed to hide his identity from the Japanese.

In early May came news of Germany's surrender – but even this did not generate much excitement in Stanley as many believed, like George, that the Pacific still faced a long and bitter struggle against an obdurate

George was pleased but echoed the doctor's concerns

enemy. There was evidence to suggest the Japanese would make a final stand at Stanley, a natural stronghold. One internee, John Charter, who knew Billie, wrote in March: "The Japanese have been working like badgers on anti-invasion defences around Stanley. They are busy tunnelling into the hillsides, not much above water level, at numerous points on this peninsula and the adjoining bays and headlands, and blasting goes on day and night."

Just as alarming was the rumour that, since food was extremely short in town, the Japanese would massacre all the POWs. This story gained currency when guards advised internees to dig trenches to hide in when the fateful hour arrived.

As camp morale sank, Billie said, "survival had now become a desperate race between starvation and liberation, with many near their wits' end."

On Billie's 29th birthday, June 14, George gave her a poem dedicated to the "unborn baby of my unwed wife":

How shall I dedicate to you, unissued life
A father's blessing; How speak my joy
Who know not whether you as girl or boy
Will enter on this world of sun and flowers
Nor know the anxious and unnumbered hours
That shall precede that great event, the birth
Of one more child to this old earth.

But, beneath this optimism, he told her in an accompanying letter that he looked forward to the baby "with equanimity only disturbed by the lack of suitable food for you, the difficulty a birth may be to you and the bearing the forcible liberation of internees may have upon your state of mind and physical condition."

Revealingly, he continued, "I haven't said much about love. We have had a great deal of each other and have meant a great deal to each other and we have consummated a union that is greater than friendship if a little below the greatest passion, in a way that is not given to all, be they blessed by Church or not."

George set about making a cradle, no easy task as wood was so scarce that internees were ripping up floor boards, tearing off skirting and pulling down doors to use as cooking fuel. George's finished product was no work of art, but it amused and touched Billie.

Needing nutrition for her baby, Billie sought food from any and all sources. She turned to Fr Meyer for his powdered egg yolk. She ate vegetables from George's efforts at gardening. She also turned to the black market, which was "going crazy," she said.

"Everything went over the barbed wire from fountain pens to watches and jewellery," she said. "We were at the mercy of our black marketeers. We ran the risk of never seeing any returns from our things once they were handed over. They, in turn, ran the risk of being beaten or executed if they were caught. But the guards usually returned after selling articles and we accepted whatever they gave us in military yen, the guard having taken his cut over and above the price fixed and the black marketeer would get his commission."

Even without funds, Billie opened a line of credit with one black marketeer. She wrote that, after the war, she liquidated a sterling cheque. She did not disclose the source, but it may well have involved her friend Vera and her boyfriend Gray Dalziel.

The Chief Justice deemed such IOUs illegal as they were signed "under duress," but Billie knew the extra food saved her.

As conditions worsened, Billie marvelled at the resourcefulness of internees. When people could not cook with fuel, they laid patties – rice flour mixed with water and pounded flat – in the sun; a few hours of solar energy produced a hard, crunchy biscuit.

When the salt rations ceased for months, internees collected seawater in bottles for cooking rice and vegetables. When rice ran out, someone put leaves from potato tops into an airtight jar of seawater for a few days to create the "Stanley pickle," which tasted sour but was palatable.

Even water became scarce. The authorities turned on the water for two hours in the morning and two hours in the afternoon every other day. "Those waterless days were frightful," said Billie. "We searched frantically for water. We tested with a water divining stick and we did eventually find one man with that mystic power. There was such excitement when his stick tipped over at a spot. They dug and dug until water was found. Queuing up at this waterhole and making water chains became a new communal activity. There would be about 50 men in the chain, leading from the water hole to the kitchens."

Nothing went to waste, she said. "We used the ash from our *chattis* to clean pots and pans, the lavatories, and our teeth. We made lye from wood ash to wash our clothes. We got a good shampoo by mixing lye with a spoonful of peanut oil."

The electricity was cut off in late 1944 and the curfew moved from 8pm to 6pm, but even this restriction produced a dividend as it led to more discussion groups, while the anonymity offered by the dark encouraged people to speak more freely and intimately.

After the defeat of Germany, the Japanese stopped bringing in their propaganda sheet, *Hong Kong News,* and there was a hunger for news of any kind.

"We were lucky to have a civil servant in the Hong Kong government who was fluent in Japanese," said Billie. "When the Japanese used him as an interpreter, he sometimes managed to get hold of some Japanese newspapers. One evening he gave us glimpses of the outside world by translating extracts from these newspapers."

Others gave "blackout talks," she said. "We heard fascinating talks on English history, from the Napoleonic wars up to the present century, elephant hunting in India, how the Burma Road was built. The most interesting talk for me was given by William Ritchie, who had been a friend and colleague of my father in the China Post Office, and he described how they laid the earliest postal routes in different parts of the country. Until that night, I didn't know anything about this.

"These blackout talks, twice a week, later branched into radio plays. It was a magnificent way of shortening our long dark and wearisome nights and we were grateful to the speakers."

Sudden danger could still emerge out of nowhere. On July 25, Billie and others had an escape from a "stray" bombing incident. A seaplane, which sounded in distress, according to an internee, jettisoned about a dozen missiles – either bombs, depth charges or mines, no one was quite sure – in their vicinity. One went through the roof of St Stephen's but caused no injuries. Others fell on or around Bungalow A, injuring a missionary and two girls.

One of the girls, Mavis Hansom, nine at the time, told the author she thought the missiles were water mines. "One fell into a partly full bath in the room next to ours and exploded, blowing out the wall between us. Mum and Dad would normally have been sitting on the bed against the wall and, had they not gone to the library, would certainly have been killed. My sister Leilah and I were hurt and taken to hospital. Leilah took longer to recover, and my hearing slowly returned, but recover we did, and we now wear the scars as evidence of our own war experience."

One diarist in camp noted, "Had they been bombs that exploded, the results would have been appalling – bungalows A and B would have been wiped out and a large part of St Stephen's, and the death toll would have been well over 100, not to mention scores of bad cases of shock and serious injury."

Some occupants moved as a result and Billie transferred around this time to an *amah*'s room in the Married Quarters.

On August 10 came another scare. Billie's friend Beryl Church told her that she and her naval architect husband Basil, along with other technicians and engineers, had abruptly been ordered to pack and be ready to leave. This sparked more fears. Why were they being taken away and what would happen to them? Were they being taken somewhere to look after Hong Kong's essential services after the war?

"We've not the slightest idea where we're going," said Beryl, as she bade goodbye. "Keep your fingers crossed for us."

Around August 14, another rumour swept through the camp – that some terrible bomb had devastated Japan and that a peace agreement might be in the offing.

In fact, the Americans had dropped atomic bombs over Hiroshima and Nagasaki, the Soviet Union had declared war on Japan and invaded Manchuria, and the Japanese Emperor had made a speech in courtly language that left many listeners confused.

Two days later, on August 16, Franklin Gimson posted a notice around camp that the Japanese had accepted the Potsdam Declaration that called for the surrender of all enemy forces. At the same time, he cautioned: "During the next few days the situation is likely to be somewhat tense and internees are strongly urged to refrain from anything in the nature of demonstration, cheering and so on. The guards are to remain on duty. They have received instructions to refrain carefully from any action likely to lead to incidents, and the hope is expressed that internces will exercise restraint in their contact with them. The danger of any attempt to leave the Camp precincts cannot be over-emphasized."

Billie witnessed all kinds of unusual activities: "Someone waved a Chinese newspaper that was brought into camp and its front page reported that Emperor Hirohito had announced Japan's surrender over the radio."

She went on, "Those of us who lived in the block of flats with a view of their offices saw the Japanese running around, tearing up papers and setting up bonfires. Some were getting into army jeeps and leaving camp. The Formosan (Taiwanese) guards were disappearing from their sentry boxes. It really seemed we were out of bondage at last."

One of the most bizarre incidents was a roll call like none other. "We were ordered to the parade ground. We had no idea what it was all about. Then, to our amazement, the Japanese commandant said we were all going to receive a present from the Emperor. It was unbelievable but each one of us went forward to receive a roll of American toilet paper which we hadn't seen in all our camp life, and a *fundoshi*, a long narrow piece of cloth that the Japanese used for underwear."

Billie and George hugged each other and cried with joy. But in this moment of celebration, Billie knew that change was coming. She and George had helped each other survive under the most trying conditions, but what would happen now?

A surreal period followed when they were technically free but not allowed to leave camp. Gangs of triads and criminals were roaming the city and the Japanese, who still had the guns, were the only group capable of keeping order.

As well as the issue of law and order, politicking was under way behind the scenes, with the Allies arguing over whether the Chinese army or the British or the American navies should arrive first. Roosevelt had made no secret of wanting Hong Kong to revert to China but, after his death in April, Truman showed little interest in the anti-colonial stance.

In the hiatus before the arrival of Allied forces, one important vacuum needed to be filled – the control of information.

On August 19, Harry Ching, the Australian-Chinese editor of the *South China Morning Post* who had been allowed to stay outside, arrived at Stanley to see Ben Wylie, the managing director. Ching had been to the newspaper's offices in Wyndham Street, but the Japanese had refused to leave.

The next day, Wylie and George Giffen headed for town to meet Ching at the office. When they asked the Japanese when they would be leaving, the occupants replied they had received no instructions and still refused to hand over the office.

Ching noted in his diary: "Wylie bold, bluffs Japs, inspects office. Building filthy. Staff gape at us and chatter. Japs say awaiting instructions but amicable. Cheeky Giffen wants car and gets it as missed bus. Take Wylie for walk around town."

On August 25, Ching wrote that Giffen called him from town and said Wylie thought "local change will be slow. China expects Double Ten, probably here middle September. Gloomy outlook."

The next day, however, Ching wrote: "Rumour British fleet to take Hongkong under Admiral Harcourt, but no date."

On Monday August 27, Ching returned to Stanley. Wylie's doctor, however, would not allow him out. Wylie was suffering from "electric feet" and heart problems, and the doctor said he needed to be sent home on the first available hospital ship.

Wylie's assistant general manager, Frederick Franklin, was in Shamshuipo military camp, so he asked George to take over the administrative side, giving him power of attorney.

It would also be agreed that, with the scarcity of resources, the *South China Morning Post* and the *Hongkong Telegraph*, George's paper, would be merged.

When George told Billie he was going to town, he assured her he would be in touch as soon as he could. There was a gleam in his eye that showed he was keen to be back in action and she could not help feeling hurt.

29

Wilting in Freedom

With the Japanese still around, George and Ching camped in the office, with George regretting he had not brought his bedding from Stanley. They were not friends, but George thought highly of the editor. "Ching was a fine chap, he had integrity and I respected him. In the office, his favourites were Australians. He liked their rough style. He had no time for the English chaps and I was the only English fellow then. He told me he had had a lousy time in the war; he was beaten up by everybody," George said.

Like all of Hong Kong, they were anxiously awaiting the arrival of military forces to end the tense, uneasy limbo where no one was fully in charge.

Although the food situation had improved, Billie watched with wonder when, on August 29, the US Air Force dropped parachutes with food and medical supplies. "While we looked on in disbelief, the first fly past of planes roared over our heads, doing the victory roll again and again. Then each of the planes released coloured parachutes with trunks full of medicines and Red Cross parcels tied to them. This beautiful heaven-sent rainfall went on for hours, the trunks landing all over the camp. We were so well disciplined by then that squads were immediately formed to collect the trunks from rooftops and places where they had landed. It was tremendous."

At the newspaper office on August 30, Ching and Giffen set about preparing their first full issue under a cloud of uncertainty. Many were still unsure which force would reach the colony first – the Chinese army or the British or American navies.

EXTRA

FLEET ENTERING

The first communique from the Hongkong Government to the people of Hongkong since December 1941 was issued this morning at 11 o'clock as follows:

"Rear Admiral Harcourt is lying outside Hongkong with a very strong fleet. The Naval Dockyard is to be ready for his arrival by noon to-day.

"Admiral Harcourt will enter the harbour having transferred his flag to the cruiser Swiftsure which will be accompanied by destroyers and submarines.

"The capital ships will follow as soon as a passage has been swept.

"The fleet includes two aircraft carriers Indomitable of 23,000 tons, and the Venerable; the battleship Anson of 35,000 tons and carrying 10 14-inch guns, the Euryalus and the Swiftsure carrying 10 5.2-inch guns; the merchant ship Maidstone of 8,500 tons, the merchant cruiser Prince Rupert, Canadian registry, and the Hospital ship Oxfordshire.

"A considerable number of other ships will follow in a day or two.

"The formal surrender is likely to follow the proceedings at Tokyo."

(South China Morning Post and The Hongkong Telegraph)
AUGUST 30, 1945.

George's leaflet on the arrival of the British fleet

It was George who spotted the warships. He had been out and about since early morning and he rushed into the office shouting, "The British fleet is coming in." George typed out his story on the arrival of Admiral Harcourt on the cruiser *Swiftsure* – it was printed as a single-page leaflet and distributed free to passers-by and was on the streets of Central by afternoon, with copies reaching Stanley later.

The next day, Ching and Giffen, assisted by fellow ex-internees John Luke and Eric MacNider, produced the first full post-war issue under the combined masthead of the *South China Morning Post* and the *Hongkong Telegraph*.

To print the paper, George had to "walk up and down Wyndham Street, asking people to turn off their fans and lights so that we could get more power and get the press to run – and they obliged," he said. "It was a wild time because everybody was celebrating. I had to go around the city in a rickshaw and visit the Chinese paper firms and try and confiscate rolls of newsprint so that we could go to press."

Franklin, the assistant general manager, arrived as Army Press Liaison Officer with an officer from the Hong Kong Police and ordered the Japanese to leave. They did, reluctantly, taking their Japanese type but leaving a large stock of rice, which Franklin found useful in paying the Chinese staff during the next few days. George would be on the newspaper's masthead as publisher for the next three months and would run the company for 10 weeks after Franklin left with health issues. In Stanley, Billie read the paper with pride but she missed George terribly. Her head was swirling with thoughts of the future, not least the baby that was due in November and needed a Caesarean delivery.

On August 31, she saw Admiral Sir Cecil Harcourt, newly appointed Commander-in-Chief and Governor of Hong Kong, arrive in Stanley with his aides and Gimson.

Billie stared at the big, strapping navy men in his party who made her acutely aware of her skeletal frame. She saw jeeps for the first time, a stark symbol of how the outside world had moved on in some ways while she had been at a standstill.

Washing had been taken down from camp buildings and a Union Jack hoisted as Admiral Harcourt addressed the internees: "The motive that has inspired my men, all the Bluejackets, to get here as quickly as possible, which we have done, has really been you people."

The assembled gathering sang *God Save the King* and other nationals raised their flags, which were lowered to half-mast as a bugler sounded *The Last Post* in memory of the departed. Internees sang *Oh God, Our Help in Ages Past* and planes flew low in salute.

Billie was finding that liberation was bringing unexpected stress.

Supplies of Red Cross parcels found in Japanese stores were distributed, but the richer diet caused those who gorged themselves on tinned vegetables and bully beef to be violently sick.

After dreaming of steak for years, Billie found the taste of beef bland and repelling and she hankered for the pungent flavour of salted fish.

Gradually, she began to regain her strength. Activities like climbing the footpath became less exhausting. Her skin shed its pallid colour and her face looked less gaunt. To her relief, her memory started to return, like an old friend.

But she encountered psychological challenges as initial jubilation gave way to anxiety about the future. For so long, she had been intent on surviving day-to-day without having to make plans for the morrow and now, suddenly, the gates opened onto a big wide world and she wondered, with many moments of doubt, whether she could summon the strength to learn to live and work all over again.

The arrival of the British fleet ended the uneasy truce between the Japanese and the POWs and the Chinese, and saw pent-up feelings erupt. Many Chinese sought revenge for years of starvation, forced deportations and random violence. After recognizing the executioner from Stanley jail on a ferry, a mob towed him across the harbour with a rope around his neck. Billie saw ex-POWs settling scores too, getting drunk and going down to the jail to beat up their former captors.

She saw Stanley's egalitarianism corrode as some reverted to patronizing the Chinese and Eurasians.

With scarcity already relegated to the past, the value of items changed dramatically. Scraps of food and cigarettes, once highly prized, were now discarded casually. Instead of "scrounging," people were littering the camp.

On September 3, internees were allowed to write one letter and Billie sat down and penned a long and lucid airmail to Mickey.

George had told her he had seen Charles and he was safe. Unbeknown to Billie, Charles had been transferred three months earlier to a miserable prison in Canton, where he had shared a vermin-infested cell. Now he was back in Hong Kong and looking remarkably well after his ordeal. He had written to Billie, asking about the last unprinted article he had submitted to *T'ien Hsia*. As Billie told Mickey, "I thought it was typical of Charles."

Billie's letter reveals her state of mind after emerging, like Rip van Winkle, from a long sleep. She took her cue from a brilliant editorial that appeared in the first full edition of the *South China Morning Post* on September 1. She thought George wrote it, but in fact Ching had penned it. Billie felt it reflected her condition well.

Under the heading "Deliverance" the editorial opened with: "How long dead? Three years, eight months and six days. Forty-four months lost from our lives – a thousand and more dreary days and nights of waiting and hoping, starving, praying and enduring. Not really dead, only buried alive, conscious of great tumult far off, wherein we could have been participating – wish-dreaming with all the phantasmagoria of delirium. Now for us, the forgotten folk, life begins again."

Billie told Mickey: "The happenings of the last three weeks have been practically beyond our powers of realization. I still cannot feel or believe that everything is over, but that is partly because I am still sitting here in the camp. But the things that are taking place every single moment are real enough and soon, I suppose, I shall really be out of these barb-wires. Even being told that one can write an uncensored, unlimited (at least 3 pages) airmail letter is something of a long almost-forgotten past. But the brain is slowly beginning to function and my first thought of contact is with you. I hardly know how to collect my thoughts on paper. I do not know whether you had heard about my little Brian. That's part of a dream from which I know I will never quite awaken. I lost him last May. He was drowned at the beach.

"I really don't know how I lived after that. Internment conditions and the struggle to exist were bad enough, but after I lost Brian, I felt I had lost everything. And I did. My mind was paralysed. But time slowly softened things and George, by his devotion and friendship, gradually fitted into my life like a beautiful pattern on a tapestry. The world before and the world outside faded. We only knew one world and that was here and it seemed that it would go on forever to eternity.

"So we decided to have a baby. Now the war is over and I am expecting this baby either at the end of this month of October or on the actual date it is due, which is November 7. The date is vague because of the state of my health and because it will have to be a Caesarean."

Billie went on: "I want very much to get away from here and give this child a good start in life with food that I have hitherto not had in my system. But the final wrench from George is going to be difficult. However, I have had a week to think about it all seriously and from this new light. He was among the first of the essential people required to go into town and for five days we have had the *Post* back with a vengeance. I have been very proud of his work these last few days, particularly as he has had to do everything single-handed. Also, his worries are going to begin and, rather than add to them, I feel I must get away and make a life for myself away from him. You remember he has a wife and daughter in Canada. They've got to be considered now. He doesn't know how the land lies until he sees them again. So that is one reason why I want to get away and leave him free to fulfil his obligations first towards them. As for myself and this baby of his on the way, I feel the future will unfold itself."

She said Harry Ching had told her all the *T'ien Hsia* staff had managed to leave Hong Kong and that Wen was "a big shot, representing China at various peace missions."

"Can you help me please, Mickey?" Billie asked. "Please let Wen know I am alive and by January next year hope to be back to normal and I want something to do in England or America. I want to get a new start in life before I come back to China. I feel as though I have been buried alive for three years and as soon as I am physically fit, I want to do things. This baby is giving me the incentive. I didn't want to do anything, but just die for a long time. Now I feel I have everything to live for."

The letter's tone was calm, but her anxiety rose over the following days as George failed to return. George was staying at the Gloucester Hotel, sharing a room, he said, with "an East Indian who had this shirt with gold buttons and a chain." He wrote to Billie on September 7: "I got your last chits when I returned to the hotel at 8.30am. I can understand how upsetting all the changes must be to you." He was referring to the hurried repatriation arrangements being made for internees.

"These were terrible days of confusion and chaos as evacuation plans were made," said Billie. "At first, we were told we would all be sent to special camps in Manila where we would be sorted out and taken to our respective homes. Then I was told I would be on the troopship, the *Empress of Australia*, which was taking internees to England."

On September 7, David MacDougall, who had a high opinion of Billie, returned to Hong Kong as Chief Civil Affairs Officer in charge of the civil administration. MacDougall had made a dramatic escape from Hong Kong in a torpedo boat on the day of surrender in 1941 and had been in

London planning for the return of Hong Kong to the British. He would later tell George he wanted to hire Billie but, by that time, she had left.

On the same day, a Friday, George wrote a letter at 3pm: "I received everything safely and am indeed grateful. I learn now that you won't be going till Tuesday. I don't think the information at your end is so reliable as it is here. I am borrowing the car to come out very early Sunday morning. I should arrive at 6.45, see room 31 till 7.30am, you till 8.30am, after which I must get back. I am quite sure of this programme so don't come into town – it is such an anxiety getting you back comfortably and getting off time to look after you here. My love, my dear, and if the most urgent thing happened and you were transported away without us meeting again, don't forget that we shall certainly meet sometime and I will always remember you and baby. With love, George."

Some of her friends such as Vivienne were leaving camp and Billie asked George if she could not see him in town if he could not come out to Stanley.

At 2am that Sunday, George replied: "My dear girl, I am sorry to say that my arrangements for coming early this a.m. have fallen flat as another party, with equal rights to it, has taken the car. Furthermore, we are bringing out 3 editions today and I shall not have a moment to spare. I know it is cruel that work should intervene but duty will prevail over sentiment, my dear, and you will be finer in my eyes if you accept the position. I can't come out unless a fluke gives me the chance on Monday and I shan't be able to spend any time with you if you come to town. Please believe that I am not stalling but am stating the cold facts. I have only spent the hours from 2am to 7am in my bed since I came out and have had no diversions."

George went on, "I am fit as a fiddle so I suppose work suits me. You must go in for being a mother and I know you will be a splendid one. I have received a pile of things from you and milk powder of all things. Please don't go without as I am getting 3 sq meals a day now. I am thinking of both of you and wishing you comfort of mind and body. Do not despair of seeing me out there as even Tuesday might not be too late. With love, George."

But they knew the time was running out as Billie was due be taken to the evacuation ship the following day.

On Monday, September 10, as Billie was to be transferred to the *Empress of Australia,* she received another message from George. It was still not too late. If he had changed his mind and asked her to stay, she would.

George scribbled that he planned to see Billie – from another vessel. "A hurried note to say farewell," he said. "I hope to see you from the *Kempenfelt* from which I have managed to get a trip with the admiral to see you off. Try and imagine that HMS *Kempenfelt* has especially come out to bring me nearer to you. Dry your eyes and rest. Believe me, there will be lovely things in store for you when baby is born and you're reunited with friends. Goodbye my dear for now. Don't regret Stanley and think not too harshly of me who have done you so much harm and brought you so little happiness. With love from George."

The internees' departure from Stanley was almost as chaotic as their arrival had been, only this time they were in high spirits as they were on their way home. Billie didn't share their exhilaration. In just a few days, the love that had bloomed in the shadow of war was wilting in the sunlight of peace. She was alone, possessing only what she was wearing and could carry. One of her biggest concerns was that she could not carry out the family mementoes Ah Chun had helped her bring into camp. She had to choose what to leave behind and, with a wrench, she gave the precious, but heavy, family Bible to Brian Fay, the police officer she had helped rehabilitate.

Clutching her belongings, she joined the corvette that carried internees to Junk Bay, outside the eastern end of Hong Kong harbour, where the *Empress of Australia* was anchored. The *Empress* was a Canadian Pacific ocean liner that had been converted into a troopship and was painted warship grey.

Billie walked up the gangway to join 1,000 ex-POWs from Stanley and Shamshuipo. It was crowded way above its capacity, with women and children squeezed into the cabins and men camped out on the decks. Billie shared a cabin with up to a dozen women and children from Stanley. At intervals, she would make her way to the deck to see if there was any sign of HMS *Kempenfelt*.

She was leaving Hong Kong without the lover who had become her rock. Even as she boarded, she thought she was bound for England, where her sister Jessie lived. She had no inkling that her voyage would land her at the opposite side of the world.

30

A Lucky Break

"George never did come out on the *Kempenfelt* with the admiral," said Billie. "The next day, we rocked our way to Manila. There were tears and confusion on board. We were over a thousand. There was litter everywhere, total disorganisation, and rumours every minute. We were packed like sardines with as many as 6 or 10 or 12 in a cabin. The lounge, the dining room, everywhere was jam-packed. Those five sailing days were like our scruffy life in camp."

Despite the congestion, the freed POWs appreciated the food piled on tables and the films put on for their entertainment, even if some found the screen dialogue too rapid to follow as their powers of concentration were still recovering.

Such amenities were lost on Billie, however, as she spent much of the journey bent over the railings on deck. "I was hopelessly seasick the entire time. It was hell for me."

Fortunately for her, Dr Smalley was also on board and he kept an eye on Billie amid the mayhem, knowing she was at a critical juncture of her pregnancy.

By the time the *Empress of Australia* entered Manila Harbour, which was strewn with wrecked vessels, Billie could not endure another moment on board.

To the dismay of the 1,000 British passengers, however, the US authorities in Manila would not allow them to land. An intense battle between Americans and Japanese a few months earlier had claimed over 100,000 lives and reduced one of Asia's most elegant cities to rubble.

"There was nothing prepared or planned for us. The American authorities were not even aware of our arrival. The end of the war had come so unexpectedly. So, the *Empress of Australia* marked time for another five sweltering days in Manila while awaiting decisions, with conditions worsening every day," said Billie.

Then an old warhorse sailed into the harbour. It was the HS *Maunganui*, over 30 years old, which had served as a troopship in World War I, a cruise ship between the wars, and was now a New Zealand hospital ship. It had come from Hong Kong and Formosa, picking up seriously ill and dying POWs and was stopping in Manila to refuel and re-stock on water on its way home.

When Dr Smalley saw the ship, he knew what he must do. The veteran doctor, who had been a brilliantly innovative surgeon in Fiji for years before being posted to Hong Kong, did what a less bold or experienced man might not have dared to do. He went in search of the captain and told him that Billie needed to transfer to the hospital ship, or she could face catastrophic consequences.

At noon, the *Empress of Australia* sent an SOS to the *Maunganui* – and received an affirmative reply soon after. The hospital ship agreed to take Billie but, since neither ship was permitted to dock, this presented a problem.

"The news that I was to be transferred to the hospital ship spread quickly and soon everybody who had a relative on the hospital ship came rushing to give me messages to take over," said Billie.

"After a delay of a few hours, the quartermaster and two aides from the *Maunganui* arrived at 8pm to accompany me for the tricky move at night. They helped me onto a small barge and I waved goodbye to people lining the floodlit decks above me as we moved away."

The quartermaster told her: "You are now a guest of the New Zealand government and our job is to take care of you." Billie said, "I felt safe for the first time in years."

After 40 minutes in the water, they approached the *Maunganui*, ringed with red and green lights. Her escorts insisted she lie on a stretcher, which was fitted into a hoist that was pulled up by a crane. On deck, she was transferred to a stretcher on a trolley and wheeled straight to an operating theatre, where a medical team was waiting.

The SOS message from the *Empress* had read: "Can you accommodate expectant mother?" and the recipients had taken that to mean birth was imminent.

"I was embarrassed when I told them I was not expecting my baby for a few more weeks," said Billie.

What happened next was unforgettable. "They wheeled me into a room that was so pretty and bright. The walls were cream and the beds and tables and chairs were pale and green, so restful looking. There was an electric fan and two portholes. The nurses brought me a cup of cocoa and biscuits. I slept wonderfully; it was my first peaceful sleep in freedom."

The next morning, she had breakfast – "porridge, with more than our camp's ten-day rations of sugar and milk, and with bacon and eggs and fruit. It was marvellous." She moved into "a bed with a mattress, clean sheets, a line of coloured towels over the cot, and a gaily-coloured wash-bag of toiletries. They gave me new pyjamas and took me to my first hot shower in four years. It was like a dream."

Two doctors from Stanley, Dr Philip Court and Dr John Loan, the young medical missionary who had diagnosed her appendicitis, came to see her and were keen to hear news from the *Empress of Australia*. Billie was stunned to see how quickly the doctors had filled out since their release from camp.

Though she was an old oil burner, the *Maunganui* had been comprehensively converted and was one of the best-equipped hospital ships in the world, with an operating theatre equal to that of a modern hospital, and a 100-strong medical staff.

Dr Smalley's intervention had quite possibly saved her life.

Billie reunited with friends from Stanley, including Rosaleen Millar, a nurse who was recovering from tuberculosis. In camp, Rosaleen had made a cushion for Billie, depicting a view of Stanley, stitching it together from pieces of a blanket and table felt. Billie would later ask her to be the author's godmother.

Their joy was dampened by the sight of invalids who were lying motionless in their cots. Some would owe their lives to the care they received on board, but others would not leave the ship alive.

As they neared their destination, Billie grew excited. "We approached Wellington around six o'clock in the morning on October 7. We passed Mount Egmont, the first snow-capped mountain I had ever seen. As the ship slowed, hundreds of seagulls flew around us, filling the air with their cawing and flapping of wings," she said.

"Wellington Harbour was not unlike Hong Kong, with its chain of mountains and houses dotted over them. The mountains looked golden – I was struck by their beauty but was told the colour was from gorse, regarded as a nuisance weed."

The *Maunganui* docked shortly after a requisitioned Dutch hospital ship, the HMHS *Tjitjalengka*. "We were the first ships to arrive in Wellington with POWs and it seemed the entire city turned out to greet us. The men wore top hats and bowler hats and the women had pretty, flowered dresses and picture hats," she recalled.

"They looked large and healthy and so well fed. There were women in all sorts of uniforms. We were greeted with a band, a gun salute and cheering. The governor of New Zealand (Sir Cyril Newall) was the first to come on board to welcome us and he shook our hands, saying something special to each one of us. He also told us we could stay in New Zealand for as long as we wished."

Their reception was well organised. Details of each patient had been sent ahead and railway ambulance cars were waiting at the wharf to carry patients to Palmerston North and Rotorua as well as locally.

"Dolly Reddish (a friend from the Married Quarters) and I were the first two to be taken off the ship, at 3 o'clock. As I went down the gangplank in my camp-made dressing gown, I could hear the movie cameras clicking; our arrival was being filmed for the news that evening."

There was a moment as they were disembarking when the rousing welcome faded into silence.

"What's the matter? Why have they gone quiet?" asked Billie.

"They're shocked at the way we look."

Only then did she notice the awe and pity on the faces of those standing on the quay. The contrast between hosts and visitors could not have been starker. The New Zealanders were giants compared to the stooped, rail-thin arrivals in ragged clothes.

A sprightly sparrow of a woman stepped forward to greet Billie. Miriam Duncan was head of a volunteer cadre of blue-uniformed women known as the Ladies in Petrel Blue, who drove their own cars to ferry patients around.

Billie took an instant liking to her "minder," who took her to a new hospital in Lower Hutt, near the capital, which had opened as an extension to Wellington Hospital.

"We were taken to Ward 8 in a new wing where each bed had soft blankets, a curtain that could be drawn around the bed, a white locker beside it and individual ear-phones for the radio. Others arrived from the Rosary Hill orphanage in Hong Kong and we had a ward to ourselves," said Billie.

A young nurse asked if she wanted a bath and opened her eyes wide when Billie said that she had been fantasizing about a warm soak for nearly four years. "Lying in that deep white bath, allowing the water to envelop me and seep into every pore, I was in a state of ecstasy," said Billie. "Every now and again, I would reach for the tap and turn on more hot water, feeling guilty about such extravagance."

Afterwards, she asked the laughing nurses, "I'm sure I am several shades lighter. Can you notice the difference?"

Billie had left Hong Kong believing she was going to England, but that unexpected delay in Manila steered her onto another course.

She was in an unfamiliar country known for immigration policies that were not friendly to Asians, but she was being pampered as never before and, if her start was anything to go by, she felt she had little to worry about. It was an excellent place to have her baby and think about the next move.

31

At the Crossroads

The doctors set a date for Billie's Caesarean and she began to count down the days. The waiting period, she recalled, was "crowded with kindness, new friends, flowers and all sorts of presents." She did not mention the anxious moments she and the doctors must have experienced wondering if and how her gestation under conditions of deprivation might affect her baby.

On October 25, 1945, nurse Margaret Mitchell walked briskly into the ward, greeting Billie cheerfully with the words, "Today's the day."

At around 9.45am, aides wheeled Billie out of the room, with others calling out "Good luck" and "Don't worry, everything will be all right."

The next event that Billie recalled was coming around after the operation and hearing nurse Mitchell saying, "It's a boy, it's a boy."

There followed a seemingly endless interval before they brought her baby to her.

"They took such a long time, I worried something was wrong."

The baby weighed six pounds and four ounces and the delay may have been caused by doctors examining the new arrival with closer scrutiny than usual. In the end, they pronounced the baby healthy.

The tricky operation had gone well except for one mistake that went undetected. The medical team left behind a stitch that would cause Billie distress for nearly two years.

Billie and George had already agreed on the name Ian for a boy, as it comprised the last three letters of Brian and the middle letters of George's daughter Dianne.

More agonizing was the decision whether to use George's surname or hers. She hated not telling the truth but important issues like legitimacy were at stake and in the end, she used her married name. If people asked any questions, she decided, she would say her husband had died in the war.

Over the following days, the kindness of strangers overwhelmed Billie.

"Our ward was filled with visitors from the Red Cross, the press and organisations created just to help us," she said. "They came with underwear, slippers, cigarettes, chocolates and toilet articles. As the doors

Billie and Ian at Lower Hutt Hospital

swung open each evening, total strangers came in and piled food, clothes and toys on my bed. Every day was Christmas."

The generosity of Kiwis extended beyond the ward. "Even after I left hospital, when I stepped into a shop, some merchants refused to accept payment once they learned I was an ex-POW."

She was soon feeling well enough to give an interview to an *Evening Post* reporter and a lengthy report appeared in the paper on November 5.

One source of frustration, however, was the length of time communications took between New Zealand and the outside world. Though Billie cabled George about the birth of their child, his congratulatory response did not arrive for over two weeks. A second telegram came from George around the same time, saying he had heard from Wen Yuan-ning in Chungking and that he "wants you back year end."

Wen also wrote to Billie saying he had tried to contact her three times after reaching Chungking in February 1942 but "special messengers came back to say it was impossible to get in touch with you in the concentration camp." Wen said he left the Ministry of Information in 1943 and Hollington Tong had resigned, too. He told her he would

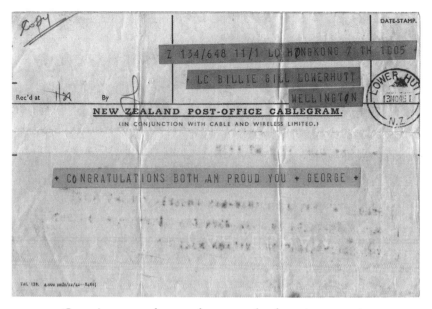

George's congratulatory telegram took a long time to arrive

always have a place for her whatever he did or wherever he went, but gave no other details. Billie was glad Wen was clearly a Very Big Shot in the government – he had spent two three-month stints in India and joined China's Goodwill Mission to Great Britain in the winter of 1943 – but *T'ien Hsia*, which had been "my baby," was gone forever and the idea of Chungking did not appeal.

Wen had also written to his friend David MacDougall, now in charge of the civilian administration in Hong Kong, to take care of her. George also told Billie that MacDougall would "take her like a shot" – if only she were in Hong Kong. However, he added, "for those who left, women in particular, [Hong Kong] is sealed off until the priority cases have gotten here from UK and Australia, and until more housing is available."

Until then, Billie had been leaning towards Hong Kong, especially as George seemed to be staying on rather than going home.

She suspected George was emotionally conflicted and that, if they met again, he might be swayed to stay with her and Ian.

She was right. It was why he rebuffed her suggestion of meeting again.

"I am fond of you and I could be fonder, but I just won't," George wrote. "It is obvious that I could not go to New Zealand if I wanted to and, my dear, you must not lose sight of the fact that I cannot rejoin my family and you. I have to choose one or the other and you know which I chose. Nothing will alter that but your letters do not seem to appreciate it."

Moreover, George now had a timetable – "Franklin, my relief, writes that he will be back in January (1946) and I shall leave immediately that happens."

Billie had also broached with George her most pressing concern – her lack of money.

This brought a disappointing rejoinder.

"I am afraid all the bad things about me have come true for you," George wrote. "Although I have not been badly paid, I have wasted every bean and shall go home in debt about a thousand dollars. I know that's a bit criminal but I have been having a hell of a merry time, disgracing myself and getting into all sorts of trouble.

"I am now just trying to stay sober till I pull out without making a big hash of anything. Brutal but frank. I have just raised $100, which I enclose, hoping it will be of some use.

"I am sorry you are in such an agitated frame of mind. There is nothing to be alarmed about, really; you will charm everybody you meet; you will finish up with the job you want and make a lovely boy out of Ian."

Exhausted, for she was still recovering from her Caesarean as well as her long captivity, Billie reconsidered her options. People in New Zealand were wonderful, but letters and newspapers took a long time to arrive from abroad and she felt cut off from the world she knew.

Then Billie got word that Paddy was still alive and in England, and she realized she needed to tell him about Brian as well as discuss their broken marriage. Around this time, she received a surprise visit from James Bertram, the New Zealand journalist, who had read her account of Stanley in the *Evening Post*. The Japanese had captured Bertram near Stanley as a gunner in the Hong Kong Volunteer Defence Corps, interned him at Shamshuipo for two years and shipped him off to Tokyo to labour in railroads and docks until the end of the war. Bertram said he had heard from Mickey Hahn, who now lived in England and was asking for her whereabouts. "When James Bertram told me Mickey was looking for me, that was a galvanizing force," said Billie.

There was another reason for her to visit England for the first time. Her father, by his influence on her in childhood and by sending her to SPG, had left a mark on her as indelible as his DNA. As she told Mickey before the war, Billie was "too foreign in her ways" and could not see herself marrying a Chinese. Her inclination had already shown itself clearly, though her timing had been unfortunate, losing a husband to the war and a lover to the peace.

The British government was offering free repatriation for its citizens and Billie, with her British passport, now stirred into action.

On November 20, Rosaleen Millar, dressed in her smart military nurse's uniform, arrived in a jeep in her new role as Ian's godmother. She drove Billie and Ian to the nearby Church of St Peter and Paul, which had been inaugurated a few days earlier, and carried Ian to the baptismal font where Fr Bernie Keegan christened him. After the ceremony, they returned to the hospital for a party for which the matron had prepared a cake. Billie's next step was to obtain a New Zealand passport for her son.

Ian's godmother Rosaleen with her daughter Signe

But she was still adjusting to "normal" life in other ways. When Miriam Duncan took her home for tea, Billie found herself unexpectedly awed by the elegance of her sitting room. When her hostess brought tea served in cups of exquisite bone China, Billie hesitated.

"What's the matter, dear? Don't you drink tea?" asked the kindly Miriam.

"It's not that," said Billie. She explained it was the first home she had visited since before the war and "it's so long since I touched such a beautiful cup and saucer that I'm afraid I might break it."

The New Zealand Government gave Billie 25 pounds and Miriam took her on a shopping expedition for clothes. Billie was exhilarated, but the one item she really needed but could not find was a pair of shoes to fit her tiny feet.

Around December 22, as Miriam said goodbye to her on the quay, she gave Billie another 10 pounds from the government and added five pounds from her own pocket.

Having arrived with only what she could carry, Billie left with four suitcases, a trunkful of clothes and a six-month supply of Cow & Gate milk powder. Her stay in New Zealand had restored her faith in humankind and she would retain a soft spot for Kiwis for the rest of her life.

She boarded the P&O's RMS *Mooltan*, named, like the company's epic ship built in 1861, after Multan in the Punjab. The latest version had been dubbed the "magnificent Mooltan" as it was by far P&O's largest ship at 21,000 tons gross when it was launched in 1923 and, with seven decks, was enormous. It was converted during the war from an ocean liner to an armed merchant cruiser with six-inch guns and then to a troopship.

In Sydney, Mavis Ming, whom George had cabled from Hong Kong, met Billie at the boat.

Mavis had had an astonishing war. She had walked out of Hong Kong, embarking on a 3,000-mile, six-week journey by river barge, truck and train before reaching Chungking. In the nationalist capital, she had worked for the British embassy before being repatriated to Australia through India in early 1944. Now she was working as a typist for the US Navy, living with her sisters in Manly, and was even giving League of

Health classes in the evenings. But Mavis was again feeling restless and would soon head back to China.

She took Billie to a David Jones department store. "It was the biggest shopping complex I had ever seen," said Billie. "To my joy, I found two pairs of child-size shoes. I also ate the biggest mango I had ever seen."

In a photograph taken with Mavis, Billie appears radiant in a smart new jacket and hat; her face had filled out even in the weeks since she was pictured looking rather gaunt with her son.

Mavis Ming helped Billie find shoes in Sydney

Back on the *Mooltan*, Dr Helen Canaval, wife of Dr Gustav who had removed her appendix in Stanley, approached to ask Billie if she would partner her at bridge.

"I would love to, but I'm afraid I have spent my last penny on shoes," said Billie.

Helen was so keen to play with Billie that she loaned her a stake to get started.

That evening, Billie played the most amazing bridge of her life, picking up so many winning hands that she began squirming with embarrassment as she picked up her cards. Bidding several grand and small slams, she made them all and won enough money to repay Helen and to keep herself for the rest of the long voyage.

At Port Said in Egypt, Billie watched boys diving for coins and beamed at the Red Cross officials who came on board to distribute soap, slippers and jumpers to the former POWs.

On February 15, 1946, the *Mooltan* docked at Southampton, only a few hundred yards from where her grandparents had left for Hong Kong and China some 80 years earlier.

By then, George had reached a very senior position in the *South China Morning Post* company. Taking official leave of absence, he left Hong Kong for Vancouver on February 13, 1946, on the SS *Suncrest,* with plans to later return to Hong Kong. At the same time, Billie was sailing to England on the *Mooltan* on a new adventure to the "mother country."

Thus, in a strange twist of fate, Ian's parents were on their separate ways to meet their spouses, whom neither had seen since before the war and neither was aware how their Stanley relationship was about to affect their plans.

32

Single Mother in England

There was no brass band or welcoming speech at Southampton when Billie disembarked under a grey sky with several hundred ex-POWs. Two months after the war had ended in Europe, British voters had rejected Churchill and swept Labour to a landslide victory with promises of a new social security system and a national health service. Britain was bankrupt, rationing and austerity were in force, and the arrival of yet another shipload of returning POWs excited little media attention in war-exhausted Britain.

Billie was looking forward to living in the putative land of her father, who had been to England only a few times on leave but had been partly shaped by his English parents. England had given Billie her mother tongue and her education.

After scrambling to get off the boat train from Southampton with Ian and her luggage, Billie was happy to see her sisters Jessie and Dolly at Waterloo station in London.

Billie hadn't seen Jessie since she left Shanghai in pursuit of Albert, nor Dolly since her departure from Hong Kong for Australia after her whirlwind marriage.

"It was a marvellous reunion, and they have both been trumps to welcome the baby and me," Billie wrote to Mickey on February 20.

"We are staying in a very modest little house and the last few days have been spent settling in," she continued. "Ian, of course, wormed his way into their hearts and now he reigns like royalty in this household. My sisters would like me to remain in England."

At 98 Holyrood Avenue, South Harrow, Jessie had rented a tiny room for Billie beside her own studio that she leased from the downstairs couple who eyed Billie warily; and Jessie had made a similar arrangement for Dolly in the house next door.

It was a cosy arrangement as the three Newman sisters from Shanghai helped each other out.

Jessie was well settled in an unvarying routine. She rose early, in the dark during winter, to catch a bus for the one-hour journey to her city job as a teletypist with Cable & Wireless. When she returned, often too tired to cook dinner, she would bring fish and chips or open a tin. At weekends, she caught up on her sleep, did her laundry and visited Edie from Shanghai, who was her best friend. Albert's name was never mentioned.

Billie dreaded the meeting with Paddy and was sure he felt the same. Stationed in Yorkshire, he came down to London and was friendly as she gave him tea at home.

She searched his eyes that had once lit up at the sight of her. "Perhaps I hoped we could still have a life together as I needed help badly. I had no money, I had a baby, I was weak," said Billie.

Paddy, who was now a captain, reminded her so much of Brian she felt a pang. But he had lost his happy-go-lucky air and his hairline had receded further. He had had a brutal war in Burma, where he caught malaria and was now feeling tired a lot.

After a while, Paddy told her he had found someone else, a Land Girl who had worked in the countryside as part of the war effort, and he wanted his freedom to marry her. It hurt to hear the words of such finality.

"That was the end of our cup of tea and I told him to go ahead with the divorce," said Billie. Seeing him off at the bus stop, she said, "Good luck, Paddy." He turned with a wave and said, "You, too," and that was the last she saw of him. Their divorce came through over a year later.

Billie was grateful for Jessie's hospitality, especially as she soon realized that, despite her office skills, finding a job was near-impossible as employers looked askance at a young mother with a child. "The situation here for mothers is appalling," she wrote to Mickey in America. "No wonder babies are just dumped. Every day in the papers since I have been in England a baby is found left in railway stations, telephone booths and even in the cinemas."

When Billie did the shopping, she encountered rationing for the first time. "You won't like it here," she told Mickey. "They tell me it's not like what it used to be. Certainly, life is grim – there are moments when I feel I am back in the camp – the queues here are back-breaking. I spend days waiting for potatoes and queuing for the weekly joint. You have simply got to queue for everything in England. No wonder the people are worn out."

Billie's one respite was to wrap up warmly and go for a walk, wheeling Ian in a pram. "We couldn't afford to stop in a café or go to the local cinema," she said. She was pleased when old ladies bent down to hug Ian, with his "sloe-like brown eyes," she said. But "after a while, I didn't want him to catch germs and I pinned a tin badge on (his) sweater with the words, 'Please don't kiss me!'"

Billie began running regular evening temperatures. "All the time I was feeding Ian, I kept a hold on myself (but) the moment he was on the bottle I let myself go haywire," she wrote. Her nerves, she thought, were shot.

Given their cramped living conditions and financial strains, it was inevitable that the relationship between the siblings began to fray.

Dolly, gentle and sweet-tempered as ever, was the first to leave. Unable to get work and finding the weather too cold, after less than a month she took a boat back to Australia.

Billie told Mickey she was disappointed that Jessie had not changed since Shanghai. "She is so empty besides being selfish," she wrote. No doubt, Jessie was also finding it difficult to live with her stressed and sensitive sister. Yet there was no escape. "I couldn't move without any money and it is not easy getting a room with a baby," wrote Billie.

Then she received a telegram from Mickey on March 19 that changed everything. Mickey and Charles were coming to England and she proposed to Billie that "you will live with us, help me run the house, do a spot of typing, sort of social and regular secretary."

What fun it would be to stay with Mickey and Charles! Billie remembered all too well the parties at Mickey's flat where she had met fascinating people from a variety of backgrounds.

Billie replied swiftly: "My heart swelled to enormous proportions when I received your cable – Mickey, you are a Saint! As if by magic, you have swept away all my problems. Now I can make plans to await your arrival."

She sent the letter from Hastings where she was staying with Helen and Bob McNeale, her father's customs friend who had sent her to secretarial school. Her letter revealed that, like many former POWs, including George, Stanley had left her with dental problems. "I am having beastly trouble with my dentures – I need fifteen fillings – all this is part of my legacy from camp, and I have got appointments with a dentist in Hendon."

As her spirits were recovering, she received a letter from George, to whom she had told her news of Paddy.

"I had a happy reunion with my wife and am charmed with my daughter," George wrote in a letter dated April 2, 1946. "I am very happy with them and my wife has forgiven my trespass. I am, therefore, distressed to learn how things turned out for you. Did you give Paddy a chance?"

Billie took it hard. "He wrote that 'my wife has forgiven me my trespass and I am sorry that yours has not' and that was the end of that. I thought that was cruel. It broke my heart," she told me.

When George added that he planned to return to Hong Kong with his wife "in a month and a half, I hope," Billie felt he was adding salt to the wound.

By June, however, she appeared to be back on track. "I am in a more normal frame of mind," she wrote to Mickey on June 18, 1946. The divorce business with Paddy was over – she was served the petition and all she had to do was wait for it to be settled. And where George was concerned, she said, "I have covered the ground too many times and I'd rather leave those wounds to heal by themselves."

On July 28, Mickey and Charles boarded the RMS *Queen Mary* in New York, occupying a spacious cabin that also accommodated a Danish-born governess for Carola. They docked at Southampton on August 2 and, soon afterwards, Billie picked up the telephone to hear Mickey's familiar drawl, inviting her to Charles's country home in Dorset.

As Billie wrote to historian Dauril Alden, author of a biography of Charles Boxer: "Mickey's offer of a home for my baby and myself came as an answer to my prayers."

Days later, Billie took the train to Dorchester, where Charles met her; he was lean and straight-backed, but his left arm was hanging limply by his side.

When Billie expressed her sympathy, Charles was dismissive. "I was such a damned fool," he said. "I found this band of stragglers and led them into battle and a sniper shot me in the back. Unbelievably stupid of me."

Ian takes his first steps at Conygar on his first birthday, 25 October 1946

In the driveway, as Conygar, the Boxers' large 19th-century mock Tudor mansion, came into view, Billie exclaimed, "This is rather grand, Charles. A real country estate."

Charles replied, "Mickey told me to warn you about the house. The Army requisitioned it during the war and I'm afraid they left it in a mess."

Mickey came out with Carola, whom Billie was meeting for the first time.

"You look wonderful, Mickey. So content and mellow. Marriage and motherhood suit you," said Billie.

This house is driving me nuts," said Mickey. "Our agent told us to leave everything as it is until the Army has investigated our claim for damages."

Charles loved the house but he had not exaggerated when calling it a mess. Some of the rooms still had broken windows and badly cracked washbasins. The walls were smeared and dented, the floors were grey with grime and splintered wood. Some of the plumbing was not working.

The Boxers had decided to occupy only one end of the house. Billie had two rooms, one for Ian, and she set about making them homely. It was agreed the nanny would look after Ian as well as Carola.

Billie told Charles and Mickey she would not accept any money and would earn her room and board by typing, an agreement she soon came to regret.

After breakfast, Charles would shout, "I'm off to the post office. Does anyone have any letters they want posting?" He always invited Billie to join his long trek to the village and, the first time she accepted, she found herself trotting breathlessly to match his long strides. After that, she excused herself, saying she lacked walking shoes. Charles had boots made for her and an embarrassed Billie had to find other excuses.

Above all, Billie was looking forward to the company of the two people who had always been the life and soul of parties in Hong Kong.

She wanted – in fact needed, compulsively – to talk about Stanley but Charles was completely the opposite. Even though he was a historian, he refused to discuss, let alone write, anything about his war experiences. When Billie asked how he survived being forced to sit cross-legged in front of a wall for much of the day, he fobbed her off by saying he had memorized poetry and meditated.

But it wasn't just that Charles was loath to discuss the war. Neither he nor Mickey seemed to be up for much conversation about anything – the two writers spent their days in their studies and, at mealtimes, would read, in silence, books propped up in front of their plates.

Charles was working on a history of Macao, *Fidalgos in the Far East, 1550-1770*, that would enhance his reputation as a leading authority on the Portuguese and Dutch seaborne empires. Mickey had just finished a book on Raffles, founder of modern Singapore and governor of Sumatra. In fact, in what was intended to be the first of a number of collaborations,

The author and his daughter Sabrina visiting Conygar in 2014

Mickey had sought Charles's advice on *Raffles*. But the two disagreed so strongly on the content and style of Mickey's draft that Charles refused to be credited in her book and they ended up agreeing they would never read each other's writing.

They also fell out over Mickey's best-selling book, *China to Me*, a devastatingly gossipy account of her affairs as well as candid portraits of her lovers, including Sinmay and Charles. Since its publication in November 1944, it had been met with near-universal outrage among the people she wrote about in Shanghai and Hong Kong. Charles had begged her to ask the publisher not to release the book in the UK as he feared it would damage his chances of getting posted back to the Far East.

Billie found no pleasure in the meals, either, a bland combination of meat or fish with boiled potatoes and cabbage, prepared by Mrs Hammond, a crabby woman who had been at Conygar for over 30 years and ruled the kitchen fiercely, resenting any interference.

Mickey, quite apart from knowing that domestic help was impossible to obtain, was afraid of Mrs Hammond – and so was Billie.

Mickey suggested to Billie that they make fudge. Astounded, for Mickey had not been known to step inside a kitchen, Billie shared the adventure of going to the village to buy chocolate and then conducting the grand experiment. They heated up the chocolate, but it failed to solidify and they ended up with a gooey dark soup. On seeing the sticky saucepans, Mrs Hammond went into a rage and wreaked her revenge by over-salting their meals for several days.

Charles had stayed behind after the war to search for his library of rare books which had been looted by the Japanese – and he had found most of them in Tokyo. Billie was at Conygar the day his books arrived. His face wreathed in a smile, he refused all help and removed the books one by one from the packing cases and lovingly dusted and examined each one.

Billie was fond of Charles but he remained an enigma to her. She knew that his father had walked into certain death on the western front and that his mother had killed herself, and Charles was an intensely private man whose tongue loosened only after several drinks.

Billie looked forward to trips to Dorchester, but they were not without incident. "People in Dorchester nudged each other, or turned around in tearooms to look at us, especially at Ian," wrote Mickey in *England to Me*. "I often forgot about her distinctive looks and I never did get accustomed to the way people stared at us whenever we went out together." Nor did it help that "some local people mistook her nationality and spoke of (Billie) as 'that Japanese girl' in Conygar," she added.

The winter of 1946-47 was one of England's coldest on record and it marked Billie's lowest ebb. For days, she huddled over a small fireplace in her room, weeping and refusing to move. When Mickey tried to coax her out, Billie cried, "I think I'm going crazy. I'm in prison, I'm in prison, and I'll never get out. I might as well be back in camp; life will always be just washing clothes, and washing more clothes, and looking after Ian."

Though she didn't know the cause, Billie's stitch was causing a sharp pain whenever she sat down or got up. "It was a moveable pain. It didn't hurt when I walked around but, when I sat, the pain was so sharp I would jump up," she said. Mickey asked two GPs to come to the house and Billie told them about "this sharp thing poking me" that was causing vaginal bleeding. But, she reported, "The doctors felt my pulse but didn't even examine me. They dismissed it as the after-effects of the war."

Billie reached the point where, as she told Dauril Alden: "I found myself trapped in a totally alien and unfamiliar world. I was not on the same wavelength as the Hammonds, nor the numerous feeble-minded nannies who came and went. I was so desperately lonely that I remember yearning for my fellow internees – even those who had made life so intolerable in internment."

In fact, Billie did meet her Stanley friends several times – invariably over a Chinese meal – and such occasions helped to keep her sane.

"We hated each other in camp, but we couldn't wait to see each other afterwards," she said. The former POWs were having difficulties adjusting to the post-war world. Some found it difficult to hold their tongues when seeing people leave food on their plates in restaurants. Others found it hard sleeping in a soft bed. Many, including Billie, hoarded rather than threw things away. All felt that only those who had been in Stanley could truly understand them.

"Our experiences were so extreme that I sometimes wondered if it was all a bad dream," said Billie. "So, when we got together, we laughed and we cried and we talked madly until the waiters were wiping down tables. It was unadulterated joy."

But, one by one, friends like Mary, Freda and Vivienne headed back to jobs in the Far East, leaving Billie disconsolate.

The turning point arrived when Billie fell out with Mickey – over Ian.

Ian was wailing a lot, which Billie put down to his teething. Nonetheless, the bawling grated on Mickey's nerves and one day she announced the time had come for what she called Ian's "great reform phase."

Every time Ian cried, Mickey smacked him on the thigh. This infuriated Billie, who thought Carola was a spoiled brat whose nanny allowed her to do whatever she liked.

Billie tried to suppress her feelings but, after Mickey slapped Ian one more time and set off another round of tears, she turned in cold fury and asked, "Have you ever in your life smacked Carola?" Clearly taken aback by the outburst, Mickey didn't reply.

Billie dispatched a flurry of letters to Wen and former colleagues in Chinese government offices in North and South America as well as China. Everyone was pleased to hear from her, but the responses were not encouraging.

Wen had been appointed as ambassador to Greece and said he wished he could take her but her British nationality excluded her from the Chinese diplomatic service. From Chicago, Fabian Chow offered her a job, but Hollington Tong had to step in and tell Billie that he was considering closing the Chicago office.

However, Holly's letter of July 10, 1947, more than hinted at promising news. "I still remember vividly your meritorious contributions to the country in Hong Kong," he wrote. "I have in mind a position of responsibility in China but I am not ready to discuss details with you."

This, of course, lifted Billie to a new peak of excitement.

Soon afterwards, Charles came into the hallway, waving a letter from China.

Holly was offering her a job in Nanking with an eye-popping salary, plus government-provided accommodation. Her full compensation package would include a salary of 5.69 million Chinese National Currency (CNC) which in early 1947 was worth about US$475, a bolt of cloth and a sack of rice, with accommodation and utilities thrown in. Moreover, the London office of the Chinese government information service would pay for the tickets and expenses of bringing her and Ian out from England.

It was puzzling that Holly was still not giving any other details. But Billie didn't mind – it sounded as if she was going to be "a little big shot."

At the same time, Wen was warning Billie that China was much changed from when she had left. "No salary that you can ever get in China will be sufficient to keep body and soul alive, unless you have private means in foreign exchange," he wrote. "A few days ago, I saw a CNC$10 bill on the road. Nobody troubled to pick it up. Ten years ago, even a 10-cent piece would disappear in a jiffy. We are living in a topsy-turvy world and no one knows what the morrow may bring. It gives me a nightmare each time I look at the papers: nothing but trouble, and all for no very good reasons."

Wen's letter did not deter Billie at all. After 18 months of frustrating dependence upon family and friends, she eagerly wanted to take back control. A flurry of activity followed as tickets and funds arrived from the Chinese information office in London and Billie rushed out to buy new clothes and provisions.

Mickey was envious that Billie was heading back east, but she was not sorry that her exasperated, and exasperating, friend was leaving.

On August 3, Billie sent a postcard from Dorchester to George with the brief message: "Both returning to China. Many thanks for past parcels. Address in future: c/o Dr Hollington K. Tong, Director, Chinese Government Information Office, Manufacturers Bank Building, Hsinchiehkou, Nanking, China."

Ten days later, she and Ian boarded the RMS *Empress of Scotland* at Liverpool, bound for Singapore and Hong Kong.

George had been right when he had told her: "You will charm everybody you meet; you will finish up with the job you want."

For George, however, things had not gone according to the plan he had outlined to Billie. Only a few months earlier, he told Ben Wylie that he would not, after all, be returning to Hong Kong.

He did not spell it out, but his wife was refusing to return to Hong Kong, where she feared many people knew what had happened between her husband and Billie in camp.

33

Little Big Shot

The *Empress of Scotland* was one of the first passenger ships to resume service to Hong Kong after the war and Billie joined two distinct groups of expatriates – returning merchants, civil servants, teachers and rubber planters (who were getting off at Singapore) and wives who were rejoining their husbands.

Billie registered on the manifest as a secretary though Holly had hinted he was offering her a "little big shot" position. She looked wistfully at the wives and their children as, at 31, she had yet to find a Prince Charming who was constant.

She was still mad with Mickey when the ship docked at Port Said and she couldn't resist sending a postcard, saying: "Everyone just loves Ian. They all take turns looking after him." It was an unsubtle dig at Mickey's Great Reform Phase.

When, four weeks later, she disembarked in Hong Kong, she found a city that was much changed from the shell she had left two years earlier. The Chinese had quickly returned, as had many of the British, and the streets were humming again.

Billie could hardly walk 50 yards in Central without seeing a familiar face – and all whom she saw were doing well. Mary Smalley, who met her off the ship, had been promoted to the administrative level of the civil service, though she had not lost her grumpiness.

Bumping into Dr Harry Talbot, Billie learned that his ear, nose and throat practice was busier than ever. Dr Talbot had famously feuded in Stanley with Mrs Flaherty, the Chinese widow of an Irish soldier, when she emerged from a spell of detention and asked him to return a chicken she left in his safe-keeping. He asked her to repay him the costs of feeding the chicken and, when she refused, he ate the bird.

"Mrs Flaherty is paying me back for eating that precious chicken," he told Billie. "Scarcely a week passes without one of the blessed Flaherty kids appearing in my clinic with one complaint or another – and their mother refuses to pay a single bill."

Billie saw a lively Eurasian friend, Janet Broadbridge, who said things were changing slowly for the better. "The British were beaten by the Japanese, so they can't be Mr High and Mighty like before," she said. "Some Chinese have moved into jobs that used to be filled by whites and others are pushing harder to move up through the ranks."

In Shanghai, her old colleague, the effervescent Jimmy Wei, one of Hollington Tong's closest aides, eyed Billie's pork-pie hat and smart English business suit and exclaimed: "*Wai kuo ren hui lai la*" (meaning "A foreign woman has come home"). This tickled Billie and Jimmy would repeat the phrase to everyone they met.

Jimmy had also brought a baby *amah* to the Bund. "Bless your heart, Jimmy," said Billie. "It was impossible to afford help for Ian in England." She handed Ian over to the *amah* and later remarked, "That was the end of my mothering days."

Jimmy gave Billie the big shot treatment, installing her in a government suite at Broadway Mansions, on the other side of Garden Bridge.

Taking the train to Nanking, Billie stepped onto the platform to be met by the information office's youthful deputy director and his wife, who was lovely, pale and had a persistent cough.

Billie had never been anywhere in China except Shanghai, and Nanking was quite different from Shanghai's cosmopolitan International Settlement. Once the imperial capital under the Ming dynasty, Nanking still had remnants of the old walls as well as temples and pagodas, but many of its roads were unpaved. Chiang Kai-shek had made Nanking his capital in 1927 and, after retreating from the Japanese during the war, returned to the city in May 1946.

Billie's first shock was her accommodation.

"The deputy director and his wife were charming and considerate," said Billie. "But when they took me to the government house we were all going to share, I was disappointed."

The rooms were bleak and gloomy, stocked with plain government-issue furniture. Worst of all, they were cold. Nanking was already entering its usual bitterly cold winter and the house's only source of heating was in the living room – a pot belly stove with a pipe that gave out noxious fumes when it clogged up and leaked.

Billie swallowed her feelings and hurried to the office to find out about her new job, which was still a mystery.

The information ministry's premises were in the downtown Manufacturers Bank Building, which was in a shabby and decrepit state. Billie saw its drab, austere furnishings – and was shocked to find the office had no heating whatsoever. The first person she saw was a tall, stooping American, Richard Lieban, who was wearing gloves and striding around, stamping his feet and moaning, "I can't stand the cold, I really can't stand it." Richard was hired as an editor from Chicago. He told her he had chilblains: "My toes are black; they look bruised all over."

Billie's new boss, Jimmy Shen (Shen Jianhong), welcomed her effusively. He was another long-standing cohort of Hollington Tong, a fellow Missouri University graduate, a senior figure in Holly's International Department and later English editor at the Central News Agency.

Only then did Billie learn about her new duties. Shen told her she was being engaged as a feature writer and that her stories would be bylined and included in a bulletin for foreign news agencies and publications. They would use the name Lee as they wanted readers to know Billie was Chinese, even if she had a British passport. Shen told her she would be the highest-paid among local staff and he was assigning her a driver, a photographer and an interpreter, the last because many Chinese from outside Nanking did not speak the local dialect.

Billie was pleased, yet puzzled. Her new position was certainly a step up from secretary, but was hardly a position of importance, and she could not imagine why Holly had considered it to be too sensitive to mention in his letter.

But she was nothing if not a trouper and, keeping on her overcoat, Billie settled behind a typewriter, though she first wrapped her hands around a cup of steaming tea to warm her fingers.

Shen, the chief editor, ran the office like a newspaper. He sent staff out on story assignments in the morning and they would write up their reports in the afternoon. Their work was distributed to foreign journalists and to the department's overseas branches.

Nanking was known as the "beautiful city with an ugly past." Its tragic history included several massacres – by Taiping rebels, by the military in 1913 and, more recently, the Rape of Nanking in 1937.

Billie discovered another dreadful side when she went to cover a memorial service held by survivors of a Japanese prison camp in the Pukou district. Its prisoners had called the camp "the Japanese Belsen" and, after interviewing survivors, Billie reported that over 4,000 prisoners, mainly Chinese officers, had had to endure starvation, bitter cold, hard labour and extreme cruelty. One survivor told her the Japanese had thrown prisoners to hungry dogs and onto barbed-wire fences. After one mass escape attempt failed, the Japanese mowed down 2,800 prisoners with machine-guns, equivalent to the entire POW population of Stanley.

Billie also interviewed Liu Weng-chin, who was campaigning to represent Nanking in the Legislative Yuan, a highly unusual action for a woman in China. Liu, who had studied at New York's Columbia University, was crusading for the emancipation of Chinese women, reminding Billie that the vast majority of Chinese women were like "small children who could not walk until they were taken by the hand and led by the government."

As she travelled around Nanking, Billie realized why she was given a jeep. The northern district, where the government buildings were located, had wide, paved boulevards and circles, but the rest of the city had earthen roads that turned to thick, cloying mud when it rained.

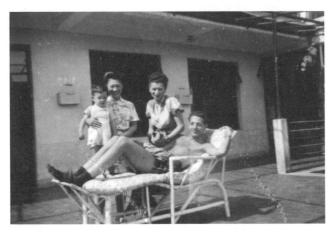

Ruth and Richard Lieban

Richard Lieban and his wife Ruth turned out to be bridge players and Billie met them often at the press hostel on Nanking Road where they lived and which was run by the wife of H.P. Tseng, head of the information services in Nanking.

Although the two-storey building was constructed by foreigners and once had central heating, the Japanese had torn out the system and taken the heavy metal pieces to a northeast corner of Nanking to transport to Japan. "The stuff just sat there and we had no central heating," said Ruth Lieban. "We had a stove with a metal pipe which ran outside and when it got blocked the room would fill with charcoal dust." Ruth loved walking but complained that she kept losing shoes in the muddy roads around the hostel.

Despite the conditions, Richard and Ruth, a charming Jewish-American couple, reduced Billie to helpless laughter regaling her with accounts of their hapless adventures. One, in particular, solved the mystery of why Holly had really brought Billie out from England.

Richard had been working for the Chinese government information office in Chicago and, after persistent applications, landed an editor's job in Nanking. Ruth had a career as a writer with one of America's top magazines before Richard asked her to give it up and join him for an Asian adventure.

"I was earning $12,000 a year, a huge salary, but Richard really wanted to go to China and when he asked the Chinese government about me, they sent a cable offering jobs to both Richard and me. I resigned my job and we went to the West Coast to get a ship to China. But there was a shipping strike and we ended up staying with Richard's parents for three months. Then a cable came from Nanking saying, 'We will have Richard, but not Ruth.' That was a big double cross, and, boy, was I mad! Richard cabled back, saying we gave up everything to go and we needed at least housing and food for me, and they agreed to that, at least."

Once they arrived in Nanking, Ruth said, an "inside source," likely Jimmy Shen, told them why they had withdrawn the offer to Ruth. It turned out that Billie had been earmarked to be personal assistant to Madame Chiang Kai-shek but, while she was en route to China, someone learned she had been living with Emily Hahn, whose book *China to Me* had included indiscretions that upset a great many people in China. Worried that Billie might inadvertently pass on information to Mickey, Nanking had changed its mind. But Billie was already en route, and it was too late to tell her to go back, so they gave her the feature-writing job intended for Ruth.

Billie listened open-mouthed to this revelation, but now she understood what Holly had meant by a "position of importance," as well as the need for discretion. She also recalled the brief conversation she had had with Madame Chiang in Hong Kong and gathered that W.H. Donald might have recommended her.

Another shock for Billie was the realization that working for the information ministry did not mean that she and Richard knew how the Nationalists' war with the Communists was going.

"I was in a barber shop in Los Angeles and read an article in *Gruen Time* magazine about a great Nationalist victory in December 1946," said Richard. "They had captured Kalgan in the north and experts estimated it would take six months for the Nationalists to complete their victory over the Communists. But when we arrived in Nanking, the journalists and the US government officials laughed and said it was all nonsense."

The capture of Yan'an by government troops on March 19, 1947, had elated the Nationalists, but the truth was that they made almost no further gains that year.

The Communists were in fact making critical inroads into central China and, even as Billie was on her way to Nanking, had caused the closing of the defensive gates at Nanking in mid-September. Two months later, in a report to the Chinese Communist Party's central committee, Mao said the Communists had taken the fight into Kuomintang territory and that this marked "a turning point in history."

In the face of such setbacks, the Nationalists sacrificed credibility. "On one occasion, we held a press conference and the Minister of Information was discussing a so-called victory in battle and said that reports were '60 per cent accurate.' What a stupid thing to say," said Richard.

Through bridge, the Liebans introduced Billie to a remarkable Englishwoman, Gladys Yang, and her Chinese husband Xianyi. They were both noted scholars. A tall, striking woman with lively blue eyes, Gladys had spent her early childhood in China as the daughter of missionaries and met Xianyi, an upper-class Chinese intellectual, at Oxford where he was reading classics and she was the first undergraduate to study Chinese.

They arrived in China in 1940, married and taught in various universities. They moved to Nanking after the war but were having trouble finding steady work, scraping by with teaching and translating Chinese classical works into English. Gladys and Xianyi smoked and drank a lot and shared an earthy humour. "They were puckish and playful," said Ruth Lieban. "Xianyi took us out to a boat that was like a gondola, with someone pushing it, on Lotus Lake. He spoke to a lovely young boat girl and told her in Chinese that Richard was Mr Lee and I was his sister. The girl cosied up to Richard and asked if she could meet him later and he was to come back at three."

The Yangs' home was without electricity or plumbing, yet Billie never heard Gladys complain. A fluent Mandarin speaker, Gladys embraced Chinese culture and way of life. She cropped her chestnut-coloured hair in the local style and wore padded jacket and pants. Their little boy had pants that opened at the back, Chinese-style, to make it easier for relief.

"Gladys, you're more Chinese than I am," said Billie, shaking her head.

"And you, Billie, are more English than me," riposted Gladys.

As Billie started work, China's rate of inflation took off on another upward climb, reaching dizzying proportions.

The Liebans told her that Richard, as an American hired from abroad, was being paid in US dollars, most of which they were able to bank as they paid no rent and their food was provided at the hostel.

Somehow, Billie, who had also been engaged from abroad and had a British passport, thought she would be protected.

But when she went to collect her pay, she found that she was paid in Chinese National Currency – and that the 5 million CNC that was worth over US$400 when she was offered the job had plummeted to US$5, barely enough to buy a loaf of bread.

She returned to the cashier and said, "Excuse me, there must be some mistake. In England, I was told my salary would be equivalent to more than $400."

The woman told her that she had given her the correct amount in CNC. "I'm afraid we're all in the same boat," she added, in tears.

"Because Billie was Chinese, they paid her an unspeakable salary in local currency," said Ruth Lieban.

It was unbelievable and terrifying. The hyperinflation gripping the country was making paupers of all Chinese, including the middle class and government employees who held secure jobs. Almost overnight, salaries became worthless and people were bartering carpets, vases, furniture and family heirlooms for food.

As prices skyrocketed, Billie saw people carrying bundles of money tied with string in wicker baskets and wheelbarrows. "People accepted them on trust as no one had time to count the notes," she said. "We had nothing to barter with so fish and meat were beyond our reach. Our *amah* scoured the market looking for the cheapest vegetables such as cabbage and bean sprouts with which to flavour the rice."

On the streets, traders hoarded and profiteered. Shops selling rice or coal or paraffin closed early so they could charge higher prices the next day. The poor begged, stole and offered daughters for sale.

The fact was that the Nationalist government was printing vast amounts of money, a short-term expedient that could lead only to disaster.

Prices rose by the day and then the hour. A hairdresser told Billie the price of her haircut had gone up since she entered the shop.

"The people who helped us were the foreign correspondents who were paid in hard foreign currencies. They would pass by our house to drop off tins of food," said Billie. "Even so, there were hungry days when I regretted leaving England and even wished we were back in Stanley, where at least we had two meals a day."

Hollington Tong felt bad as he had brought Billie out, thinking she would be protected by Madame Chiang.

On a visit to the United Nations office in Shanghai, he asked whether they had any vacancies. China was one of the "Big Four" signatories when the United Nations was set up at the end of the war and the UN had some agencies in Shanghai.

Calling on Dr Chu Pao-hsien, deputy director of the United Nations Information Centre (UNIC), Holly learned he was looking for a secretary of British nationality – and promptly recommended Billie. Dr Chu cabled her application to Lake Success, New York, along with references from Holly, Wen, Jimmy Wei and George K.C. Yeh, the Vice-Minister of Foreign Affairs.

The application took weeks to process before Holly called Billie.

"The UN has accepted your application," he told her. 'We shall be seconding you to them for three years."

Billie hesitated. "Does this mean I can come back if I wish?" she asked.

The hardship had brought all the staff closer together and it was painful to think of deserting them like a rat leaving a sinking ship.

She said goodbye to Richard and Ruth, who had started teaching at a new college set up by the Yangs. "I taught two freshman classes with 200 Chinese in each class," said Ruth. "The school wasn't finished and it was

January and very cold. The wind blew in through the windows which had no panes."

From a train steaming out of Nanking in February 1948, Billie waved goodbye to her friends with tears in her eyes. She had returned to China to do her part to help the Nationalists rebuild after the war, but instead had watched them ruin the economy.

For her new move, she was again indebted to Holly, who had come through with his promise of making her a little big shot, if not quite as he had intended.

34

Turmoil in Shanghai

Billie's return to Shanghai marked not just the start of a new career but, extraordinarily, considering all that they had been through, a reunion with her friends from Shanghai Public School for Girls.

Mavis Ming was back, once more working for the Chinese Industrial Cooperative and Pilan Petigura was secretary to Palamadai Lokanathan, the Indian head of the recently formed United Nations Economic and Social Commission for Asia and the Far East (ECAFE).

In fact, Mavis had written to her sister Edna in Australia on January 20, 1948, that one of her friends, Alice Chow, "now has a fat job with the United Nations Emergency Appeal for Children Fund…and Mary Lou (Billie) has a job in UNO so she will be able to live happily ever after."

When Billie stepped off the train in Shanghai, her SPG friend Lois hugged her, stepped back and exclaimed, "My dear, you're so thin. You look like hell."

Lois was the only one among the SPG women who had stayed in Shanghai during the war and survived, due to her resourceful now-husband Joe Larcina who obtained Spanish passports for his family to keep them out of internment camps and ran a casino for the Japanese military in the upstairs room of his brother's home.

Lois was living with her family at 19 Columbia Road in a tree-lined neighbourhood and had no hesitation inviting Billie to stay for as long as she needed. Billie was grateful for a bed on the couch, as new waves of refugees were making accommodation in Shanghai so scarce that landlords were demanding enormous down payments known as 'key money'.

When Billie mentioned she was having vaginal bleeding, Lois said, "I know just the man to take care of you. He's a brilliant gynaecologist and all the mothers adore him."

Soon afterwards, Billie sat across the desk from Dr Amos Wong (Wang Yihui), a small, vital man whom they also called the luckiest doctor in Shanghai because he had never lost a baby. Demand for his services was so high that he charged US$1,000 for a delivery at his clinic, known as the Stork Club.

When Billie described her problem, Dr Wong frowned and said he would schedule a full examination the next day. When she asked what he thought the problem might be, he said he couldn't be sure yet but needed to rule out the possibility of cancer.

Cancer! People so feared the disease they were loath to mention its name.

Billie's first thought was of Ian and who would take care of him if something happened to her. She wanted him educated in England and thus avoid the issues facing Eurasian children in Shanghai or Hong Kong. Ironically, she thought of the woman she had quarrelled with over her treatment of Ian. Despite her spat with Mickey, she knew that she and Charles could be relied on to bring up Ian. She went home and wrote to Mickey, making her unusual request and including a will, leaving everything to the Boxers. She even mailed it off immediately in case she did not survive the procedure.

The next morning, recovering from the anaesthesia, Billie opened her eyes to see Dr Wong waving a small glass bottle. Inside was what looked like a U-shaped piece of catgut. It was the stitch left behind from her Caesarean. "I felt better immediately," said Billie. "I stopped crying. I used to cry every day and I didn't know why."

Tuberculosis was rampant in Shanghai and the authorities sent out mobile radiology units to provide free tests. When a van arrived in the neighbourhood, Lois took her children and Ian along. That evening, when Billie returned from work, Lois had to break the bad news. An X-ray had found a small white patch on one of Ian's lungs. It was surprising as well as distressing, until Billie remembered the coughing of the deputy director's wife, who doctors later diagnosed with consumption, as tuberculosis was known.

Fortunately, Shanghai had an excellent sanatorium run by American doctors, but it was not cheap. The UN's medical insurance scheme covered much of the US$350 monthly cost of Ian's hospitalization, but Billie's share consumed most of her salary.

Billie and Pilan lunched together, and Billie told Mavis she could help her get a job with the UN, but Mavis preferred work that she considered had more direct impact on the needy of China.

At Whangpoo Road, Billie was helping Dr Chu publicize the work of the UN's specialized agencies, including the International Refugee Organization, headed in China by Jennings Wong. Billie would have been amazed had she known the IRO was trying to help her father's Russian "second wife" who was in dire straits four years after Frank's death.

One of the IRO's major concerns was the tens of thousands of White Russians who fled to Shanghai from other parts of China under the Communist advance. These stateless Russians knew the fate that awaited them in Stalin's Russia, but now they faced the prospect of China turning Communist, too. In 1941, Nina Kovaleva, 38, married Michael "Misha" Reuter, a compatriot from Irkutsk who was just under six feet tall and had scars on both cheeks caused by burns.

Both were lucky to be working as janitors and hoping desperately that the IRO would help them leave China. Nina's daughter Kira – the half-sister Billie did not know about – found her mother overly strict and was rebellious. At 19, Kira married an American soldier in Shanghai and was pregnant with his child when he was killed at Iwo Jima. Towards the end of the war, Kira was working as a secretary with the Armed Forces Services radio in Shanghai when she met a dashing American broadcaster named Malcolm Riddle, later marrying him and sailing to America with her daughter from her first marriage in 1946.

As Nina and Misha were struggling to get by, Billie had the rare opportunity to move into a mansion. Ruth and Richard Lieban had left Nanking and were in Shanghai on their way back to America. "There was a strike at the port and we couldn't get a ship out," Richard said. "The China Relief Mission asked us to work for them, so we worked with the Economic Cooperation Administration; Ruth was working with refugees and I was in public information."

After several housing moves, the Liebans heard that a magnificent house and garden would be available for the summer. The tenant, the Panamanian ambassador, had gone on leave. They asked if Billie would share the rent with them.

It was a fabulous offer. Along with the house, which was in Holly Heath, along elegant Amherst Avenue, they would have use of the ambassador's staff, which included a cook.

Each evening, she and the Liebans enjoyed a sumptuous dinner in a large, ornate dining room under a glittering chandelier.

Living in such style, albeit temporarily, Billie celebrated her 32nd birthday in the mansion, inviting a wide variety of friends. Lois and Joe, and Mavis were there. Mama's friends like the Doodhas and Hans Kellner and his wife,

Billie and Ian in the garden of the Holly Heath mansion

were among the guests. Also there were Jimmy Wei from the information ministry and Zau Sinmay and poet William Empson from the *T'ien Hsia* crowd. The first thing Sinmay said to Billie was, "Why did Mickey write those things about me?" He was referring to Mickey's references to him in *Mr. Pan* and *China to Me* which he thought made him look ridiculous. Among the photographs in the *North-China Daily News* the next day,

June 14, was one of Billie looking radiant in a long black dress, standing between Alice Chow, Jennings Wong, the IRO China chief, Sinmay and Empson.

Billie with Alice Chow, Jennings Wong, Zau Sinmay and William Empson

One Sunday soon afterwards, Billie held a small party at Holly Heath for Lois and other friends and their children. After lunch, they were chatting in the garden when Billie dozed off. She slept in her chair for an hour and, when she woke up, Lois chided her, saying, "Billie, how can you go to sleep at your own party?"

Still drowsy, Billie began to dress up, as she had to go to a local radio station to deliver a United Nations announcement. She asked Lois to accompany her to the studio, as she was feeling dizzy and alternately hot and cold. In front of the microphone, Billie somehow managed to get through the script but, immediately afterwards, fainted. Lois helped take her home to bed where, despite the warm summer evening, she shivered uncontrollably beneath layers of blankets.

The next morning, when Billie's temperature rose sharply, the Liebans called in Dr Wong, whom they also knew from bridge.

Billie and Ian with birthday party guests Lois, Mavis and Alice

"As soon as Dr Wong saw Billie curled up and facing the wall because she couldn't bear the light, he suspected spinal meningitis," said Richard Lieban.

Spinal meningitis was a dreaded disease that was highly contagious and often fatal. "Everyone was terrified because we all had contact with her," said Ruth. "Our office was immediately placed under wraps."

Dr Wong instructed the ambulance driver to take Billie to his private clinic, but he mistakenly took Billie to the Stork Club, where news of the arrival of a spinal meningitis case caused pandemonium among the mothers-to-be who fled as fast as they could.

Since Billie had to be isolated, Amos Wong installed her in the attic of his house, next door to the hospital. For days, Billie tossed and turned deliriously, her life in the balance. The only person she saw was Dr Wong, who remained steadfastly calm and reassuring, never seeming concerned about the risk of being infected.

Fortunately, an injection of penicillin every few hours proved an effective, if painful, antidote.

Billie was unaware that she had become a celebrity – in the worst way – after the radio announced that Shanghai had a case of spinal meningitis. She was later told that the newscaster advised all who had been in contact with her to get inoculated. This triggered widespread alarm for Billie had had contact with a large number of people. As well as attending an official reception, she had been at the microphone in a talent contest for amateur singers. All her UN colleagues rushed for vaccinations and her boss, Dr Chu Pao-hsien, insisted on a double dose and ran a fever as a reaction.

Billie remained in isolation for weeks and her only diversion was going to the attic window and waving as Lois held Ian up in the street outside.

She left Dr Wong's care to find the city in turmoil. In August 1948 the government abolished the currency and replaced it with the gold yuan, pegged at four to the American dollar. The government fixed prices by decree and required all Chinese, under penalty of death, to hand over gold, silver, Chinese or foreign currency, to the Central Bank in exchange for gold yuan. In Shanghai, they sent out a large force of police and spies to implement this policy.

However, the programme proved disastrous, the rate holding for only a few weeks before the gold yuan became worthless. Millions of people were ruined.

The Nationalists were throwing away their last chance of holding on and rumours of a Communist takeover grew louder each day. At the UN agencies, the bosses were sending frantic cables to headquarters, urging a transfer to another regional base.

Billie's colleagues and friends had difficult decisions to make.

In November, 1948, with news that Communist forces had advanced around Shanghai, the UN instructed Dr Chu and Billie that they should leave for Hong Kong.

Dr Chu adored his wife and three sons, and he was also intensely patriotic. He became increasingly conflicted between concern for his family and the desire to stay and help his country.

Billie took Ian, not to the Bund as on previous occasions, but to Lunghwa airport for their first trip on an aeroplane. Billie was excited but nervous, too, as flights were not always straightforward in those early days of commercial aviation; only a few days later, a China National Aviation Corp (CNAC) DC-4 arriving from Shanghai crashed in poor visibility into a hill on Hong Kong's Basalt Island, killing all on board, including Quentin Roosevelt, grandson of American president Theodore Roosevelt.

Adding to the tension, Dr Chu and his family did not show up. Billie waited until the last moment before boarding the plane for Hong Kong. It was one of the last flights operated by CNAC before the Communists nationalized it.

Billie was more fortunate than Nina and Misha Reuter who were in a desperate race against time. The IRO was asking countries to provide temporary shelter for White Russians but was drawing no response until the new Philippine president, Elpidio Quirino, agreed to make the small island of Tubabao in eastern Samar available as a Russian refugee camp. Soon, Nina and Misha were among the 6,000 Russians trying to reach the Philippines by any means, even rusty vessels.

As the bamboo curtain came down, Billie's friends, including Gladys and Xianyi Yang, Zau Sinmay and Dr Amos Wong, decided to stay to see what would happen.

Pilan moved to Bangkok with ECAFE and Lois and Joe fled to Hong Kong. The Liebans left in early 1949, the US consulate evacuating them with six hours' notice in the middle of the night, forcing them to leave many of their belongings behind.

The feisty Mavis stayed and witnessed the occupation of Shanghai by the Communists. She said the troops, mostly peasants from the countryside, were well-behaved and lived and ate on the street, without looting, and that students and workers greeted them enthusiastically.

35

Coup de Foudre

In Hong Kong, while waiting for instructions, Billie did something that illustrated her methodical character. Now that she had recovered her health, and was in British territory, she changed her will and registered it with the Supreme Court on November 22, 1948, stipulating that, should Ian die before her, her estate would go to Jessie and Dolly rather than Mickey. Whatever differences she may have had with Jessie, family came first.

The UN told her to fly to Manila, even without Dr Chu and, in the city that had barred her ship from docking four years earlier, Foreign Ministry officials accorded her VIP treatment.

They escorted her to a waiting car and drove her along the palm-lined Dewey Boulevard (now known as Roxas Boulevard), following the curve of the bay where Dr Smalley had made his timely intervention.

White-capped bellboys opened the doors at the elegant Manila Hotel, and as she checked in at the opulent lobby she noted a sign requesting patrons to deposit their firearms at the desk.

Soon after, in her room, Billie heard several sharp retorts that sounded like gunfire. Alarmed, she rang the service bell and asked the room boy what was happening.

"Don't worry, Ma'am," he said. "It's just one man shoot another man."

"What?" cried Billie. "What was the reason?"

"This other man was dancing with his girl," was the reply.

When Dr Chu arrived with his wife and their three teenage boys, he told Billie their mission was to set up UNIC in Manila. Given that one of the UN's main tasks was to rebuild a war-devastated Asia, this appeared an easy sell. A short walk from the Manila Hotel, the old Spanish capital of Intramuros still lay in ruins.

While nationalist movements were springing up around Southeast Asia, America had already given the Philippines its independence and Elpidio Quirino was the second home-grown president in this new era. Hosting a United Nations agency would help the country access assistance from the international community while Manila would be a good base for the UN, with its well-educated, English-speaking workforce.

Billie recalled that she accompanied Dr Chu daily to the Foreign Ministry in Malacañang Palace to discuss this opportunity. These commutes were hot and dusty, with horns honking and radios blaring from the *jeepneys*, the public utility vehicles converted from American jeeps left behind after the war.

Dr Chu and Billie had to adjust to the local timetable as officials started work late in the morning, took a siesta after lunch and resumed work in the late afternoon. They also had to accept the unhurried culture of *mañana* (tomorrow), meaning that matters could always be deferred.

To his dismay, Dr Chu found it difficult to find anyone to take the UN proposal seriously.

As well as being frustrated by the lack of progress, Dr Chu was obsessed with what was happening back in China. He scoured the Chinese-language newspapers and wondered aloud whether he should return and help the revolutionaries.

"We are Chinese, Billie," he would say, his eyes glistening. "We cannot run away from our country. We have a contribution to make. Our country needs us."

Billie found much to like about Manila, which was likely to be her next permanent residence. The people were warm and friendly and she had struck up a relationship at the Foreign Ministry with Isabella, a slim, pretty *mestiza,* the Spanish term for the offspring of Spanish and Filipinos and other children of mixed parentage. Far from being treated as second-class citizens, *mestizas* were well regarded, especially for their physical beauty.

But Dr Chu and Billie were concerned over the exorbitant costs of staying in the Manila Hotel, which consumed not only their *per diem* allowance but a chunk of their salary, too. The hotel charged such a hefty fee for using the swimming pool, for example, that Billie had to restrict her use to dipping Ian into the water. Even a trip to the movies over-stretched her budget.

To solve the problem, Dr Chu and Billie decided to move to apartments. Dr Chu and his family had barely moved into their flat when a group of men paid a visit and demanded money to protect them from the Huks.

"I don't understand what they want. Who are the Huks? And why would I need protection from them?" Dr Chu said to Billie. A Foreign Ministry official explained that the Huks were Communist rebels in the countryside fighting against the powerful oligarchy, and this had been an attempt at extortion.

Shortly afterwards, the UN told Dr Chu and Billie to pack up immediately and move to Bangkok where ECAFE had established its new headquarters. Everything was in a rush, and they forfeited the deposits on their apartments.

When they landed at Don Mueang airport in February 1949, Thai immigration officials sat behind wooden desks at an open-air shed under a corrugated roof. Pilan, working for the ECAFE head, met Billie and took her to the Rattanakosin Hotel, which had opened a few years earlier.

Alone in Southeast Asia, Thailand had not been colonized and the Thais were a proud, gracious and easy-going people with a distinctive culture. Though the Japanese had used Thailand to access other countries, the country had largely escaped the horrors and destruction faced by its neighbours. Food was abundant and seeing farmers tilling their fields with ploughs and water buffaloes and the saffron-robed Buddhist monks walking in ornate temples, Billie felt that she had found an oasis of tranquillity.

She was settling Ian to sleep at the hotel when she heard gunfire that sounded remarkably close. The noise was coming from machine-guns mounted outside on Ratchadamnoen Avenue and pointing towards the government radio station.

She rushed to the lobby, where guests were milling around, some in their night clothes. Hotel staffers were telling them, "This is nothing serious. We are quite safe. There is nothing to worry about."

The guests returned to their rooms and the firing gradually petered out. The next morning, Billie found the staff serving breakfast and acting as if nothing had happened. The UN station wagon arrived as usual to collect her, and the streets were full of people going about their business.

At the office, a colleague greeted her: "Congratulations on your first coup. You aren't considered a proper resident until you have been through three coups."

This "palace rebellion", an attempt by the Navy to replace Prime Minister Pribul (aka Phibun) with its own candidate, Pridi, was suppressed by the Army.

Colleagues assured her that, while coups in Thailand were often bloody, they involved only rival factions, rarely affected the public and had negligible impact on the running of the country. Thailand's unifying influence was a young King Bhumibol, revered as a deity, and a government bureaucracy that stayed in place no matter which political group was in power. Beneath the apparent volatility, close links between politicians, generals and bureaucrats made Thai politics a game of musical chairs, where people changed seats and took their turn at the helm.

Billie found a place of her own for the first time, renting a new two-bedroomed bungalow with a garden of mango and banana trees on Kasemsanta, a dusty street off a major road, Rama I, near the national stadium. Her landlord was a Thai prince, who lived next door.

At the office – the government loaned ECAFE Paruskawan Palace, a comfortable though not palatial building – Billie joined a close-knit group of 80 regular staff who were enthusiastic about helping to create a new peaceful world order, though it would not take long before harsh realities set in.

A birthday party for Ian at the first home Billie could call her own

A shortage of skilled staff opened one door after another for Billie. She worked for the chief of the research and statistical division and, with English proficiency in short supply, they needed her precis-writing skill at ECAFE meetings. When the Chief of Registry became ill and flew back to England, Billie took charge of the Secretariat's typing pool and records of outward and inward correspondence and cables. Later, she took charge of the documents section and her bosses would recommend her for promotion to professional staff.

Billie tried to acclimatize to Bangkok's tropical weather before air-conditioning was available. Sweltering nights under a mosquito net made sleep difficult and, when the monsoon brought cooler weather, she sometimes screamed when snakes slithered into the house after a flood and the gardener would come running in with a rake.

In the office, fans were of little use against the oppressive heat, and staff worked from 7am to 2pm, after which Billie would drop by the Royal Bangkok Sports Club to cool off in the pool or play bridge. Through bridge, she met David Spriggs, a younger man who worked for the Bombay Burmah Trading Corporation; and Johnny Sutherland, a dapper ex-Royal Air Force pilot, and his Eurasian girlfriend, Lulu Smith. A besotted Johnny wanted to marry her but Lulu, older by a few years, declined his proposals, saying that he would one day leave her for a younger woman.

The foursome spent weekends visiting temples or floating markets on the Chao Phraya River and taking trips to the ancient royal cities of Ayutthaya and Bang Pa-In or the mountain town of Chiang Mai.

Billie reconnected with the Stanley network, too. Vivacious Patti Mace, whose husband Rupert represented the Swedish match company, lived in a sprawling house across from a kindergarten run by a German woman, Mrs Schaller, and helped get Ian into the school. Ian's godmother, Rosaleen, wrote to Billie saying she was divorced, her mother had died, and she was looking for work. She came to Bangkok and Billie helped her find a job with the British Embassy, where they would hold birthday parties for Ian. Billie also enrolled her son in the Klong Toey pony club, run by another German, Mrs Koch, and he took part in gymkhanas at the Royal Bangkok Sports Club.

Billie organised Ian's sixth birthday party at the British Embassy

Billie was finding life pleasantly routine but it did include disruptions. She woke one night to see, through the mosquito net, a man in black shirt and trousers standing by her dressing table, picking things up and handing them out of the window. Suddenly, the man turned, and Billie saw he had a knife in his hand. He approached the bed as Billie lay still, suppressing an urge to scream. She saw the man cut through the cord of the electric fan, which disappeared out of the window.

The man stepped out of the side door leading to the veranda. After a while, Billie got out of bed and, in the gloom, could see two men kneeling on the grass, piling objects onto a white cotton counterpane. Suddenly, someone began screaming. It took Billie a few seconds to realize it was herself. The startled men hurriedly wrapped up the counterpane and ran off. Billie found herself shouting plaintively, "Come back, please come back!"

The noise woke up her household and that of the prince next door and the police soon arrived. Billie found the robbers had taken every stitch of her clothing, leaving her with only the nightgown she was wearing. A seamstress had to come to her house the next day to make up new clothes.

The incident prompted ECAFE to complain to the Thai authorities, who provided Billie with a night watchman.

Dr Chu had an unnerving experience, too. He and his family slept upstairs and came down one morning to find their living room and kitchen stripped bare of appliances and even large pieces of furniture. It was common for thieves to use incense, which induced a deep sleep, and police suspected this was the case with Dr Chu and his family.

Dr Chu kept Billie updated on China, waving news clippings, often about how some measure of the new regime was improving the lot of the workers.

Billie arrived at work to find Dr Chu, arms akimbo, but smiling.

"I've done it, Billie. I've resigned. I'm taking my family back to China," he said.

In addition to her regular duties, Billie took verbatim notes of ECAFE meetings

Even after seeing Dr Chu wrestle with his conscience for months, Billie was surprised as she never thought he would go home to an uncertain future. She and the other staff held an emotionally charged farewell for their well-respected colleague.

Meanwhile, the cracks were showing at ECAFE. The commission's task was to gather and analyse data to deal with the economic problems of the region's vastly disparate countries. But politicking from the start was a huge obstacle to regional cooperation.

The Soviet Union objected to almost every proposal, treating the forum as a front in the rapidly emerging Cold War while the Western powers, still wearing colonial lenses, focused on their own areas of interest to the neglect of Asia as a whole.

In 1949, the UN's Expanded Programme of Technical Assistance offered a great opportunity to channel funds through ECAFE. But New York controlled the funds as well as making all the big decisions, leaving Asian governments feeling that ECAFE "was a mere talking shop and of little practical value," as one report noted.

Pilan vented her frustrations to Billie over lunches and quit her job.

Billie told Mickey she had given Pilan her number in case she turned up in London. "Pilan quit last week and bought herself a ticket to Bombay, then on to Rome, and I think she will land in London sometime next month. She is a wonderful girl and has plenty of guts," wrote Billie on April 11, 1949. "Believe it or not, I have got a credit balance in my account at last and feel wealthy for the first time in my life. If I wasn't so earnest in trying to stack up another thousand dollars, I would have gone with her, with things as they are in this set-up."

Billie confessed to Mickey that the one thing missing in her life was romance. "Yes, I remember telling Irene [a mutual friend] that I was going to look for a rich husband," she wrote. "I don't know why I said it except perhaps that I had just been told that the Giffens have had another baby. The chances are that I will probably never find that rich husband. Up till now, anyway, there's no one in sight, not even a very poor one."

Billie routinely attended cocktail parties hosted by the UN or the British Embassy to mark events like the Queen's birthday or to welcome special visitors, but the men she met were almost always married.

A month later, Billie learned that Jessie had died in her London office, slumped over her typewriter, at 46. Like Mama and Frank, she had succumbed to heart failure. Billie could not help wondering if she, too, would die alone.

Then the horizon brightened. "The doctor said I was mad to burn up so much energy in this trying weather and said I needed a good, long holiday. Actually, in spite of the diagnosis, I have never felt better even though I have a stupid temperature every evening," she wrote to Mickey on August 11, 1949. "Perhaps the truth is I have been too rapturously preoccupied to notice anything. I really meant to tell you all about it last month. But it seemed that everything was over just as it had scarcely begun. I expect I am talking in riddles. What I should have said is, 'I met Leslie last month…' He's nice, Mickey, awfully, awfully nice. I am quite sure that you would agree.

"Anyway, he kept me happy for fully three weeks and then he had to leave Bangkok for Hong Kong, and now I am simply straining at the leash for his return. He is here on a year's contract with United Nations to audit all the UN books in the Far East. I really don't know how things will turn out, Mickey. I am not even sure how he really feels about me. But it seems so long ago that anyone ever made a fuss about me that it's nicer than I can ever remember it being. Anyhow, Mickey, wish me luck."

As it turned out, Billie never mentioned Leslie again, but the letter showed that she was once more open to amour.

On December 23, 1952, the *Bangkok Post* ran a brief news item that a British Council representative, Dr James Noonan, a London University lecturer, would be coming to Thailand to advise on methods of language teaching and the training of teachers.

Jimmy Noonan

Billie took no notice of the report as she had bigger issues on her mind. Excitingly, at 36, her bosses were proposing to promote her to the professional grade, a big jump. Her once unlikely plan to send Ian to school in England was actually taking shape. On an earlier 'home leave' to England, she had taken Ian to a Catholic public (i.e. in British usage, private) school in the Midlands and reserved a place for him, starting in 1953. Like other British expatriates, she planned to continue her job and fly Ian back from boarding school for the holidays.

She received an invitation from the British Council to attend a dinner to meet Dr Noonan and, on February 13, 1953, found herself seated next to him at the table. In his early forties, Dr Noonan looked distinguished, with black-rimmed glasses and swept-back, grey-flecked hair; his sparkling smile and dapper white suit suggested he was no dry academic. Clever and scholarly, without a trace of pedantry, he reminded Billie of her father.

Jimmy, as he insisted that she call him, was a lecturer in linguistics at the University of London but travelled frequently for the British Council and was on a tour that included Burma, Indonesia, Malaysia and Singapore.

Although he said it was his first trip to Asia, he seemed remarkably well informed about the region. He did not explain why a linguistics lecturer should visit these countries, but it was well known that the British Council provided information on local politics to the Foreign Office.

"Jimmy was a witty conversationalist and showed keen interest in my background. I couldn't recall when I had enjoyed a dinner more in Bangkok," said Billie. She noticed his eyes had grey irises, flecked with white.

A few days later, Billie was renewing her passport at the British Embassy when she bumped into Jimmy, who was calling on the ambassador.

Jimmy asked Billie to join him for dinner. She told him she was disappointed that she had something on that night, but Jimmy, who was leaving for Burma the next day, said they could meet in a week upon his return.

After learning that the British Council was giving Jimmy another dinner when he got back, Billie arranged pre-dinner cocktails for him in her garden. Jimmy called from the airport and, after a quick change at the hotel, arrived at the bungalow.

Over dinner, they found themselves side by side again. Conversation rippled between them to the point where Billie felt they were anticipating each other's remarks. When a gramophone record began to play, Jimmy took Billie's hand and led her to the floor, where she was thrilled to find he danced divinely. Whatever the music, they fell effortlessly in step. By the small hours, they were staring at each other in bemusement.

When Jimmy said he was falling in love, she laughed, replying, "It must be the champagne."

She recalled later, "We danced all night and by dawn we knew it was a *coup de foudre* for both of us. He was off to Kuala Lumpur at noon the next day and I vaguely remember seeing him off at Don Mueang airport, where we embraced passionately, and returning home on cloud nine. I stayed quite dazed for a long time."

36

Into the Flames

Two days later, Jimmy's first letter arrived, penned in flight on a Comet, in his small, cramped scrawl that was difficult to decipher.

"I'm still in the daze and haze of the last 24 hours," he wrote. "What did happen to us, my darling? It will be a few days yet before I get it all sorted out – but this I do know, that for both of us a wonderful miracle, the kind of miracle that occurs to very few people, has happened for us, and I thank all the gods that exist for bringing it to me. Because you see, my darling, I love you. That, now and forever, is and will be the supreme fact of my existence. To start to try to explain or to analyse all this would be like explaining the glory of a sunset or dissecting the beauty of a flower. The miracle has happened, my dearest, and we mustn't question its reality."

Billie thought it was all too fantastic to be real. It seemed surreal, but she knew Jimmy was no fly-by-night chancer; he was a respected London University lecturer, endorsed by the British Council.

Sensing her doubt, Jimmy wrote, "This is the real thing, dearest – don't ever doubt that and I'll just live until I hear from you again. Write soon, Billie darling, very, very soon because all my happiness is in the scope of your hands."

Jimmy said he needed a few days to sort out his feelings and, when his second letter arrived from the Majestic Hotel in Kuala Lumpur, Billie found herself opening it with trepidation.

"I no longer have any doubts about what happened to us both, no doubts and no fears and I pray that you have none either, my darling," he wrote. "When you write, my darling, please tell me all the things I want most to hear, that for you, too, a miracle has taken place, transforming the whole of life and giving it new meaning."

Every few days brought a new letter, each more passionate than the last. Then from Jakarta came a startling invitation: "I have to go by Constellation from here to Singapore and then on to Colombo. Could you possibly come to Singapore for three or four days, my darling? The idea sounds absolute heaven to me. Do try to make it possible, my sweet. I love you, my dearest, and I want you so much that I've got an intolerable ache inside me all the time."

Billie knew what this meant, and asked if he was sure.

From Bandung came a swift

London Educator Coming To Bangkok

Bangkok Post

LONDON—(BIS)—Dr. J.A. Noonan, lecturer at the Institute of Education in London University, is coming to the Far East early in 1952 for the British Council to advise on methods of language teaching and the training of teachers.

Dr. Noonan leaves for Thailand on December 31 and on January 17 goes to Burma where he will remain until February 13, *when he will come to life.*

Billie kept the news item about the event that changed her life

reproach. "Am I very, very sure that I want you to come? What an extraordinary question, my dear! Why not ask me if I am very sure that I breathe, that I get up in the morning, that I go to bed at night or even that I occasionally think? Because, darling mine, since our miracle happened, I breathe-Billie, I get up-Billie, I go to bed-Billie, I think-Billie. I find you at the most probable and the most improbable moments and I haven't even got a photograph to remind me of what you look like."

Billie knew this was a turning point. At 36, she had seen the best and worst of humanity, survived terrible losses, and considered herself worldly wise.

"I didn't hesitate to accept that lovely romantic idea," she said. "Always, always, I grasped whatever it was that presented itself to me, never regretting, never wishing otherwise, never even imagining that things could have been totally different. And so it was with our love. Our chemicals were absolutely right. Jimmy was so intense and compelling and my feelings for him totally overshadowed all my earlier emotions which in my naivete I had foolishly mistaken for love."

She flew into Singapore's Kallang airport on Good Friday, April 3, 1953. She went to the Adelphi Hotel, unpacked and tidied up before going back to the airport to meet Jimmy. As soon as he appeared on the landing steps, Jimmy waved and ran across the tarmac, leaning over the barrier to kiss her.

"Every moment from then on was very precious and very beautiful," Billie recalled. They had a candlelit dinner at the Prince's Hotel, with violins playing at their table. The following night, they dined and danced at the Sea View Hotel. "I was ecstatically happy," she said. "I wore a dress of pillar-box red tulle, yards and yards of it with two large feathers."

Jimmy told her he was married. He said he met his wife when he was a student, staying at her guest house. She was a much older woman who helped him out and he married her out of gratitude. He said it was a big mistake, for it was a sham marriage and they had no children together. He had not known love until now, he told her, and spoke of a future with her once he sorted things out. He made her promise she would have no doubts about this.

"He asked me to believe in him," said Billie. "Love asks no questions, nor does it have any doubts. My trust and belief in him were as total as my love for him."

Jimmy, who was 43, didn't talk much about his past. He said he was Scottish by birth, that he had adored his mother, who had died, but did not mention his father, who was a schoolmaster six years younger than her. He had done very well at Oxford, which she could well believe.

In Singapore, after three days and nights together, Billie and Jimmy parted on Easter Monday, she for Bangkok and he for England. She was going to England in September to put Ian into prep school, so they faced a separation of several months.

In his next letter, Jimmy wrote: "I haven't the slightest recollection of what time we emerged from our room for dinner on Good Friday, or what we ate or drank. But the turn of your head, the movements of your arms and hands, the breathless kisses, all those things are very real. I don't remember a great deal about the views of Singapore. But I remember vividly the drops of perspiration on your upper lip and forehead, I remember the touch of your hand as I helped you up and down that grassy slope."

Over the next several months, he penned a sheaf of letters which Billie read and re-read countless times. He wrote from a Qantas flight: "Even though the seat beside me is empty of you, I'm not in the least unhappy because the real you is here right inside me, never to go away again, and I am praying, my dear one, that you feel exactly the same."

His next letter, however, contained the news that his wife was seriously ill. "Please don't worry, my own sweetheart. There's nothing I can't stand now that I know beyond all doubt that you are in my heart forever," he said. "My body may be here in a plane but the real me is not here – it's in Singapore in the place of our own heaven and there it will remain, reliving the ecstasy we found until we are together again. Have you, too, my dearest, got that mystic feeling of belonging, utterly and irrevocably, as I have?"

His wife's condition remained uncertain for weeks. The doctors said she needed an operation, which had to be postponed until an inflammation subsided. Jimmy said they suspected his wife had cancer and he could not ask for his freedom under the circumstances.

"Can you wait for me, my darling?" he asked. The question was unnecessary as he knew her answer.

For Billie's birthday on 14 June, Jimmy gave her a pair of marcasite earrings that he had taken from his mother's brooch and reset in silver to match a dress Billie had worn in Singapore.

Towards the end of June, Jimmy said his wife had had her operation which was successful, but she needed to remain in hospital for several weeks, followed by a lengthy period of recuperation.

Jimmy went to Daniel Neal, the school outfitter, to ask about Ian's wardrobe and shoes. "It was so exciting, my darling, making all these arrangements. It will be lovely to go there with you and Ian to try everything to see that he's the smartest little boy that ever went to prep school."

Though his personal situation was unsettled, Jimmy repeatedly said he wanted her to join him in London on a permanent basis.

This was a huge step. If she resigned from the UN, Billie would miss out on her promotion as well as the educational allowances for the rest of Ian's schooling; but she calculated she had enough in her pension fund to take care of his school fees until things sorted themselves out.

She handed in her notice and, at a farewell party, Mr Lokanathan, the ECAFE executive secretary, presented her with a Chinese hand-carved teak bar.

Billie flew out of Bangkok with Ian on September 10, 1953, via Beirut, Rome and Amsterdam and it was late when they touched down at London airport. Jimmy took them to the Russell Hotel in Holborn, near the university. In their room was a bouquet of flowers and a poem entitled *Waiting*, which Jimmy had composed for her. He also wrote, "This I can promise you, my own dearest darling. Never, never, never in my life or in my actions will I ever do anything consciously to cause you a single second of unhappiness."

They found a furnished one-bedroom flat in Crouch Hill, overlooking Alexandra Palace, and she made it homely with her Chinese pieces.

"I always wanted to be a wife and mother," said Billie. "I never intended to be a career woman. I was forced only by circumstances to earn a living."

With Jimmy, she lunched at a city oyster bar or watched a West End play or the cinema in the evening. She met two of Jimmy's colleagues, Valentine and Edna. A tall, well-built man with blonde hair, Valentine was Jimmy's closest friend; Billie soon realized that Valentine was married and that red-haired Edna was his girlfriend. The four would often lunch over white wine at the National Liberal Club, where Jimmy was a member.

In between his lecturing, the British Council kept Jimmy busy with assignments abroad but he kept their passion alive with telegrams and

Jimmy and his London University colleague Valentine

letters sent through the diplomatic bag. Billie was bemused by the new ways he found to express his feelings and, more than once, she wondered if it was his frequent absences that kept their relationship at a high pitch.

They celebrated their first anniversary on 13 February, 1954, by dining and dancing at the Piccadilly Hotel and Jimmy gave her a silver dressing table set from Greece.

Whenever Billie asked about his wife, Jimmy would say that she was dying and made it clear he was loath to discuss the matter. Anxious not to spoil their moments together, she stopped asking.

Financial problems began to crop up. Although he earned a good salary, Jimmy said his wife's nursing home bills and their Oxford home consumed almost all of it, which meant he could not contribute as much as he wanted to. Billie began to dip into the savings she had set aside for Ian's schooling.

Billie found shift work at the BBC as a typist, but the pay was low and hours were often at night. She applied to the United Nations' European headquarters in Geneva and was rewarded with a summer contract with the Economic and Social Council (ECOSOC) conference.

The temporary job introduced Billie to a charming French-speaking city at the foot of Lake Geneva.

Jimmy and Ian joined her during the summer, strolling around the cobbled lanes of the old town, boating on Lake Geneva, and visiting Billie's office at the white marbled Palais des Nations.

Billie found it depressing to return to London and begin another search for accommodation among gloomy, overpriced flats with gas heaters that devoured piles of shillings while giving out minimal heat.

The winter of 1954 was long and dreary, with Jimmy away for three months in West Africa and, upon his return, spending Christmas with his wife who, he said, was in a nursing home.

In early 1955, she was sipping tea at a friend's home in Hampstead when a neighbour dropped by and, hearing that Billie was looking for somewhere to live, offered her a one-bedroom flat in the house next door.

The basement flat was cosy, drawing its light from large windows opening up to a garden. Billie was sure the rent was beyond her budget but the abstracted landlord had little inclination for business and had trouble coming up with a figure. When he mumbled, "How does five guineas a week sound?" Billie could hardly believe her luck. She and Jimmy celebrated their second anniversary by moving into 6 Frognal Gardens.

In Hampstead, Billie found a cosmopolitan group of friends and entered her happiest period. Bettina Lanigan, a vivacious American actress who always had a hilarious story to share, became a special friend. Her

Australian husband John was a Covent Garden opera singer. Vida Hope, an actress and director of the long-running play, *The Boy Friend*, and her director-husband Derek Twist lived in the flat above. Another neighbour was Maggie Kraus, a pretty, excitable and disorganised Irish woman who spent money as fast as her globe-trotting Jewish businessman husband could earn it. Such friends eased Billie's loneliness when Jimmy was away and shared in the celebrations when he came home.

That winter, Billie was ecstatic when Jimmy had no overseas assignment and would spend Christmas with her and Ian. It was their first Christmas together and she cooked a turkey. Carollers came to the door and Billie held Jimmy's arm tightly as they listened to *Hark! The Herald Angels Sing!* She wished the moment would last forever.

In January 1957, after Jimmy left for yet another trip, Billie felt unusually tired and started to haemorrhage. The doctor sent her to hospital and Billie didn't know what was happening until the doctor told her she had had a miscarriage. She was despondent over losing the baby, as she knew Jimmy had no children and adored Ian. Jimmy, however, took the news in his stride.

Jimmy never failed to bring gifts after a trip, such as a ring from Cairo or a jewellery box and plate from Damascus and, as he breezed in from Hamburg, he gave Billie another beautifully-wrapped present. She smiled when she saw three pairs of nylons, but then she noticed the size.

"They're lovely, darling, but these are size 10½ and I am 8½," she said.

Jimmy knitted his brows in annoyance. "That stupid girl in the shop made a mistake. I was in such a hurry to catch the plane I didn't check whether she had given me the right size." Billie shrugged it off.

A few weeks later, the landlord came down to see Billie and, obviously embarrassed, handed her a cheque from Jimmy. It was stamped with the words, "Insufficient funds – return to sender." When Billie told Jimmy what had happened, he reddened with anger.

"Those idiots at the bank don't know what they're doing," he said. "My pay cheque goes in there every month. It's obviously a mistake. Just send it back."

With Jimmy in Trafalgar Square, September 1953

Billie did as he advised, but the cheque bounced again. When she called the bank, she was told there had been no error. Moreover, she could not discuss it with Jimmy as he had left on a long trip to Japan and India.

That summer, Billie did another stint with ECOSOC in Geneva, but found it difficult to keep her mind on work. Jimmy's letters continued to arrive, though less frequently than before.

She and Ian returned to Hampstead in mid-September. The British Council called, requesting Billie to tell Jimmy to come and see them as soon as he arrived the following day.

"There must be some mistake," said Billie. "Jimmy's not coming back till the end of the month."

There was a pause while the man from the Council checked his schedule. "No," he said, "Mr Noonan is due to arrive tomorrow."

The next day, Billie wrestled over whether or not to meet Jimmy. The BOAC plane was due late that evening and the airport bus would arrive at the Cromwell Road terminal around midnight. Despite the late hour, she took Ian with her. Ian asked if she was looking forward to seeing Jimmy. Billie didn't reply. She wanted to see Jimmy, but she didn't want to catch him out in a lie. As the airport bus rolled into the terminal, Ian spotted Jimmy sitting on the top deck.

They waited for Jimmy to walk into the terminal before Billie stepped forward. As soon as he saw them, he walked towards her, arms outstretched, his face a wreath of smiles. "Why weren't you at the airport to meet me?" he asked. "And what is Ian doing up at this hour?"

Jimmy did not ask how Billie knew he was on that flight. They were tired and Billie didn't want to question him in front of her son and the taxi ride was spent in silence.

The next morning, Jimmy went upstairs to the bathroom. After a restless night, Billie waited to talk to him. Just as she began to wonder why Jimmy was taking such a long time, he appeared at the bedroom door, white as chalk, clutching his stomach and groaning. He collapsed on the bed.

The doctor diagnosed a perforated stomach ulcer and summoned an ambulance. Billie went with Jimmy, holding his hand, to the hospital.

The next day, when Billie and Ian went to see Jimmy, they were surprised to see that he had a visitor on either side, a large, ruddy-faced middle-aged woman and a tall young man. Jimmy had tubes coming out of his mouth and nose and was unable to talk. He could do little other than switch his eyes between Billie and the other woman.

Billie realized this could only be Jimmy's wife, a hale and hearty woman who was purported to have lain at death's door these past few years. The other woman remained calm and self-possessed. With her arms folded, she gave Billie a look of contempt.

Blind with tears, Billie stumbled out of the ward. She and Ian reached the High Street before they noticed a young man walking rapidly behind them. Apologetically, he introduced himself as Jimmy's stepson.

He told Billie that Jimmy lived with him and his mother in Oxford. Billie stared at him, open-mouthed. "But that's not possible. He's been living with us for four years."

It was the young man's turn to look incredulous.

"Are we talking about the same man?" he asked.

Ian had a few more days of his holiday left, but there were no more outings. Oblivious to him, Billie spent hours bent over her dressing table, her chest wracked with deep sobs.

Slowly, Billie unravelled the extent of Jimmy's deception. Some of his trips might have been genuine but others were fictional and he had arranged for friends to send her letters through the diplomatic pouch.

She remembered how Jimmy would go out every evening, even if it was raining or foggy, to buy cigarettes. It struck her as odd that he should habitually run out of cigarettes, and she assumed he liked his nightly stroll. Now she believed he had been calling Oxford.

But the crucial question remained: Had he loved her? Did he love her still?

She could only answer with another question: Why else would he go to such lengths to share his life with her?

Jimmy had lied to Billie for years, but she could not accept that his passion had been a pretence.

Then she found letters to him from a woman who was evidently one of his students. Their intimate tone made it clear that Jimmy had another lover, and the affair had been going on for some time. She re-read the letters to make sure she was not mistaken. Then she stood still for a long time, tears rolling down her cheeks.

"He's a con man," Bettina said to Billie. "A first-class con man."

Billie had never heard of the expression and, when Bettina explained it, she laughed and cried at the same time.

The truth about Jimmy would only emerge much later in a bombshell message received by Ian.

37

The Silver Corridor

At her lowest ebb in Stanley, the fortune-teller had told Billie, "You will rise superior in spirit to the difficulties of your life and career and you will gain a victory after a long fight, long initiation and tests of determination. There is promise of success, help from superiors and protection from those in high places, with honours, elevation in life."

If such a scenario was unbelievable in camp, it still seemed far out of reach as Billie prayed for a miracle in nearby St Mary's Church, built by Huguenots fleeing persecution from France.

Jimmy had broken her spirit and blown a hole in her savings for Ian's schooling. She remembered Martin Hill, her gallant, charming Irish boss at the ECOSOC conference in Geneva. "He was outgoing, full of fun, a gentleman of the old school," she said. "He used to give me a box of chocolates and take me out for a farewell dinner at the end of every ECOSOC session."

She wrote to the now Under-Secretary Hill, explaining her situation, and he sent a message to the UN Deputy Director in Geneva, Georges Palthey, saying: "If you help Billie Gill, you will find your reward in Heaven."

The timing was fortunate. The UN was preparing for another major conference at the end of October and Mr Palthey's secretary, Janet, called Billie with the news that she would be recruited.

On October 31, 1958, Billie started work in Geneva on a preparatory meeting for the Conference of the Discontinuance of Nuclear Weapons Tests. Since the first atomic bombs had brought the Pacific war to an abrupt end, there had been over 50 nuclear explosions and a Cold War arms race posed a terrifying threat to humanity.

She joined a small team from New York, headed by the personal representative of the Secretary-General, T.G. Narayanan, an urbane, soft-spoken Indian, who brought his secretary, Gaby Gervais, a warm French-Canadian.

Gaby Gervais (left) helped secure Billie a fixed-term contract

Narayanan was a deeply spiritual man who would become a friend. He stood with Billie when her schoolboy son rode his red-and-black bicycle into the Palais des Nations for the first time and he treated Ian to lunch at the UN executive lounge after he passed his 'O' level school examinations. A former special correspondent for *The Manchester Guardian* in Madras, Narayanan knew Ian wanted to be a journalist.

Billie sat behind Narayanan in the council chamber as the conference opened with much fanfare for a trio of diplomatic heavyweights, James Wadsworth (US), Semyon Tsarapkin (USSR) and Sir Michael Wright (UK).

The three met twice a week and conference days were hectic, with Billie and Gaby dealing with a torrent of papers, letters, telegrams, documents and diplomatic pouch material from New York.

Billie (top centre) at the disarmament conference in Geneva, 1958

After the conference resumed in 1959, Billie bent over to baste a chicken in the oven – and cried out in agony. She had slipped a disc, which meant weeks of treatment with a physiotherapist. The experience was costly since, as a temporary staffer, she was not covered medically by the UN.

Narayanan and Gaby came to her help. "We knew she was a wonderful worker and, after her injury, Narayanan and I spent hours with personnel suggesting Billie be hired on a fixed-term basis. But once the contract was arranged, Billie for some reason was reluctant to go down to personnel to sign it. She was like a zombie, and I didn't know why," said Gaby.

The reason was that Billie thought that, if she committed to the UN, it might be a problem should Jimmy reappear and ask her to go back to him.

From this uncertain start began an 18-year career in disarmament that would see her effectively run the secretariat for one of the UN's longest-running conferences.

Its offices were along a corridor of silver metal doors called "Millionaire's Row" and were adjacent to the council chamber where meetings took place under monumental baroque murals by Spanish artist José María Sert, representing human progress through health, technology, freedom and peace, and united by five colossal figures clasping hands at the dome.

Although unity was the goal, disarmament, critical for world safety, was inevitably controversial. Many placed high hopes on the brilliant Dag Hammarskjöld who had, since taking over as Secretary-General in 1953, resolved diplomatic crises and improved the organisation's morale and efficiency.

In September 1959, the United Nations General Assembly declared its goal to be general and complete disarmament and Soviet premier Nikita Khrushchev had a new programme on the table.

But on May 1, 1960, the Soviets shot down an American U2 plane, piloted by Gary Powers, over their skies. The US claimed it was a weather monitoring plane gone astray but the Soviets retrieved film that indicated it had been on a spying mission.

This led to the collapse two weeks later of the Paris Summit between Khrushchev and Eisenhower who had been due to discuss a Test Ban Treaty.

In June, the conference of the Ten-Nation Committee on Disarmament in Geneva fell apart after the Soviets and Eastern European delegations left. The future of the disarmament talks looked in the balance.

In the midst of this tense atmosphere at work, Billie picked up the phone and instantly recognized Jimmy's voice. It had been more than two years since their abrupt separation, but she still felt an ache like a lead bar over her left breastbone.

"It's nice to hear your voice again. How are you?" Billie heard herself saying and, to her surprise, she realized it was true. In lonely moments, she still replayed scenes of her happiest times and wondered what would have happened had Jimmy not collapsed. She had never been able to still a nagging voice in her head: *Did he ever really love me?*

"I am much better and have been back at work for some time now." A pause. Then: "I was wondering if you would like to meet me in London some time."

Billie could not quell a fluttering sensation in her chest.

During the plane ride to London, her mind was full of contradictory questions. *Am I being a complete fool even to consider giving Jimmy another chance? Yet why did he call after so long? Could the magic still be there?*

As she stepped into the foyer of the National Liberal Club, Jimmy strode towards her, arms extended, just as before. His eyes even had their old sparkle as she allowed him to take her in his arms.

Jimmy took her to the Piccadilly Hotel, where they had celebrated their first anniversary. When, by the middle of dinner, Jimmy had made no reference to the past, she became uneasy. He was trying to pick up from where they had left off, but she had expected him at least to explain what had happened.

"I need to ask you something, Jimmy," said Billie.

"Of course, my dear," he said, refilling their glasses.

"Why did you lie to me? Why couldn't you tell me the truth about your wife?"

Perfectly composed, Jimmy looked straight into her eyes: "Because I was certain that, if you knew the truth, you would leave me. And I wanted to keep you at all costs."

She paused. "And how is your wife, Jimmy?"

"Same as ever," he said, with a shrug.

The scales fell from her eyes. She realized Jimmy had no regrets and had not even thought about what she had gone through. Now the fuss had died down, he thought he could pick up the pieces again.

For the first time, she noticed that Jimmy's chin was small and weak, that his eyes were lustrous, but without depth.

They passed the rest of the meal in polite, but strained, conversation. After dinner, Jimmy took her to the Apollo theatre to see Peter Cook's *Pieces of Eight*. He reached for Billie's hand, but she pushed him away. They went by taxi in silence to the airport terminal, where Billie climbed aboard the airport bus and sat on the top deck. They waved to each other before she passed out of his life forever.

As she turned the key to her Geneva flat, she noticed that the pain under her breastbone had gone. Jimmy was a Walter Mitty, she decided. He lives in a fantasy world, does what he wants without heed of consequences. He wings his way through life with charm and empty promises. Taking a deep breath, she told herself, I don't care if I never see Jimmy again. I can get on with my life once more.

She had barely recovered her old form at work when she became embroiled with another disruptive character.

The Cold War dealt disarmament one blow after another. The civil war that erupted in the Congo after independence in 1960 became a proxy Cold War, with the Soviet Union and United States supporting different factions. Khrushchev attacked Hammarskjöld at the 1960 General Assembly, accusing him of siding with the "colonialists" in the Congo affair and demanding his resignation and replacement by a *troika* (council of three), representing Communist, Western and neutral nations.

This proposal caused sharp divisions within the UN and the tense atmosphere in the Geneva office took a toll on Billie's boss, Narayanan, who had a close working relationship with Hammarskjöld and was also beset with high blood pressure and heart problems.

The crisis took a tragic turn in September 1961 with Hammarskjöld's death in a plane crash while en route to broker cease-fire negotiations. Billie saw Narayanan turn ashen and retreat to his room, too overcome to speak.

In 1962, when the Committee on Disarmament expanded to 18 countries, Omar Loutfi of the United Arab Republic, a non-aligned member, ousted Narayanan as Special Representative of the Secretary-General. Narayanan remained as deputy and a Canadian, William Epstein, was appointed second deputy.

Suspicion and jealousy among the three men – and their staffs – ratcheted up tensions in Millionaire's Row. Epstein started arguments with Loutfi and the mild-mannered Narayanan became a buffer between the two.

The son of a Russian Jew, Epstein's flashing eyes, high cheekbones and a shock of grey-white hair created a powerful presence. An abrasive man of huge ambition, he challenged the gentle Narayanan on many issues. Simmering tensions broke out into shouting matches that became so heated Billie thought they would lead to fisticuffs.

The fractious atmosphere spread to fights over the allocation of offices and the division of labour and even to squabbles between New York and Geneva staff.

When the newly-expanded Eighteen Nation Committee on Disarmament opened in 1962 with foreign ministers Andrei Gromyko of the USSR, Dean Rusk of the US, Lord Home of the United Kingdom and India's Krishna Menon, Narayanan and Billie raced behind the scenes to deliver the countries' positions to the chamber and into cables and reports and official UN records.

After one exhausting Saturday at the office, Narayanan collapsed at his hotel with a heart attack. When Billie heard the news of his death on the following Monday, she fainted and regained consciousness in the UN Infirmary.

For days, Billie could not drag herself to the office to cope with the anxieties that had pervaded the secretariat. She sought a transfer, but New York wanted her to stay with the disarmament work. She was the only one familiar with the conference's history, special procedures and documents. Just as importantly, she knew her way around the UN bureaucracy in dealing with administrative, budget and documentation matters.

In early 1963, Loutfi had a heart attack and M.A. Vellodi from India replaced him to become Billie's new boss. But Vellodi, even-tempered and considerate, was soon recalled by New Delhi to head India's Atomic Energy Commission and his replacement, Dr Dragoslav Protitch, a tall, smooth diplomat from Yugoslavia, brought his own secretary.

Billie was assigned to Epstein, now Deputy Special Representative.

With his eye on the top job, Epstein worked around the clock and expected the same of others. With no private life – he was separated from his wife – Epstein gave no thought to the staff's personal needs.

When Billie wanted to attend her son's university graduation ceremony, the culmination of years of sacrifice on her part, it was in doubt whether Epstein would let her go for the occasion.

Billie needed to fly over on a Tuesday to attend Ian's graduation the following day but there was a conference that day and Epstein told her she could not leave if there were any speakers at the meeting. Billie knew this was unlikely. However, as word of her problem spread, the Burmese delegate came to see her. "Bring your suitcase to the office and, if there are no speakers, I shall drive you to the airport," he said. When the meeting opened on Tuesday, the chairman asked if anyone wanted to speak. No one responded and the chairman closed the meeting. The Burmese delegate jumped up, ran with Billie to her office and grabbed her suitcase to carry it to his waiting car. As she ran out, Epstein called out that he wanted her back for the next meeting on Thursday.

In the spring of 1970, Protitch died suddenly in New York and Epstein was appointed Acting Special Representative of the Secretary-General. This was his long-awaited chance and Billie typed letter after letter as he lobbied the Canadian government and other delegations for the top job. The entire secretariat dreaded the prospect.

News of the appointment arrived as a press release in Billie's in-tray. She braced herself to read it. It announced that the new Special Representative of the Secretary-General was Ambassador Ilkka Pastinen of Finland, a complete unknown in disarmament circles. She almost felt sorry for Epstein.

Billie was busy on both her phones when she heard a knock on the door. A well-built man in his early 40s, impeccably dressed in a dark suit, came in and stood by the door waiting for her to finish her conversation. As soon as she put down the phones, Billie sprang up to greet Ilkka Pastinen, apologizing for not doing so earlier.

"Not at all, Billie. I am very impressed," said Pastinen, blue eyes twinkling under bushy red eyebrows. The Finnish ambassador had a strong, intelligent face that often broke into a wry smile and his manner was suave and cultured.

Pastinen disarmed Billie by putting his complete trust in her. "I have heard all about you while I was in New York," he said. "As I am the new boy, I shall have to ask you to take care of all the arrangements for me to meet people. Just keep me busy."

From that day in February 1971, she knew her nightmare was over. Pastinen would restore tone and dignity to the office.

Billie's workload kept rising. After one budget cut and the axing of several staff, she was tasked, in addition to her regular duties, with overseeing the conference records before they went to the editors and translators of the four language groups and then into the final records. Maddeningly, the delegations frequently changed their written statements, often for minor reasons, and each change had to be reflected in four languages. Billie became a familiar figure in the basement where the printing unit was housed.

Pastinen used his prerogative to recommend her to the professional grade, the promotion she had missed in Bangkok. Just before the recommendation letter was placed in the pouch, however, an accountant friend of Billie discovered a curious anomaly. Billie was intending to retire in Geneva, and the accountant calculated that her US dollar-based pension as a Professional would be less than her pension in Swiss francs at her current level. Billie asked an incredulous Pastinen to withdraw his letter.

In 1974, the disarmament club expanded to 31, but the UN still did not increase its tiny secretariat staff.

Billie's career peaked with the mammoth Review Conference of the Parties to the Non-Proliferation Treaty in May 1975, the most important event in 30 years of disarmament. It was so huge – drawing nearly 100 parties, including government delegations, NGOs and observers – that a new wing of the Palais des Nations was built to hold it.

For three weeks, Billie waded through a river of documents to the Final Declaration. What kept her going was that she would be flying to Hong Kong afterwards to meet Ian for the first time since he had left England for New Zealand in 1971.

Billie had not told Ian that it was anything more than a holiday but in fact she had a plan that would change their lives.

38

At the Palace

In the summer of 1975, Billie flew into Hong Kong for her first reunion with Ian since he had left England four years earlier for New Zealand. At 59, she was soon to retire from the United Nations and Ian, 29, had settled into his newspaper job in Wellington.

It was her first time back since the war and she found the city much changed. Her flat had disappeared but the Hongkong and Shanghai Bank Building where she had worked was still there, though it was now one of a thicket of tall buildings. Hong Kong had pulled through the riots of the 1960s sparked by China's Cultural Revolution, and was booming as never before.

Ian, on his first trip to the British colony, was overwhelmed. He had panicked momentarily at the exit of Kai Tak airport, wondering if he could pick out his mother among the sea of Chinese faces. In the taxi to the hotel, he had stared at the densely packed streets of Tsim Sha Tsui, the garish Chinese signs, the pushcarts and red double-decker buses, feeling the city's pulsating energy but also somewhat claustrophobic.

He soon had cause to feel even more discombobulated.

Billie had an agenda but did not tell him of her plan. First she had a personal mission. She had left Hong Kong 30 years earlier wearing a housecoat made from a blanket and with rope slippers on her feet. Suddenly, as she and Ian were jostling among the throng near Nathan Road, she disappeared into a hole-in-the-wall shop. He watched her bargain and emerge with a wide grin – and her first mink coat.

In a Chinese restaurant, Billie proudly introduced her British-educated son to her best friends from school in Shanghai. 'Auntie Lois', elegant in a long flowing dress, had come up from Manila for the occasion and 'Auntie Mackie' was a widow living in Hong Kong with her two daughters. China had been shuttered to foreigners for years but, over hot tea and dim sum, Ian listened to them talk about their Shanghai of the 1920s and 1930s with a mixture of nostalgia for the old days and horror at what they had heard the city had become.

Billie was eager to locate her old network – and a phone call to Jimmy Wei, a walking *Who's Who* of China, did exactly that. Lin Yutang was in Hong Kong; however, when she called him he was pleased to hear from her but could not meet as he was unwell, devastated by the suicide of a daughter.

Billie took Ian to Taipei, where the effervescent Wei, still a director of the Central News Agency and an advisor to President Chiang Ching-kuo, son of Chiang Kai-shek, took them to the Grand Hotel, a vermilion and gold temple-like structure on a hill. They went to the home of Wen Yuan-ning who, despite being paralysed by a stroke, had insisted on being dressed in a three-piece suit to meet the woman he called his "right-hand assistant." They drove up the hill in Yangmingshan to see John Wu, mandarin-like and gently humorous, who gave Ian, his godchild, a crystal rosary.

Her former colleagues had occupied senior positions in the Nationalist government before and after they had moved to Taipei as the Communists came to power and Ian was deeply impressed by the warmth and respect they showed Billie. She had clearly been far more than a fiercely protective mother.

At the American Club, they met Spencer Moosa, her mentor at Reuters, who had another kind of effect upon Ian. Moosa and George Giffen had been fellow members of the press corps in Hong Kong and Billie told him that George was Ian's father.

Moosa's eyes widened, then narrowed as he looked at Ian intently. "Yes," he said, after a pause. "Yes. He looks just like George." Ian had never met anyone other than Billie who had known George and something stirred inside him.

At the National Museum, full of artefacts the Nationalists had brought with them from the mainland, she pointed out the bowls and vases that were like those in Frank Newman's collection.

Before they parted, she took Ian to the still-existing buildings of Stanley internment camp in Hong Kong, where some 2,700 internees had lived behind barbed wire. They went to the cemetery and found Brian's grave, a small milestone marker, at the top of a slope. Billie told Ian, "You were two sons rolled into one," a remark he fully understood only a few years later.

The whirlwind trip left Ian unsettled. When Billie proposed they put together an account of her life, he readily agreed, though with reservations. Conflicts had arisen between them since his adolescence, when he found her too controlling, but he knew her exotic and horrific story was also his and hoped that understanding where she came from would heal their rift.

Back in Geneva, Billie received recognition in surprising ways.

The British ambassador to the United Nations Conference on Disarmament, Mark Allen, hosted a reception to mark her retirement, itself an unusual gesture, and at the party he presented her with a unique gift – a Union Jack from one of the Far East internment camps that a friend had left to his family.

Billie told the gathering that it brought back the day they had raised the British flag in Stanley. "I remember standing there, with my fellow internees, with tears of relief and joy rolling down our faces. This flag was not only a symbol of my king and my country, but also a symbol of peace and freedom and a second chance at living."

Then, in January 1977, she answered the doorbell to find, to her astonishment, Finnish ambassador Risto Hyvärinen, the new Special Representative of the Secretary-General, holding a bottle of champagne and roses.

With a sheepish expression, he explained that they had recruited three people, including the daughter of Secretary-General Waldheim, to replace Billie – and they all needed training.

"Would you please come back as a consultant for eight weeks?" he asked.

Billie had turned down a two-year extension, but this was different. Apart from the handsome fee, she was flattered at being offered a consultant's contract, which referred to her as "the only person with the necessary knowledge."

Her biggest surprise, however, was still to come.

A call from John Taylor, counsellor of the United Kingdom delegation, woke her up. Drowsily, she heard him say that he was calling on instructions from Buckingham Palace to ask if she would be willing to accept the award of Member of the Most Excellent Order of the British Empire (an MBE).

Billie wondered if she was dreaming or if Taylor had taken leave of his senses.

As Taylor pressed for an answer, it dawned on her that he might be serious.

Billie could only ask, weakly, "What would you do if you were me?"

"I would accept."

"Alright, I shall accept," said Billie.

After this, Billie knew no rest. She pinched herself when she saw her name among the Queen's Jubilee Honours list on June 11, 1977.

Now came the joy of going from one boutique to another in search of the perfect outfit and hat for the Queen which, thanks to her consultancy, she could choose without thought to the cost.

She settled on a Nina Ricci navy-blue cape suit.

Allowed to bring two guests to Buckingham Palace, she invited Ian to come over from Honolulu where he was having a break from journalism by taking a master's degree at the East-West Center.

On November 15, 1977, a watery sun cast a thin light over London as Ambassador Allen and Ian donned morning coats and black top hats, Ian having shaven off his moustache and trimmed his hair in deference to Billie's wishes.

Billie's friend and colleague from ECAFE, Tony Gilpin, drove them to Buckingham Palace, where a policeman inspected their invitations before waving them through the wrought-iron gates. In the inner quadrangle, Tony took photographs of Billie in front of the John Nash portico and columns.

Passing between two Household Cavalry guards, standing like statues, holding heavy swords with their arms straight out, they walked down a long corridor, with priceless oil paintings and tapestries on the walls.

The band of the Royal Air Force played as they entered the ballroom, which seemed as large as a football field, with massive white pillars and a high ceiling from which hung six pendulous chandeliers like glass moons.

An official came on stage to address the guests. "After the Queen enters, the National Anthem will be played and you will stand until the Queen bids you sit. You are allowed to talk during the ceremony but, please, keep your voices at a low pitch. And, of course, there will be no applause."

At 10.55am, the Yeomen of the Guard trooped in. Founded by Henry VII in 1487, they wore scarlet, gold and black livery, with flat-topped black hats, and carried pikes. They formed a semi-circle in front of two gilt thrones beneath a canopy of crimson velvet.

The ceremony was due to start at 11am and everyone knew the Queen was never late.

Ian looked at his watch as the small hand reached 11, but nothing happened. As the minutes ticked by, everyone looked expectantly at the side of the stage, but there was no sign of Her Majesty. It was all highly unusual.

Then at 11.10, the Queen arrived, with the Lord Chamberlain, her equerry and two Gurkha guards.

"I'm afraid I'm a bit late," she said. "But I've just had a message from the hospital – my daughter has a son."

Immediately, the guests broke into applause.

As the ceremony got under way, the recipients, their names called by Lord Maclean the Lord Chamberlain, approached the Queen. The knights were the first to be honoured, dubbed on the shoulder with a sword. The awardees came in walking, on crutches and in wheelchairs. They came singly apart from one pair of double scullers. They were from all parts of the Commonwealth.

After half an hour, as the ambassador and Ian were straining their necks, Billie finally appeared.

While Billie was waiting, she had whispered, "I hope you're watching, Mama. This is a long way from Boundary Lane in Shanghai."

Entering the ballroom, her one thought was that she might trip. Reaching the Queen, who was standing, Billie curtsied and froze as the Queen bent down to pin a pink-and-grey-ribboned medal onto her lapel.

"And what do you do?" asked the Queen.

"I worked for the United Nations, Ma'am."

"That must have been very interesting."

As Billie walked towards the other side of the ballroom, a childhood jingle ran through her head. "Pussy cat, pussy cat, where have you been? I've been to London to look at the Queen!"

Lunch followed at Quaglino's restaurant with friends from the different chapters of Billie's life – they included Charles Boxer (Mickey was in New York); Flossie Kellner, whose husband Hans had been a pallbearer at Mama's funeral in Shanghai; Stanley ex-POWs Vivienne Locke (née Blackburn) and Mary Smalley; and her Hampstead neighbours Bettina, who had comforted her after the split from Jimmy, and her husband John, the Covent Garden opera singer. Tony Gilpin and Mark Allen gave eloquent tributes and John Lanigan sang the rousing drinking song from La Traviata.

"No-one could have asked for more," said Billie.

That evening she told Ian, "I was thinking of Brian this morning. He would have been 37 this year. I thanked God for his most wonderful gift to me – you."

But she added, irritably, that she wished he could appreciate her the way others had done.

She was telling him that recognition from others was all very nice, but what she really wanted was for their bickering to stop, something he very much wanted too.

Not long afterwards came a major step towards exploring their past when Ian landed a job on a news magazine, *Asiaweek*, in Hong Kong in 1978. As it had been for his father 45 years earlier, Hong Kong would be a turning point.

39

The Proposal

Billie had seen the shallowness behind Jimmy's charm at their final meeting in 1960 but she admitted to her son that, in lonely moments, she still wondered what might have happened if Jimmy had not fallen ill in their London flat. Would they have been able to continue a life together, even if it had been based on a lie?

The answer came in a series of messages Ian received in 2017 from a fellow researcher. It turned out that Jimmy had indeed been brilliant – he had obtained a first-class honours degree in modern languages at St Catherine's, Oxford, in 1930, followed by a doctorate. In 1937, he was a private tutor when he boarded with Gladys Cowper, a divorcee who was 14 years older than him. Despite his brilliance, he didn't, for some reason, receive a full-time post but was kept at Oxford and fed 'coaching' work, probably giving private lessons to not-so-bright students.

Then came the bombshell email.

It contained details of a court case heard before Justice Charles at the Oxfordshire Assizes on January 19, 1942, in which the defendant was James Aloysius Noonan, 32.

According to press reports, which appeared in many newspapers, including *The Times*, Jimmy had been out of work after leaving Oxford in 1941 and had run up an overdraft of £380.

He had written a letter to the university, purporting to be signed by Mr E.C. Yorke, an acting junior bursar of New College, Oxford, claiming that £750 was due to him from Oxford University for arrears of salary.

Noonan pleaded guilty to intent to defraud and the judge described his offence as a "skilfully thought-out plan" – and sentenced him to six months' imprisonment.

By a remarkable coincidence, Jimmy was incarcerated at the same time as Billie was entering Stanley internment camp in Hong Kong.

After Jimmy left jail, his career in ruins, he returned to Mrs Cowper's lodgings and married her in 1945.

But evidently, the smooth-talking Jimmy re-invented himself for he was working for both the University of London's Institute of Education and the British Council by the time Billie met him in Bangkok in 1954.

That was not the end of the story. After his affair with Billie, Jimmy and his friend Valentine had seized on opportunities that arose in the early 1960s with the independence of African countries like Nigeria and Uganda and the resulting exodus of expatriates.

Jimmy became the Dean of the Faculty of Arts at the University of Nigeria, Nsukka, and Valentine was appointed to a teaching position at Makerere College, University of East Africa in Uganda.

Billie might have chuckled if she had read that, in 1964, Jimmy was awarded a CBE (Commander of the Order of the British Empire), presumably for his services to academia.

Jimmy's wife Gladys led a long life and was with him until she died in 1971, aged around 76, in Roma, Lesotho, when Jimmy was Dean of the University of East Africa.

But then came the coup de grâce.

According to Gladys's grandson, when Ian spoke to him, Jimmy met "a wealthy woman in Johannesburg who took him for what little he had left" before he died in 1978, aged 69. It seems the old rascal had finally met his comeuppance.

Billie kept a cache of photographs of Brian, her beloved first-born and thought about him often. When she was alone and penniless in London, she had held out a hope that she and Brian's father might get back together, but Paddy had found someone else.

Paddy went on to have his own family and, in 2014, Ian received a call from Paddy's daughter Karen who was enquiring about her discovery that her father had had a son before the war. Ian confirmed this was so and, as they talked, it turned out that Paddy, whom Billie had asked to switch to civilian life after the war, had never left the Army.

He had contracted malaria in Burma which "hounded him for years and years," said Karen, and had a series of heart attacks after the war.

Paddy never settled back in Ireland but was a strong patriot and told his daughters that he wanted to die in Ireland. He almost made it. In February 1970, Paddy set off on a trip from his home in North Berwick, Scotland, to Dublin to watch Ireland play Scotland in a Five Nations rugby match.

He arrived in Stranraer on February 24 to catch the ferry to Belfast the following day but, that evening, he had a heart attack and died, aged 64.

There was one lover Billie had hardly given a thought to since the eve of the war, but in 1981, Billie, then 65, picked up the phone in her Geneva flat and was transported back forty years to Hong Kong.

"Billie, is that really you? I've been searching for you for a very long time."

She instantly recognized the soft-spoken voice of Cromar Mitchell, the tall, auburn-haired soldier with whom she had had an intense affair in the last weeks of peace.

"Good heavens, this is incredible." she said. "Where are you calling from?"

"From England," he said. "I have been searching for you in all the Hong Kong telephone directories and finally found you through Charles Boxer, whom I found in *Who's Who*. I have thought about you so often through all these years."

Cromar had been interned in the military camp at Shamshuipo and was later transferred to Japan, spending time in two POW camps. He returned to his family after the war and his wife had died recently. He was now 74.

"Now that I have found you, may I come to see you in Geneva?"

"Yes, of course," she said, keeping her voice light.

In the days before Cromar's arrival, the story spread among Billie's friends that a long-lost admirer was returning to see her after forty years. Several offered to drive her to the airport to meet him.

When Cromar came through the arrival gate at Geneva's Cointrin airport, he had snowy white hair and a goatee, looking like a trimmer version of Kentucky Fried Chicken's Colonel Sanders.

Cromar's face creased with delight as he stooped to kiss her cheek. "You look absolutely wonderful," he said.

Over the next few days, Cromar told her stories of his military life and his grown-up family. His passion, he told her, was Shakespeare. He could quote extensively from the great man's plays and he had chosen to live in Stratford-upon-Avon. For years, he had pursued a research project to try to settle a controversy over the authorship of some plays that had long been attributed to the Bard. The research included counting the number of times certain words cropped up in the plays.

He didn't take long to broach the reason he had come to see her. Sitting at her dining table, he said, "Billie, I have carried a torch for you all these years and seeing you again has fanned the flames. Will you marry me?"

Billie was not surprised and found herself moved by the first proper proposal she had ever received. She asked to think about it overnight.

Cromar was sweet and kind, even if he was given to repeating his favourite stories. If he had played a sound game of bridge, she might have found him more companionable, but he didn't.

The next day, when they met over lunch, his expression of eager anticipation almost made her change her mind.

She chose her words carefully. "Your proposal has made me happier than you can imagine and I am very flattered," she said. "Had you asked me to marry you after the war when I was sick and abandoned and penniless, I would have accepted you like a shot. But I have brought Ian up and have had an extraordinary career with the United Nations and my recent retirement has given me a new freedom and, quite honestly, I don't want to take on another new responsibility at this stage of my life."

One more lover from Billie's past would return to her life.

In 1985, Billie experienced two more instances of what she called "a rounding of the circle." She learned that her son was changing careers and joining the Manila-based Asian Development Bank, which had been started by the United Nations Economic Commission for Asia and the Far East, for which she had worked in the 1950s.

And then in August that year, Billie received a phone call from Ian in Singapore.

"I've found George," he said. "He's alive and sounds pretty good. He's agreed I can go over and see him."

40

Mynah the Cow

Billie had mixed feelings when Ian called to say he had spoken to George and was planning to visit him on Denman Island in Canada. She had felt bitter when she was penniless in England and Paddy had asked for a divorce while George had told her he was very happy with his wife and daughter in Canada. It had been a twist in the wound when she later heard that George and his wife had had another child.

But Ian had sounded so excited at the prospect of meeting his father that she had stilled her apprehension and said she was happy for him. Nonetheless, she worried about how George's family might react to a reminder of his wartime infidelity and she wrote to George asking him to receive a son who was eager to meet him.

At Ian's request, a friend had gone to Denman Island – George's last known address of decades earlier – to see if he was living there, and had found him in the island's pamphlet-sized phone directory.

Soon after, on September 26, 1985, Ian was about to land at Comox Valley airport on Vancouver Island and wondering if he would solve an enduring question. He had taken after his mother in many ways but had also differed from her. Would the man he was about to meet provide the missing half of his genetic jigsaw? George had agreed to meet him, but he was unsure how his wife and daughters would react to him. Had they even heard of him before he called?

Ian was turning 40 and once again facing changes in his peripatetic life. He had come out of a painful divorce and was about to change jobs – and countries – for the seventh time in 14 years. The last thing he expected from meeting his father, however, was any advice or direction.

He knew his father was in his mid-70s and was expecting to meet someone frail. His first surprise was to see a stocky stranger, who looked oddly familiar, stride briskly towards him, shake his hand firmly and take his suitcase. George Giffen had a leathery, tanned face and a slightly protruding jaw.

Seated behind the wheel of his old station wagon, George asked after Billie and, on learning she was enjoying her retirement from the UN, said, "Always knew Billie would do well. A very competent woman, your mother."

Their conversation was desultory, but not awkward. Ian felt as if they were catching up after a long absence. After a while, George asked if he wanted to stop for a drink. Ian said he had given up smoking and drinking at the same time the previous year. If George was disappointed, he didn't show it. He, too, had given up drinking years earlier at his wife's insistence though, clearly, he was prepared to make an exception for a special occasion.

Their journey took them to Buckley Bay for a ferry across to Denman Island, then down a tarmac road for a couple of miles and finally onto a dirt path to a modest wooden bungalow beside a field. As the car tyres scrunched on the loose pebbles, George said, "My wife is prepared to like you." As if on cue, a small, wiry woman, her white hair tied back in a bun, came out onto the veranda with a wide grin. Ian sensed, however, that Erma had a no-nonsense nature.

In this isolated spot, Ian wondered whether George had known what awaited him after leaving Hong Kong in early 1946. Despite her discomfort in talking about herself, Erma described their post-war situation as they sat in the living room beside a log fireplace and George's history books on a side table.

She had been raised on nearby Lasqueti Island but in 1946 she was living on land on Denman Island that had belonged to her mother. George had arrived at a sparsely populated island with no running water or electricity. They used oil lamps, drew water from a well, grew vegetables in the garden and drove to the wharf to collect groceries delivered once a week by a Canadian Pacific Railways vessel.

"My mother had a cow called Mynah and George milked it. He'd never milked a cow before and he got on the wrong side of the cow," said Erma. "But I got on the right side of my mother-in-law," interjected George. "Mynah was very fond of George and would follow him around like a dog," said Erma. Ian laughed, as animals had an instinct for someone who would treat them kindly.

It turned out that George did know what he was coming home to, but he had expected it to be temporary. In the immediate aftermath of the war, he had held the newspaper together almost single-handedly – with the title of publisher – for months as other senior personnel were unwell or had not yet come back. He had not only expected to return, but anticipated a senior position.

Hong Kong, after all, had been the making of George. It had rescued him when he was nearly down and out. He had been laid off by the *Derbyshire Times* during the Depression and had gone to London, drawing the dole and selling fruit drinks to soccer teams on the field at half time.

He was desperate enough to go to an Army recruiting station. Fortunately, despite being in excellent health, he was turned down on trifling grounds.

"I was rejected on account of having one or two molars missing. I was so horrified that I asked if I would be accepted if I got a bridge," said George. "They said yes, so I pawned my good coat and bought a bridge."

Then George spotted an advertisement for the *South China Morning Post*. Against the advice of friends, he went to the Strand Hotel to meet Ben Wylie, the company's jowly managing director.

The interview changed his life. Giving him money, Wylie told him to go to Reuters to pick up a ticket on a Japanese ship, the *Suma Maru*.

"It was the lowest type of passenger boat," said George. "I borrowed a few pounds from a friend. We called at Naples and went through the Mediterranean, the Suez Canal and Ceylon, a great experience for a young man in those days. An English girls' band travelled with us as far as Ceylon, elevating the morale of the whole ship's company for a delightful month. We played poker dice for beer and deck tennis to acquire a thirst. It was probably the best time of my life. I had to be bailed off the ship by the *SCMP* staff because I over-spent in the last hectic week."

In 1933, George found Hong Kong like another planet. In a colony where a few thousand Europeans lorded it over a million Chinese, he was an underdog no more. For the first time, he earned a decent income. "I started off with 100 Mexican dollars a month [a currency commonly used in Hong Kong then] but doubled it with freelance work as the Hong Kong representative for Exchange Telegraph. They paid one guinea per message and I was always sending items about China, taking most of them from the Chinese newspapers. At 9pm, I would turn on the radio for news from England and hear my own stories coming back."

George took full advantage of the chit system. "All white staff immediately went into debt, signing chits at the hotels, tailors and Lane Crawford, the elite store, and seldom managed to make back their debts at the weekly poker games."

Hong Kong was "a romantic city though the work was humdrum" and reporting involved "a lot of waiting, drinking, rickshaw riding and boredom." Interestingly, he encountered an unusual type of discrimination – as an Englishman.

The editor of the *South China Morning Post* was Harry Ching, an Australian Eurasian – he had a Chinese father and an English mother – who had been raised in Australia. He came to Hong Kong with his father after their family – Harry's mother and five siblings – had been murdered on a farm.

Harry's Chinese background counted against him in Hong Kong. "He was a fine chap, but he had no time for the English and as I was the only Englishman, I was anathema to him. He always liked Australians and his favourites in the office were Norman Stockton and Jim Kelliher, both from Australia," said George.

Nonetheless, George thrived at the group's sister paper, the *Hongkong Telegraph,* and would rise to deputy editor. He got along with the down-to-earth Aussies and joined his Australian colleagues in the ANZAC company of the Hong Kong Volunteer Defence Corps, particularly enjoying the after-practice booze-ups.

In a sports-mad city, George played badminton and joined his editor Stewart Gray (an Englishman) in cricket matches at the Kowloon Cricket Club and "defended stoutly," according to a press report, when he and Gray teamed up for a European press soccer team. The journalists played hard off the pitch as well and George said, "We generally got drunk after the job but as long as you turned up in the morning and did your job..."

George and Aussie colleague Stockton overdid the champagne at the opening of the Hongkong and Shanghai Bank building in 1935. "I trundled Norman around in a money wagon through the crowd," recalled George. Stockton passed out in the office and had to be splashed with water to read his shorthand. "The next day, I had to write a letter to the bank, apologizing for my reprehensible behaviour."

George met Erma, a pretty girl who was working for the Hong Kong harbour master. In a city where European men hugely outnumbered white women, Erma once received a proposal every day for a week. She thought George looked like the film star Tyrone Power and they married at St Andrew's Church, Kowloon, on June 27, 1938. For 18 months, they lived in a flat near the Peak tramway before Erma was evacuated to Canada as a precaution against any expansion in the war across the border.

Ian was shocked to learn the reason George had decided against returning to Hong Kong. In 1947, when his boss Ben Wylie asked when he was coming back, he explained the reason for changing his mind.

"I, too, feel regretful at not rejoining the *SCMP,* especially as I know that my newspaper experience here has developed me and that the sober habits I have adopted – permanently – would fit me to do the job better than I did. However, I blotted my copybook in camp and have to atone for it here so I shall make the best of it."

It turned out that he had told Erma about Billie and Ian, and Erma was adamant that she would not return to Hong Kong because many people would know that George had fathered an illegitimate child during the war. She thought Billie might also return to Hong Kong, which would make a bad situation intolerable.

George did not adjust to the change of plan easily, however.

"He came back from the war a changed man," Erma told Ian. "The war knocked the spirit out of him, and he was drinking and didn't work for quite a long time."

He also had trouble adjusting to family life. His daughter Dianne was six when she met her father. "I was kingpin until Dad came home. He wanted me to do things his way," said Dianne. "He insisted that I cut up the carrots and other veg and put them on a fork together and, if I didn't, he would lean across the table and slap me." However, George learned his lesson and was much kinder to his second daughter, Linda, born in 1947.

Having decided to stay, he found journalism in Vancouver was having its own problems.

As he told Wylie in his March 1947 letter: "I have now been nine months with the *Vancouver News-Herald*, a morning paper of some 50,000 circulation which is sadly handicapped by lack of newsprint. Men come and go quickly here – I have been under notice to go twice but union action stopped it once, then shortage of staff stopped it again. The reasons for sacking men are mostly economic. The business manager suddenly feels he must cut down so he tells the editor and he cuts off the last three, four or five men who joined. Another reason is inaccuracy. One mistake of any magnitude and out you go. Then you join *The Province* or the *Vancouver Sun*, afternoon papers where the routine is pretty much the same."

From George's home, Ian called Billie.

"Is everything all right?" she asked, anxiously. "I wrote to George and asked him to receive you."

Ian said the visit was going well, and Erma was nice to him.

"Has he said anything about me?"

"Only that he's not surprised you did very well."

"Did he really say that?" Billie sounded pleased.

Not only was George's wife unexpectedly pleasant to Ian, but George's daughters would also surprise him.

Dianne and Linda, both teachers and married with families, were visibly startled when they met Ian in Victoria.

Linda, his younger sister, told him, "You and Dad are so alike in the way you look, walk and talk, it makes my scalp tingle." His older sister, Dianne, said, "I've not seen Dad so happy in a long time and it must be due to you. You are the son he always wanted. Why didn't you come sooner?"

The resemblance between father and son was more than physical. George gave Ian a silver cigarette case on which he had engraved the names of the newspapers he had worked for in England. An astonished Ian told George that he, too, had started his journalism in England, including in the Midlands, near the same location as George. Even more remarkably, Ian had followed George to Hong Kong.

Meanwhile, Ian was learning what made his father tick. As they went for long walks along a pebbly beach, George would call over his shoulder, "Are you all right?" as Ian struggled to keep up. They entered some woods, ducking fir tree branches and crunching pine needles underfoot. A spiky branch had poked George in the eye months earlier, causing injury, but when Ian asked if he had seen a doctor, George replied "No", as if the question was strange.

As they passed one house, George warned that a woman might come out and yell at them for trespassing. The woman had never worked and lived in squalor with her mother. She would stand by the roadside, said George, thumbing a ride to the store, but people ignored her as she had powerful body odour as well as mental issues. As an aside, George said that he generally stopped and gave her a ride.

On Sunday, George dressed up in a light jacket with white shirt and red tie and matching handkerchief in his breast pocket. Erma, too, was in her Sunday best as they took Ian to church on the mainland.

*George and Erma in their Sunday best, on the porch of the
house that George built*

George was the only male in the congregation of elderly ladies and he introduced Ian as "my friend from Hong Kong." Had the ladies looked more closely and noticed the family resemblance, they might have been scandalised.

As it was, they regarded George with obvious respect as he read from a podium and acted as usher, smiling and bowing gently like a courtly Southern gentleman.

Ian knew his father was far from religious, but he clearly supported Erma in her faith.

George had left Billie pregnant at the end of the war and, when Ian learned that George's mother had also been pregnant with him when she was abandoned by his father, he wondered whether George was following a family pattern.

But after a while, Ian realised he had the wrong end of the stick. It was true that George had deserted Billie, but only to return to his wife.

"I'm very proud of my association with your mother," George told Ian. "And if Erma hadn't been there, no doubt we would have stayed together. But Erma was very strong and very committed."

George's mother had raised him until he was three and a half. At that time, she was working long hours as a cook and was paying a family in the village to look after George. When her son developed rickets, however, it was clear the family was under-feeding George and she placed him in the care of the Society for Waifs and Strays.

That was why George could recall seeing his mother only a couple of times before they met to say goodbye before he left for Hong Kong. Ian asked George whether he had felt any resentment towards the woman who had given him away.

"No," he replied. "I felt sorry for her. Her family was fairly well respected, but she was born in the wrong time and trapped by the wrong man."

That meeting with his mother had left George with a deep compassion for women, as Billie – and the singer, Betty Drown – had witnessed in Stanley. On Denman Island, George was notorious for giving away household appliances to elderly women in need – which Erma would have to go around and retrieve later.

Erma and George were very different. She was a rural girl with traditional values who derived comfort from her faith in Christian Science. George was a journalist, an avid reader with a world view, and was sceptical about religion.

Yet, to build a life with Erma, George had given up Hong Kong, forsaken drinking, and had retired to Denman Island where he had built her a home and supported her religion.

Ian found that George's extended family of sons-in-law and grandchildren thought the world of him and said he would do anything for his family. George, who had grown up without a family, was a devoted and much-loved patriarch. It was no coincidence that Ian would follow his example by remarrying and starting a family.

"It's nice to have a son in the family," George told Ian, who would return to visit his father several times, so much so that Billie grew jealous of the vacation time he spent in Vancouver when she wanted him in Geneva.

George died in Vancouver on December 23, 2006, aged 95. His old newspaper, the *South China Morning Post*, wrote a lengthy obituary under the headline 'Champion of the Press', to which Ian contributed.

George's memorial service was a small, intimate affair and Ian's sisters asked him to deliver the eulogy. It went smoothly until Ian, remembering his father's malodorous neighbour and, incongruously, Mynah the cow who followed him around, mentioned George's kindness – and he choked.

41

A Vanished World

Billie wanted to see Shanghai again but was scared in case, somehow, she would not be allowed to leave. In 1993, she changed her mind, deciding that if her son accompanied her, all would be well.

They met in Hong Kong, which had already begun the countdown to its handover back to China in 1997, four years away. The prospect of change was not causing an exodus – the city was still a beacon of laissez-faire capitalism and many Chinese were hedging their bets by staying and buying another property in cities like Vancouver.

When they landed at Shanghai's Hongqiao international airport, Billie was bowled over by its size and modernity in an area that had been largely farmland in her childhood. As they were driven to the Hongqiao Hilton, Billie remarked that the Bubbling Well Road cemetery, where she had buried Mama, no longer existed.

The next morning, Ian called her at 7 and found she had been up for hours. "I am too excited," she said. "I wanted to see Shanghai at first light. Seventy years ago, a coolie had to carry pails of hot water to our house and was paid two dollars a bucket and this morning, I had a hot bath at a hotel." Over breakfast, she added, "I was too frightened to come. I wouldn't have come back without you but now I see how easy everything is, I want to come back for a longer stay."

Although her rusty Chinese was coming back, Ian took the precaution of asking reception to write down in Chinese the places Billie wanted to visit. She planned, sensibly, to start from the parks of her childhood – Jessfield Park, French Park and Hongkew Park – and find her bearings from there.

It was cold and raining as their driver, Mr Wu, a pleasant 30ish young man, greeted them with a "Good morning!" It turned out his English didn't extend much beyond that.

They went to Zhongshan Park, which had been Jessfield Park, and from there proceeded to Yuyuan Road, or Yuyuen Road as it had been known before the war. But when they arrived, Billie could see no trace of the quiet, leafy street bordered by manicured lawns in front of large houses.

Instead, she confronted a dense thoroughfare packed with cacophonous traffic, with shops, not gardens, on either side. She looked intently out of the car but after the slow crawl she pronounced, firmly, "This is not Yuyuen Road, which was wider."

Mr Wu stopped at Shanghai No. 1 Normal University, which he said used to be Shanghai Public School for Girls. Billie got out of the car, took one look, and said, "No, it wasn't."

After all their anticipation, this was a terrible comedown and Billie's frustration began to show while Mr Wu continued being patient and helpful.

They returned to the park and started all over again. They could feel Billie's anxiety rising until, finally, she gave a cry. She pointed to a small balcony with a green railing. "That's where I stood when Pembroke Stephens shouted that the Japanese were encircling the area," she said.

She saw the number on the building, 1283, which was the address of the *T'ien Hsia* offices.

Now they had a point of reference, they drove a little further and stopped at a lane fronted by an electronics workshop, with a large brick house behind it. They got out of the car and, her iron-grey curls quivering, Billie pointed to the house with its off-white walls, brown shutters and a red-tiled roof.

"That was our home, but the walls were yellow and the window shutters blue. We had a front garden, but it's been replaced by that," she said, gesturing at the single-storey building with the sign, "Shanghai Kaili Electronic Equipment Factory."

A few people stopped to ask what was happening and Mr Wu explained that Billie was returning after a long absence. Just then, a woman who had been walking up the lane stopped at the edge of our group. She was tall and white-haired, with an air of refinement. Then she asked, in perfectly accented English, if she could be of any help.

When Billie said she lived in the lane over 60 years ago, the woman looked at her carefully. She said softly, "Yes, I remember you playing hopscotch."

"You do? You really do?" Billie's eyes widened. Margaret Lin turned out to be 82, though her handsome face was remarkably unlined. Five years older than Billie, she had lived in the lane all her life.

"Where did you learn your English?" asked Billie.

"I'm a McTyeire girl."

"Are you indeed? I was at Shanghai Public School."

They were speaking in a code familiar only to those from an earlier era. McTyeire School had been established by American Methodists for Chinese girls from wealthy families and its alumni included the three Soong sisters.

Incredibly, had Billie arrived at this spot five minutes earlier or later, they would have missed the one woman in Shanghai with whom Billie could connect and would still remember the pre-war city.

"What are you doing right now?" asked Billie.

"I was just going out to buy toothpaste."

"Why don't you join us? I'll make sure you get your toothpaste." The women laughed and Margaret agreed to fall in with them.

Margaret knocked on the door of Billie's old house at 3 Lane 520 Yuyuan Road and a somewhat bemused resident let them in.

It was soon clear that several families had occupied the house for many years. Adjusting to the gloom, Billie and Ian could see bare floors and grimy walls. As they climbed the creaking staircase, and went from floor to floor, they could see that spaces once used for dining or family meetings were now used as multiple-purpose rooms by the families that occupied them.

With her eidetic memory, Billie could detect some architectural features disguised or buried by dereliction. In the drawing room, partly concealed by wooden boards, she saw a familiar wrought-iron fireplace. In the corners of one ceiling, she discerned the faint outlines of ornamental mouldings. She stepped out onto the semi-circular balcony that used to overlook her garden.

Billie's face reflected both the joy of nostalgia and the sorrow at the state of a home once scrupulously maintained by Mama and her servants. The elderly woman accompanying them asked a question with concern, and Margaret told Billie she was worried that Billie might reclaim the house.

Margaret accompanied them back to Normal University and this time they proceeded to the rear where they found Shanghai Shi Xi Middle School, formerly SPG. It had been extensively rebuilt and Billie would never have found it without Margaret. When they reached the grounds, Billie at last recognized the field on which she played hockey and had been the last full stop in an exercise when the girls formed the letters S.P.G.

Margaret, who had once taught English and singing at middle school, took them to meet the principal, Yang An Lan, who greeted them warmly. During a brief tour, she told Billie that the classrooms and laboratory she recalled were still in use. They also saw, on a wall, a black-and-white photograph of the school as Billie had known it.

Over lunch, Margaret told them her story. After McTyeire, she had studied languages including Japanese, French and Russian. She had graduated from university, become a teacher and married a banker, who had died a few years ago. They had three children, and her youngest son worked for a hotel in New York. During the occupation by Japan, she recalled, the Japanese took away her radio but otherwise left her and her family alone. After the Communists took over, she thought Mao was wonderful but had made a mistake with the Cultural Revolution. "The Red Guards came to our home on August 31, 1966 and took away some furniture and also my dining room," she said. She had fallen ill during the

Cultural Revolution but had recovered and was keeping fit with tai chi, shadow boxing and other exercises.

In the afternoon, with the aid of Billie's hand-drawn maps, they went in search of the mock Tudor-style house they had occupied at 10 Holly Heath off Amherst Avenue, and 19 Columbia Road, where she had lived with the Larcinas. Heavy rain hampered their efforts and they gave up after driving fruitlessly around Amherst and, at Columbia, only Ian got out to take a photograph.

In the car, Margaret, a singing teacher, burst out in her old school song:

Near the mighty Yangtze River,
In the heart of old Shanghai,
There's a school for China's daughters
Bringing truth and freedom nigh.
May she live and grow forever,
Scatter knowledge far and near.
Till all China learns the lessons
That we learn at old McTyeire.

They headed towards the Bund and Northern District but clogged traffic on Nanking Road reduced them to a snail's pace and they were tiring and decided to put it off until the next day when the weather might clear up.

But the following day brought an icy wind in addition to the rain.

Driver Wu was more relaxed and Margaret Lin was buoyant, nudging Billie to point out various sights. They drove through North Szechuan Road up to Hongkew Park. In the park, they saw men in their 70s and 80s and some would look at Billie and smile and wave knowingly, as if they shared a secret. They didn't know her, but they recognized her as of their generation – one that had been through Japanese war and the Cultural Revolution. Triumphant in just being alive was writ large in their faces.

After a search starting from Hongkew Park (now Luxun Park), they found the house at Kiangwan Road (Jiangwan Lu) where Jessie's ill-fated wedding reception was held. Recognizing the ground-floor veranda, Billie exclaimed, "The Scharnhorsts lived next door in the biggest house on the street and we played in their big garden. She had about eight children and one daughter, Joanne, was very pretty. We had a wonderful street. I remember Mrs Scharnhorst, but we never saw her husband, I didn't know what he did. The family lived off coolie food, rice and vegetables, to save money and used to invite me for meals but I would prefer to go home."

At the old Boone Road School, with its elegant row of arches in rose-and-black brickwork, they went inside and Billie showed Ian the hall where errant students once stood before a grandfather clock as punishment.

There was a long hunt for their flat in Dixwell Road (Liyang Road), which they had to flee in a hurry, leaving Mama's belongings, but driving through the lanes yielded no definitive success. "Dixwell has completely changed," said Billie. "I feel I'm in a brand new world. No landmarks. One house looked like ours – the position was perfect – but I know it wasn't the one."

The futile search did produce a new memory, however. "Our house was close to the tram line and one All Saints' Day, November 1, I was going to church and ran for the tram. Somebody pushed me and I fell down and broke my arm," she said. "I went home, howling. Mama took me to the doctor who put my arm in a splint. I was out of action for three months. I couldn't go to school and my mother engaged a private tutor. After three months, the doctor finally took the splint off. I was so happy. The other children were happy to see me, too. The boys had a wooden go-kart and they decided to give me the first ride. They sat me in the cart and I was riding it and there was a rock in front and I didn't know how to manoeuvre around it. I crashed into it, somersaulted over – and broke my arm in the same spot! My mother couldn't believe it. She took me back to the doctor and he couldn't believe it, either. My arm was V-shaped after the fall and I was put back in a splint and was out of action for another three months.

"That's why I didn't want to learn how to drive. I didn't know how to manoeuvre, how to twist or turn."

And another story: "I entered a handwriting competition sponsored by Lactogen and I was at home with my tutor, who was Jewish and her name was Miss Mordecai, when the message came through that I had won. The prize was a pink fountain pen with the word Lactogen on it. No one can read my handwriting today."

As Billie grew weary, they gave up on an attempt to look for St Joseph's Convent, her first school. Ian felt her enthusiasm was also waning as she had had enough of faded glory.

It struck her that Margaret Lin and Yuyuen Road were perfect metaphors for the changes in her beloved city. Billie acknowledged that, in her time, refugees had died in their hundreds in the streets from cold or starvation and that the Communists had ridden the city of such horrors. In fact, all over China, the lower orders had been largely freed from the grip of poverty. But the open society that had embraced interchange with the west, that had enabled her to meet brilliant people like Lin Yutang, Dr Amos Wong and Mickey Hahn, all that had gone forever. In the places they had revisited, colour and distinctiveness had been replaced by a grey uniformity.

Her homecoming was like visiting a parent who was now ailing after a long absence – she had found little resonance and had been affected more by loss than nostalgia.

Margaret asked when they would meet again and Billie replied she didn't think she would return. "Shanghai," she said, "is one..." – she paused to find the right word "...great big bazaar."

For some years, Ian sent letters and photographs to Margaret Lin, but received no reply. In 2002, he went to her Shanghai home, where her daughter opened the door. Her mother had told her all about their visit, she said, and Margaret had been most happy to meet us. But not long afterwards, she had sickened and died. It seemed extraordinary to Ian how she had appeared like a guardian angel at the very moment Billie and Ian needed her, only to vanish soon after.

Seeing Shanghai again gave Billie a keener appreciation for Geneva, which she had chosen to make her home after retirement. As the European headquarters for the United Nations and base for dozens of other international agencies, Geneva was cosmopolitan and tolerant ("They have never heard of the word 'Eurasian' here," she said), without the cacophony.

Billie kept up the bridge she had learned at Stanley, joining local clubs and playing in a few international tournaments, including one that featured film star Omar Sharif.

She visited England, often accompanied by Ian, to see Mickey and Charles, Freda, Vivienne and Mary. She and Ian went to the reunion of veterans and POWs in Hong Kong in 1995 to mark the 50th anniversary of Liberation. Later that year, she attended the London wedding of Ian and Jean, happy that her son was settling down.

A year later, with Billie full of bounce on her 80th birthday, Ian told her friends at the party in Geneva that his mother seemed to have a special gene that enabled her to survive upheaval and loss with undiminished optimism and wonder.

In 1999, Ian and Jean brought their new-born twins to Geneva and Billie was at the airport to greet her grandchildren, Brian and Sabrina. Her grandson looked like her first-born, she said, her cheeks wet with tears.

Parenthood also deepened Ian's appreciation of Billie, who had been his breadwinner, mother and father all at the same time. They finished a draft of their book though they decided to shelve it for further improvement.

In her 80s, two strokes left Billie partially paralysed, but her mind lost none of its acuity. Her son visited her on his own, taking her around in a wheelchair. She delighted in placing two photographs side by side – one of her wheeling Ian in a pram and the other of Ian pushing her in the wheelchair. At night, he helped her on and off with her stockings and slept in a camp bed near her. She treasured such moments, she told him.

Ian was with her when she died, after a third stroke, in Geneva on February 22, 2006 at the age of 89. She had outlived many friends but the service at the church of St Jean XXIII was packed with people who remembered her. Ian spoke of the side of Billie that few had known – the Shanghai girl who had ridden the city's crests and troughs to become a woman of exceptional bravura and resilience.

Billie had also told him her "secret for survival." She considered herself the luckiest of people because, at every crisis, she had always found a friend to help her through it.

EXPLORE ASIA WITH BLACKSMITH BOOKS

From bookstores around the world or from *www.blacksmithbooks.com*